FIELD BOOK OF SNAKES

The Rainbow Snake (*Abastor erythrogrammus*)

FIELD BOOK OF
SNAKES
of the United States and Canada

BY

KARL P. SCHMIDT

Chief Curator of Zoology

CHICAGO NATURAL HISTORY MUSEUM

and

D. DWIGHT DAVIS

Curator of Anatomy

CHICAGO NATURAL HISTORY MUSEUM

With four colored plates and 103 drawings by

ALBERT A. ENZENBACHER

and 82 photographs from life

G. P. PUTNAM'S SONS

NEW YORK

Second Impression

Manufactured in the United States of America
By The Cornwall Press, Inc., Cornwall, N. Y.

To

OUR RESPECTIVE WIVES

CONTENTS

ILLUSTRATIONS

PREFACE

Snakes have always been of more than casual interest to the layman, and the extensive literature dealing with them witnesses the more than ordinary appeal they have to the professional naturalist. The United States is fortunate, compared with Europe, in the richness of its snake fauna. Yet until recently there has been no book to which the interested amateur could turn with confidence for answers to his questions as to identification, habits, or behavior. Very recently there has been a burst of interest in handbooks of snakes, and no fewer than two have appeared while the present volume was in preparation. We believe, however, that our book differs so greatly from those in scope or nature of treatment, or both, that there is surprisingly little duplication.

In the past, study of American snakes has dealt chiefly with taxonomic problems. We believe that as purely taxonomic problems become less productive, interest will gradually shift to topics of broader biological interest. With this in mind, we have placed particular emphasis on life history, habits, behavior, and ecology. Description has been restricted to what is necessary for identification of specimens.

This book is quite naturally largely a compilation from the hundreds of individual studies and notes of observations that have been published by those interested in snakes. It rests on an extensive card index of this literature, which is widely scattered through technical journals and scientific publications of institutions and learned societies. Inclusion of references to authorities for all statements would have made the text cumbersome and unreadable, but nearly every statement of fact is based on careful consideration of all that is known on that topic. References have been included where it seemed desirable, and these are supplemented by complete citations to important or comprehensive papers, which will serve to introduce the serious student to the technical literature.

The fourth (1939) edition of Stejneger and Barbour's *Check List of North American Amphibians and Reptiles* has been followed in matters of arrangement and nomenclature, except that the Lower California forms have been omitted. The few deviations from the check list are usually explained in footnotes. Twelve forms described since the appearance of the check list have been included. These are: *Leptotyphlops humilis utahensis* Tanner (1938), *Leptotyphlops humilis segregus* Klauber (1939), *Opheodrys vernalis blanchardi* Grobman (1941), *Salvadora lineata* Schmidt (1940), *S. hexalepis deserticola* Schmidt (1940), *Coluber constrictor priapus* Dunn and Wood (1939), *Phyllorhynchus decurtatus nubilis* Klauber (1940), *P. browni lucidus* Klauber (1940), *Elaphe williamsi* Barbour and Carr (1940), *Elaphe vulpina gloydi* Conant (1940), *Thamnophis ordinoides gigas* Fitch (1940), and *Natrix harteri* Trapido (1941).

Unfortunately there is no "check list" of common names of snakes, and these names, which are likely to be most used by the amateur, have presented the usual difficulties. Our policy has been to use names that have become established through usage wherever possible, even when they are somewhat inappropriate or misleading. Thus some may object to our use of "worm snakes" for *Carphophis* instead of for *Leptotyphlops,* or to the term "milk snake," but experience has shown that "book names" seldom gain wide acceptance.

We consider ourselves fortunate in having secured the services of Mr. Albert A. Enzenbacher, of Chicago, as artist. Snakes are notoriously difficult to draw and paint convincingly, and we believe that Mr. Enzenbacher's work is an outstanding contribution to the illustration of these creatures. Miss Elizabeth Story has contributed a number of drawings, especially to illustrate technical details, and her aid has been invaluable in lettering and preparing the illustrations for the press.

The photographs (by the junior author, except where otherwise credited) were made on a ground-glass background in order to eliminate anything that would obscure the outlines or pattern of the snake. A 4 x 5 Graflex with an f 6.3 Bausch and Lomb Protar lens was used for all but a few. In most cases where it was desirable to show the belly pattern the snake was lightly anesthetized. Mrs. Dorothy Foss has been helpful on many Saturday afternoons in the course of the photographic work.

Many persons have aided in the preparation of this book, and we take this opportunity to thank them. Our museum associates have been helpful, and the Chicago Natural History Museum collections and library have been drawn upon constantly. We are particularly obliged to the Chicago Zoological Society; to Mr. C. B. Perkins of the Zoological Society of San Diego; to Dr. H. K. Gloyd of the Chicago Academy of Sciences; to Mr. Ross Allen of Ocala, Florida; to Dr. C. S. Smith of San Marcos State Teachers College; to Dr. Leo T. Murray of Baylor University; to Mr. J. E. Johnson, of Waco, Texas; and to Mr. C. M. Barber, of Hot Springs, Arkansas, for gifts or loans of living snakes for photographing. Dr. Gloyd has also kindly supplied photographs from his albums, and we have consulted him on various topics in the course of the work. Mr. L. M. Klauber of the Zoological Society of San Diego generously supplied the photographs credited to him, and Mr. Charles T. Vorhies of the University of Arizona supplied the specimen of the rare *Oxybelis microphthalmus* from which the drawings were made.

For aid in the preparation of the manuscript we are indebted to Miss Margaret Bauer and to Miss Peggy Collings, and to Miss Merle A. Quait, who has retyped the entire manuscript in its final form.

We are much indebted to L. M. Klauber, E. R. Dunn, Roger Conant, M. Graham Netting, and Reeve M. Bailey, and to other colleagues who have called our attention to errors of fact and of omission, to misprints, and to the lapsus whereby we recorded the boa constrictor from Iowa.

KARL P. SCHMIDT,
D. DWIGHT DAVIS.

Chicago, Illinois
May, 1944

INTRODUCTION

THE PLACE OF SNAKES IN NATURE

The dangerous nature of a few poisonous kinds of snakes so powerfully affects the popular imagination that many people have difficulty in thinking of snakes as anything *but* dangerous, and, by association, loathsome. This is not at all the naturalist's attitude toward them. His interest in them is not different from that of a student of birds in his birds. Snakes, when dispassionately observed, prove to be beautiful and graceful creatures; and while it is true that they feed on other animals, so, after all, do the robins.

"Natural History" consists of studies of animal and plant life from the point of view of rather general and popular interest, and in recent years the value of studies of the relations between animals and plants and their surroundings, or with each other, has come to be recognized as a distinct science, *ecology;* this is really rather directly derived from the somewhat old-fashioned natural history. A naturalist (or an ecologist) trying to formulate his ideas of the place of snakes in the vast economy of nature might think somewhat as follows.

Snakes give the impression of a group of animals that has had an evolutionary success. In the first place, there are a great number of living species. Secondly, these species prove to have invaded all of the principal kinds of environment; there are tree snakes that rarely come to the ground, burrowing snakes that rarely appear above it, water snakes that outswim even the fishes, and of course the great central group of terrestrial snakes that live mainly on the surface of the ground but may climb or burrow or swim in varying degree. In all these different modes of life they compete successfully with other forms of life or prey upon them, and thus, thirdly, they are successful in that they exhibit great numbers of individuals. It may be pointed out also that they are considerably more abundant in the northern parts of the temperate zone than are lizards, or indeed, any other reptiles. Finally, they persist in regions greatly modified by civilization.

The great abundance of individual snakes is not usually conspicuous, but anywhere where an intensive search is made for them they are likely to be discovered in some numbers. These populations increase greatly toward the tropics, as does the variety of different species, and also, in a broad way, the maximum size.

The fact that snakes are all carnivorous and predatory fixes their role in the general economy of nature. The existence of great numbers of snakes depends on an available food supply. Snakes are, in fact, specifically adjusted to swallowing whole animals that are considerably larger than their own diameter; and this, with their efficient locomotion, enables them to feed on a host of small vertebrates—on mammals of the size of rats and mice, on small birds and nestlings of larger ones; and on frogs and toads, lizards, and, finally, other snakes. The great majority of snakes the world over are of medium size, or small, and only a few of the tropical giants (the boas and pythons) are able to take prey as large even as a half-grown pig. It is true that a good many of the small snakes feed on insects or other invertebrates, sometimes exclusively on some special group, such as snails.

Snakes, with their considerable number of individuals, do of course provide food for other predators, and a considerable number of species of snakes have even turned to eating other snakes. This attracts great popular interest, especially when a harmless snake is observed to feed upon poisonous ones, as is the case with the king snakes of North America.* Animals that habitually prey upon snakes are especially certain hawks, and the skunks and their allies among the weasel tribe. In other parts of the world other distinct types of animals are well known as snake-eaters—the hedgehog in Europe and the mongoose in the tropics of Asia and Africa.

The larger poisonous snakes are dangerous to hunters and

* We do not refer to such snake-eating habits as cannibalism; this term should be restricted to the eating of one's own *species*.

other outdoorsmen, and children may be killed by the bite of even the smaller poisonous species. Accidents from snake bite are relatively rare, but it is not surprising that relentless war is waged by man against the poisonous forms. The naturalist's regret is that the killing of such snakes is largely indiscriminate, including the harmless little insect-eating green snake equally with the banded rattlesnake. It is remarkable that a few poisonous snakes persist even close to great cities—the copperhead along the Palisades of the Hudson and the massasauga within fifty miles of Chicago. Extermination of poisonous snakes is often promoted by the payment of bounties. In the United States these bounty payments are often made for any snake-head brought in, so that statistics about the abundance of poisonous snakes from this source would require discount. In older and more thickly settled countries the offer of a bounty is likely to lead to some form of snake breeding. Active campaigns of extermination against rattlesnakes are most effective when directed against their hibernating dens.

Far more effective in the reduction of the numbers of snakes than active campaigns of snake killing are the changes of environment brought about by the agricultural operations of man. Modern mowing machinery, for example, is especially destructive to the larger and bolder snakes, such as the blue racer or rattlesnake. Such snakes raise their heads and face any oncoming mower or reaper to their inevitable destruction. As another example, the prairie region of northern Illinois has undergone a major change of the environment brought about by tile draining of the land, which has brought with it the draining of the prairie sloughs. The drainage of the sloughs has wiped out their great populations of frogs and salamanders, and thus also destroyed the snakes that preyed upon these creatures.

Increase of a few kinds of harmless snakes under agricultural conditions may be suspected from the abundance of small secretive species such as De Kay's snake and the smooth green snake in the vacant lots and defunct subdivisions of our cities. This abundance even extends to the larger earthworm-eating garter snakes.

The direct importance of snakes to man is relatively

slight, though there may be chains of cause and effect in which they affect human life more or less remotely. The larger snakes unquestionably do play a part in restoring the so-called "balance of nature" (which is so much unbalanced by agricultural man) in the control of the host of field mice which live in grain and hay fields. The abundant bull snakes of the western prairies and plains are perhaps the most important single group of such rodent eaters.

A relation between snakes and man that affects man adversely depends on human psychology and not on the snakes. Even after a generation of effort on the part of naturalists to combat the popular prejudice against snakes and to educate the public to the distinction between harmless snakes and dangerous ones, there is still widespread fear and horror of the most harmless forms in the minds of the majority of people. This is plainly a useless and harmful burden for the human mind. The absence of fear and the obvious interest displayed by young children who are shown harmless snakes contrasts extraordinarily with the hysterical behavior of those who have been frightened by their elders.

Snakes form a part of the great web of animate nature, and should no more be killed wantonly than should birds, or any other living creatures.

FOLKLORE OF SNAKES

The widespread fables about snakes are of considerable interest and importance to anyone genuinely interested in the study of these creatures. The student of snakes is certain to be confronted with the choice between offending someone who tells him one or more of the familiar snake stories in perfect good faith, or failing to speak up for his conviction that the story is not true. The counter-contradictions of the scientific attitude with reference to the story of a snake rolling like a hoop and provided with a poisonous sting in its tail once grew so acrimonious in a newspaper column, during a controversy in which we were involved as the skeptics, that we finally closed the argument by offering a cash reward of a thousand dollars for a snake with such a tail sting and an additional thousand if it should roll like a hoop. Rewards were never claimed, and the argument languished.

There is a great body of popular misinformation about snakes that borders upon folklore. Thus it is widely believed, but certainly not true, that all snakes are poisonous;* that snakes are "slimy"; that they "sting" with their tongues; that the killing of a snake will be avenged by its mate; that the age of a rattlesnake in years corresponds to the number of rattles; that snakes "charm" their prey; that whisky is a cure for snake bite; and so on. There is a host of other beliefs regarding remedies for snake bite; and an equally astonishing number of uses of snakes and parts of snakes in medicine. The use of "snake oil" for rheumatism, for example, persists to the present day.

The more elaborate and widespread snake stories which assume the proportions of myths are the milk snake story, the story that mother snakes swallow their young for protection, and the glass snake story.

The first of these myths tells of snakes sucking cows in

* Actually, of the 223 snakes of the United States and Canada, only 52 are poisonous and only 36 of these are at all dangerous.

the pasture, so that the cows fail to give their proper quota of milk at milking time. The story rests, apparently, simply on the presence of snakes in pastures and the all too-frequent failure of milk in cows. Snakes have been observed to drink milk set out for the cat, and occasionally enter barns for mice. When the belief that snakes suck milk from cows, based on this inadequate background, has once arisen, witnesses to the actual sucking of the milk from the cow soon follow. These "eye-witness" accounts almost invariably have an evidential defect—they relate an event long past. A number of objections to the story have been raised by scientists who do not believe it. The presence of rows of needle-sharp teeth in the mouth of all of our larger snakes tells against the possibility that a cow would permit herself to be sucked. The snake of the eastern states most taxed with this story, which is in fact usually known as the "milk snake," is far too small to hold sufficient milk to account for the amounts in question in the story in its familiar form. A remarkable version of the milk snake story known from Brazil tells of the snake's entering the huts of country people and taking milk from human mothers.

The story that mother snakes take their young into the mouth and throat for protection from approaching danger is even better attested by eye-witness stories than the milk snake fable. It is attached to a great many different species of snakes, and is as well known in Europe as in America. There are some obvious objections to the story, but the most significant seems to be that it breaks down precisely because there is so much evidence for it. If this phenomenon were actually as common as the stories about it, there would be no difficulty in subjecting it to genuine proof. In many of the instances offered as evidence, inspection shows that a mother snake about to produce her young had been killed and her body so ruptured that the young could escape. Uncritical persons, and especially persons who were not aware that there are many snakes that bear their young alive, have then concluded that the young had been "swallowed." Other supposed observations are quite evidently due to hallucination, in which the observer sees what is in his mind. The excitement that snakes arouse in the minds of many persons

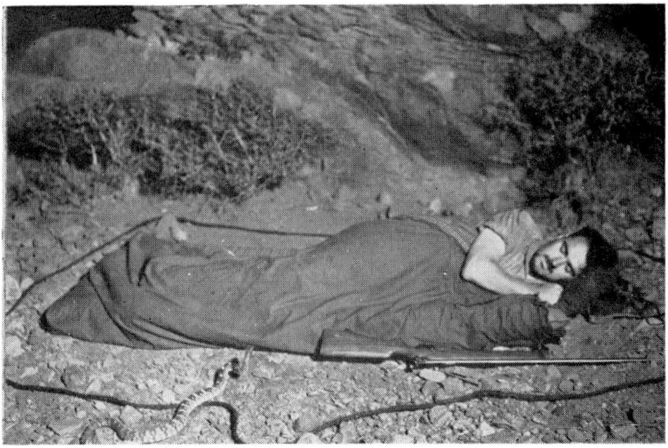

A false snake story. Black-tailed Rattlesnake crossing horse hair rope (photo by W. L. Necker).

A true snake story. Hog-nosed Snake "playing 'possum" after being annoyed.

would certainly make them quite incapable of critical or accurate observation. The writers know of no purported observation of this phenomenon which is not reported as a childhood or otherwise remote recollection.

The glass snake or joint snake story tells of a snake that flies to pieces when struck and later quietly reassembles its parts. There is an extensive basis in fact for this story, which is correctly attached to a snakelike lizard. This lizard is entirely without limbs, and has a tail about twice as long as the body. As in many lizards, the tail is fragile and when broken its convulsively jerking sections occupy an enemy and thus afford opportunity for the owner to make a get-away. Since the tail is so long, the glass snake may apparently be broken at the middle. This is remarkable enough, and it is further true that a new tail will grow out from the stump. It is *not* true that the parts of the tail reassemble.

More especially American fables report a snake that blows a deadly, or at least a violent, poison—the blow snake, puff adder, or spreading adder; and one with a poisonous sting in its tail—the stinging snake or hoop snake. The tale of the rattlesnake fang in the boot is, of course, also purely American.

The blow snake proves to be due simply to uncritical observation and nervousness. The snakes of the genus *Heterodon* all spread their necks flat (whence the name spreading adder), inflate their lungs, and hiss and puff while lunging at an attacker (whence puff adder). This behavior can readily be shown to be purely a bluff. The conclusion that a poisonous vapor is blown out may rest on an occasional case of illness induced by nervousness and fright. It is highly remarkable that the blow snake, when still further molested, and especially if actually injured, gives up the blowing and menacing tactics altogether, and plays dead. (See p. 117).

The hoop snake story is pure myth with a much more slender observational basis. In the southern states it is now regularly attached to two conspicuously colored but rarely observed large snakes, the rainbow snake (shown on our frontispiece) and the mud snake. These snakes have a sharp conical scale at the tip of the tail, and when held in the hand may be seen to make exploratory pricks with this spine. This, together with the rarity of the snakes, seems to be the sole background of fact for the stories of a stinging snake, with a deadly tail sting, on which is built the elaboration that it takes its tail in its mouth and rolls like a hoop. The senior author once traced these stories through all the available historical records, and found the hoop snake story developed at a much later date than that about the stinging snake.

The story of the rattlesnake fang embedded in the boot of a man who died from being bitten in the foot goes on to relate that the man's infant son grows to manhood, and finding a pair of his father's boots in the attic, puts them on and in turn dies from the venom remaining in the fang. In the most elaborate form of the story, the fang is not discovered until the grandson in his turn is poisoned by it, but recovers and pieces the story together. It may be doubted if anything but a very slight case of snake poisoning would result from the scratch from a venom-filled fang. Even here there is the slight factual basis that snake venom preserves its poisonous properties when dry.

The collection and critical study of the folklore of snakes may be made an interesting by-product of more serious studies of snakes. The reader may be referred to the senior author's pamphlet, "The Truth about Snake Stories," in which he will find a few further bibliographic references; or to Rheua Vaughn Medden's scholarly, but very readable, history of the extensive folklore of the peculiarly American rattlesnakes. Miss Medden's study is provided with a very extensive bibliography.

Medden, R. V., 1929-1931, Tales of the rattlesnake: from the works of early travelers in America. *Bull. Antivenin Institute Amer.*, vols. 3-5.—**Schmidt, K. P.**, 1925, The hoop snake story. *Nat. Hist.*, vol. 25. pp. 76-80; 1929, The truth about snake stories. *Field Mus. Nat. Hist., Zool. Leaflet*, No. 10, 19 pp.

HISTORY OF THE STUDY OF SNAKES IN THE UNITED STATES

The reader will find the names of the various naturalists who have contributed to the description of the snakes of the United States appended to the technical names which appear in our list, in accordance with an accepted rule of scientific nomenclature. A glimpse of the history of this phase of the study of snakes will help to make these names something more than dead letters, and will introduce the reader to the historical interest that herpetology shares with every branch of science. The specific names themselves often honor some colleague or patron, or the collector of the original specimen on which the description is based. Such names, like the names of the describers, are clues to the history of the zoological exploration of North America.

Knowledge of the snakes of North America was extremely scanty before the time of the Swedish naturalist Linnaeus, who invented our system of naming animals and plants. His simple scheme of giving each kind or *species* of animal *two* names, like our own given and surnames, automatically provided the beginnings of a classification, and established a list of names on permanent record, to which additions could be made by subsequent students. The establishment of nomenclature on a permanent basis stimulated travels for the purpose of collecting specimens to be studied and named. Linnaeus' *Systema Naturae* was reprinted in successive editions; the date of the tenth, 1758, has been adopted as the beginning of our system of naming. Linnaeus himself contributed the descriptions of sixteen species of snakes in our list. In spite of the active interest in descriptive natural history following his times, only fourteen additional species from North America north of the present boundary of Mexico had been described by 1820, with nine more during the succeeding decade. The first genuinely American students of snakes (and of herpetology in general) were at work in the eighteen-twenties, Thomas Say (1787-1834) and Richard Harlan (1796-1843). Their work, published in part by the Academy of Natural Sciences of Philadelphia, reflects the importance of that institution in early American science. Say was one of the founders of the Academy. Though best known as an entomologist, he described seven well-known species of snakes. He accompanied the government expedition to the Rocky Mountains under Major Long in 1820, and took part in the foundation of the famous socialist colony at New Harmony, Indiana.

In the succeeding decades, John Edwards Holbrook (1794-1871) attempted the first complete illustrated account of North American amphibians and reptiles in his *North American Herpetology: or a Description of the Reptiles inhabiting the United States.* The colored plates in the first edition of this remarkable work, in four volumes (1836-1840), received some unfavorable criticism, and Holbrook destroyed the edition in a bonfire in his Charleston backyard, failing to recall only a few copies. His second edition (1842), in five volumes, is well known, and may occasionally be purchased through second-hand book dealers for about $200.

As we look back over the first hundred years of descriptive herpetology, our list of names of American snakes is seen to include those of most of the authors of general works on reptiles. The early "complete accounts" of Lacépède (1788-89) and Daudin (1802-1803), are in French and form parts of the ambitious project of the great French naturalist, the Comte de Buffon, for a natural history of the world. It is natural enough that the next compendious account of the reptile group, the ten volumes of the *Erpétologie Générale* of Duméril and Bibron (1834-1854), should be by Frenchmen. An important work of this early period especially on snakes is the *Physionomie des Serpents* (1837) by the Dutch zoologist, Hermann Schlegel. This was also written in French.

With the arrival of Spencer Fullerton Baird (1823-1887) at the Smithsonian Institution in Washington, D. C., in

1850, as assistant to the first secretary, Joseph Henry, the exploration of North America for its vertebrate animal life underwent a burst of activity. Baird seized the great opportunities provided by the government surveys of the West to promote collecting for the infant National Museum at Washington. His own work and his encouragement of promising young students, like Robert Kennicott and Charles Girard, added no less than fifty-seven species of snakes to the forms known. Kennicott's premature death in Alaska, in 1865, and Baird's preoccupation with such large affairs as the foundation of the U. S. Commission of Fisheries, left the field of herpetology more and more to others. The life of Baird by his pupil and associate, Dall,* affords a history of this period of American biology. In its pages we find reflected the young enthusiasm of Kennicott and learn to respect the indomitable and greatly unselfish character of Baird.

Among others who continued the study of North American reptiles in the eighteen-fifties by means of the collections of the Academy of Natural Sciences in Philadelphia, we may mention Edward Hallowell (died 1860), and especially the brilliant but erratic Edward Drinker Cope (1840-1898). Cope is known equally for pioneer studies on vertebrate anatomy, on fishes, and on the paleontology of the American West. Innumerable papers flowed from his facile pen, mostly at first in the *Proceedings* of the Philadelphia Academy (his first paper was printed in 1859). He described no less than twenty-seven of the forms of snakes in our fauna. The reader is referred to the monumental but unhappily dull *Cope: Master Naturalist* by H. F. Osborn. Cope's fat volume *Crocodilians, Lizards, and Snakes of North America,* which was published by the United States National Museum in 1900, two years after his death, is still an important reference work; it should be remembered, however, that manuscript notes left by the careful and accurate Baird compose large sections of this work. Samuel Garman, better known for his studies on fishes, produced an important work on North American snakes in 1883 as the first part

* Dall, W. H., *Spencer Fullerton Baird,* 462 pp., il. (Philadelphia: J. B. Lippincott Co., 1915).

of *The Reptiles and Batrachians of North America,* of which no further volumes were published.

The contrasting character of Leonhard Stejneger (born 1851), whose first paper on American reptiles appeared in 1889, ushers in an essentially modern period in the study of North American herpetology. In that year he became Curator of Reptiles at the United States National Museum. Stejneger's early papers were thorough and meticulous, and set the standard and to a large extent the form still followed for descriptive studies. His careful bibliographic researches form the background for the first "check-list" of North American amphibians and reptiles, published with Thomas Barbour in 1917. This authoritative establishment of nomenclature (which had fallen into great confusion in Cope's era) greatly stimulated renewed herpetological studies; the fourth edition of the check-list (1939) is followed in the present work, deviations from its system being explained in footnotes.

Mr. A. E. Brown, Director of the Philadelphia Zoological Gardens, interested himself especially in snakes, and, while his *Review of the Genera and Species of American Snakes North of Mexico* (1901) is now entirely obsolete, it was a useful work for two decades and he is remembered here for his descriptions of several remarkably distinct snakes.

The single species of snake in our list described by G. A. Boulenger (1858-1937) affords an illustration of the extent to which North American herpetology had fallen into the hands of American students in the latter part of the nineteenth century. Boulenger's long career at the British Museum (1878-1920) was a most fruitful one for the study of amphibians and reptiles. His *Catalogue of Snakes* (1893-1896), an account of the snakes of the world, was especially weak in its treatment of the snakes of temperate North America, and modern American students will have no concept of the renown of Boulenger in Europe, or of the respect entertained for his work by his European colleagues.

The work of Alexander G. Ruthven (born 1882) on the familiar garter snakes, published in 1908, may be regarded as founding an essentially new school of herpetology in the United States. The work was a revision of a genus, carried

S. F. Baird

E. D. Cope

J. E. Holbrook

Leonhard Stejneger

EARLIER STUDENTS OF NORTH AMERICAN SNAKES.

A. G. Ruthven

F. N. Blanchard

G. K. Noble

L. M. Klauber

CONTEMPORARY STUDENTS OF NORTH AMERICAN SNAKES.

out by the examination of large numbers of specimens, and evaluated largely in geographic terms. Ruthven's influence at the University of Michigan, where he first became director of the University Museum and later president of the University, attracted students of reptiles, and numerous more or less direct descendants of the "garter snake paper" have appeared. Through Ruthven's most brilliant pupils, Frank N. Blanchard and Helen T. Gaige, students of herpetology continued to be attracted to the University of Michigan. The preparation of a comprehensive account of North American snakes, embodying a great amount of original investigation, was interrupted by the death of Dr. Blanchard in 1937. It is hoped that this work may be carried to completion by Howard K. Gloyd, who was long associated with Blanchard in the project. Under Blanchard's influence the careful study of habits and of life histories of snakes came into deserved prominence.

Others influential in the conspicuous modern rise of herpetology are Thomas Barbour, Director of the Museum of Comparative Zoology at Harvard; Mary C. Dickerson (1866-1923), formerly Curator of Herpetology at the American Museum of Natural History in New York; John Van Denburgh, who contributed the first summaries of the herpetology of the western states; and Albert Hazen Wright, Professor of Vertebrate Zoology at Cornell University. One of the first to attempt to popularize snakes and other reptiles in this country was Raymond L. Ditmars, Curator of Reptiles at the New York Zoological Gardens. His famous *Reptile Book,* first published in 1907, was for many years the only non-technical reference book on the snakes of the United States, but it has long been out of date.

Mr. L. M. Klauber, of San Diego, beginning his studies on the rattlesnakes and other snakes of the southwest as an amateur in 1924, has introduced exactness of record and observation into field studies and has turned his engineering training to account in the application of statistical method to the study of snakes. He is subjecting problems of variation and growth to a searching analysis from which we shall certainly derive more exact ideas regarding the definition of our species.

The name of Roger Conant appears frequently on the following pages because of his many contributions to our knowledge of the habits and behavior of snakes. Conant has been associated successively with the Toledo Zoological Park and the Philadelphia Zoological Garden, and his studies are an excellent example of the unique additions to our knowledge of snakes and other animals that a competent zoo man is in a position to make. His *Reptiles of Ohio* (1938) is a model state herpetology.

The great modern development of the experimental biological sciences has only begun to impinge on the study of snakes. We may mention the important experimental studies of snakes undertaken in the Department of Experimental Biology at the American Museum of Natural History by the late G. K. Noble (1894-1940) and others working under his direction. These afford checks on observational studies, and relate observations of skin shedding, mode of feeding, breeding behavior, etc., to physiologic factors. The discovery of the novel function of the pit of the pit vipers as a heat detector may serve as an example of such studies.

The history of the investigation of the anatomy, embryology, and physiology of snakes is beyond the scope of the present outline. Studies of the venom of snakes and the preparation of antivenins for the treatment of snake bite require mention; the work of Dr. S. Weir Mitchell was of fundamental importance, especially his volume (with E. T. Reichert), *Researches upon the Venoms of Poisonous Serpents*, 1886. The reader is referred also to the *Bulletin of the Antivenin Institute of America* (1927-1932).

Herpetology had no journal of its own in North America until *Copeia,* which includes the field of ichthyology also, was founded in 1913 by John T. Nichols. At first privately published by Mr. Nichols as a small monthly pamphlet, it was taken over by the American Society of Ichthyologists and Herpetologists in 1924 as its official organ. In 1930 it was enlarged and revamped into a quarterly journal. In 1936, Major Chapman Grant and Walter L. Necker founded the journal *Herpetologica,* which is issued irregularly and is devoted exclusively to amphibians and reptiles.

DEFINITION AND CLASSIFICATION

The snakes are regarded by the authors of the present book as forming one of the principal groups of living reptiles, an Order, the *Serpentes*,* of the Class **Reptilia.**

The reptiles form one of the main divisions of the backboned animals, which include, in addition, the fishes and their relatives, the amphibians (frogs, salamanders, and caecilians), the birds, and the mammals. Reptiles appear to have originated from ancient types of amphibians in the age of coal, and to have given rise to the birds and to the mammals during the "Age of Reptiles." Modern forms represent only six ** of the great number of distinct orders of reptiles, which include the gigantic dinosaurs, the flying pterodactyls, dolphinlike marine forms, and many others, most of which flourished during past geological ages and are now long extinct.

WHAT IS A SNAKE?

The snakes are so closely allied to the lizards and monitors that it is somewhat difficult to frame a formal definition that completely and readily distinguishes them. This difficulty rests primarily on the fact that many different types of lizards are limbless or nearly so. Snakes are distinguished from all lizards by the fact that the two halves of the lower jaw are separated, connected only by an elastic ligament; and the great majority of snakes are at once distinguished by their transverse ventral plates.

Snakes may be defined as elongate, scaly reptiles without limbs or with the vestiges of hind limbs only, without movable eyelids, without ear-opening, with an elongate, deeply forked, and retractile tongue, with a transverse vent and

* The term *Ophidia* is obsolete, but is still familiar in popular writings.

** Turtles, sphenodons, crocodilians, lizards, monitors and mosasaurs, and snakes.

paired organs of copulation, and with the two halves of the lower jaw independently movable, connected in front by an elastic ligament. Most snakes have straplike transverse scales, the *ventral plates,* extending from side to side on the undersurface of the body.

The structure of a typical snake enables it to move rapidly, with a sinuous gliding motion, and to swallow whole prey much exceeding its own diameter. Locomotion is accomplished by throwing the body into lateral undulations, by movement of the transverse ventral plates, or by both. The swallowing of animals of relatively large diameter is accomplished by the extremely loose architecture of the skull, in which the lower jaws are not only separately movable, but are hinged to the skull by three joints instead of one, and in which the tooth-bearing bones of the upper jaw are also independently movable. This structure makes possible the great expansion of the gape; the absence of the breast bone and the elasticity of the skin between the scales, together with elongation of the heart and other internal organs, permits the further passage of the food to the stomach.

MAJOR KINDS OF SNAKES

Since the deadly venom of certain types of snakes makes so profound an impression, it is not surprising that the early classifications of the snakes were primarily into poisonous and non-poisonous. It is now clear that this leads to an artificial grouping, and that some of the poisonous snakes are only very slightly poisonous, while, of the extremely poisonous types, the cobras and coral snakes are very different from the vipers and pit vipers. Employing what we regard as the more fundamental anatomical characters (essentially following the classification of G. A. Boulenger), the Order Serpentes is found to be divisible into eighteen * families, of rather unequal importance and very unequal in their number of species. These families are:

* This number of families is arrived at by the elevation of several of Boulenger's subfamilies to family rank. The ending of subfamily names is in *-inae* instead of *-idae;* hence the reader will find the colubrid snakes of our system referred to as the *colubrine* snakes by many authors.

Typhlopidae ....Blind Snakes (Tropics of both hemispheres)
Leptotyphlopidae ....Slender Blind Snakes (Chiefly Africa and America)
Boidae ....Boas (Chiefly tropical America)
Pythonidae ....Pythons (Chiefly tropical Old World)
Anilidae ....False Coral Snakes (South America and East Indies)
Uropeltidae ....Shield-tailed Snakes (South India and Ceylon)
Xenopeltidae ....Mud Snakes (Southeast Asia)
Achrochordidae ....Oriental Water Snakes (Southeast Asia and East Indies)
Colubridae ....Typical Harmless Snakes (World-wide)
Amblycephalidae ....Slug-eating Snakes (East Asia and tropical America)
Dasypeltidae ....Egg-eating Snakes (Africa)
Homalopsidae ....Rear-fanged Water Snakes (Southeast Asia and East Indies)
Boigidae ....Rear-fanged Snakes (World-wide, mainly tropical)
Elachistodontidae .....Rear-fanged Egg-eating Snakes (Southern India)
Elapidae ....Cobras and Coral Snakes (World-wide, mainly tropical)
Hydrophidae ....Sea Snakes (Marine [absent in the Atlantic])
Viperidae ....Vipers (Old World)
Crotalidae ....Pit Vipers (Eastern Asia and the Americas)

Vestiges of the hind limbs, or at least of the pelvis, are present in the first five families; the families Homalopsidae, Boigidae, and Elachistodontidae are the so-called rear-fanged snakes (the "Opisthoglypha"). The family Colubridae, the "colubrid" snakes proper, includes the great majority of the harmless forms and the great majority of snakes in general. The last four families are the groups with a fatally potent venom.

Modern studies of the rear-fanged snakes seem to show conclusively that enlarged and grooved posterior teeth have been developed independently in various forms from different colubrid ancestors. While most of the families of snakes seem to be natural groups, this means that our family Boigidae is an unnatural or artificial assemblage. It is retained here simply as a convenient partition of the otherwise unwieldy series of colubrid genera, and because no new subdivision of the family Colubridae is yet current. The partition of the combined Colubridae and Boigidae into natural subfamilies is obviously a major problem in the study of snakes, and one which requires much further study.

Only seven of the eighteen families are represented within our limits. These are the Boidae (three forms), the Leptotyphlopidae (6 forms), the Colubridae (162 forms), the Boigidae (16 forms), the Elapidae (4 forms), the Hydrophidae (1 form), and the Crotalidae (32 forms).

CLASSIFICATION OF SNAKES

The classification of animals is based on the recognition that there are kinds, or **species**, in which the individuals are obviously alike. Interbreeding takes place freely among the individuals of a species and parents pass on their characteristics to their offspring, so that the colors and pattern, or other characteristics, of that species are maintained at a relatively constant level; "freaks" or other deviations from the normal are soon bred out of the population. The biologist expresses this by saying that a species has "genetic continuity."

Many species are immediately recognized by the layman. A person who knows nothing about "species" would unfailingly recognize the copperhead and the water moccasin as distinct from one another. Other species, though scarcely more closely related to one another than are the copperhead and moccasin, are very similar in superficial appearance and close examination is required to tell them apart. In the Chicago area, for example, there are two species of garter snake—the common garter snake (*Thamnophis sirtalis*) and the plains garter snake (*Thamnophis radix*)—but they are never distinguished by the layman because superficially they are almost identical. The student of snakes has learned to discount such deceptive similarity. He has learned that these two garter snakes *never interbreed,* and hence that the seemingly trivial differences between them are really fundamental and constant.

All the garter snakes (or water snakes, or rattlesnakes) are more closely related to one another than they are to any other snakes. Such a group of species is therefore gathered together under a common name to form a **genus.** The species of garter snakes together form the genus *Thamnophis.* The name of the genus, together with that of any of its species, forms the **scientific name** (*Thamnophis radix,* for example). The scientific name is always written in italics to set it off from the rest of the text.* In a general way, the scientific name of an animal may be compared with our own surnames and given names. All the members of the "Smith" family have Smith for a surname (just as all the garter snakes are called *Thamnophis*). But just as there may be John Smith, Mary Smith, etc., in the Smith family, so there are *Thamnophis sirtalis, Thamnophis radix,* etc. in the garter snake genus.

It has been found, furthermore, that several genera will have characters in common (i. e., they are more closely related to one another than to any other genus), and genera are therefore grouped into larger units called **families.** Thus the copperhead, the water moccasin, the massasaugas, and the rattlesnakes all have a highly developed poison apparatus with a pair of long retractile fangs, a special sensory pit on each side of the face, and undivided plates under the tail. These snakes are therefore placed together to form the family Crotalidae (the pit vipers). Finally, all the families of snakes together form the **Order** Serpentes.

* The reader will note that the name of a person always follows the scientific name. This is the name of the man who first described, or "discovered," the species, and technically it forms a part of the scientific name. *Thamnophis megalops* Kennicott means that the species *megalops* was discovered and named by Robert Kennicott, who described it in 1860.

Modern study of snakes (and other animals as well) has revealed that even the species are made up of still smaller units, the **subspecies.** A wide-ranging species, like the common banded water snake which covers the whole eastern half of the United States, may be made up of several subspecies, each occupying a segment of the total range of the species. The subspecies are designated by adding a third name to the generic and specific names. Thus the eight subspecies of the banded water snake are:

Natrix sipedon sipedon	The northern banded water snake
" " *insularum*	The Lake Erie water snake
" " *pleuralis*	The midwest water snake
" " *fasciata*	The southern banded water snake
" " *confluens*	The Mississippi River water snake
" " *pictiventris*	The Florida water snake
" " *compressicauda* .	The flat-tailed water snake
" " *clarkii*	Clark's water snake

Subspecies differ sharply from species in that they are *geographically* distinct populations. Subspecies can and do interbreed freely, so that two subspecies *cannot occupy the the same area,* since they would promptly lose their identities because of interbreeding. This actually happens in the area where two subspecies come together; individuals from such areas are intermediate in character, and are known as "intergrades."

The beginner is likely to be somewhat confused by the fact that specimens cannot always be identified down to subspecies by means of their characters, and that he is repeatedly asked to determine them by means of their ranges. In the case of a subspecies the characters apply only to a majority of specimens, sometimes even in the center of its range, and break down completely (by definition) in a more or less wide "area of intergradation." We must assure the student who is disgusted to find that a single specimen may have to be identified by its geography rather than by its characters that the shadowy subspecific category has proved of very great value in descriptive zoology, making possible a far more detailed and intelligible arrangement of the multitude of living kinds of animals than was possible without it.

EXTERNAL CHARACTERS AND COLORATION

The external characters of snakes are so much used in classification, and hence in identification of specimens, that some acquaintance with these characters is necessary for any introduction to this group of animals.

BODY PROPORTIONS

While all snakes are elongate creatures, the relative slenderness or stockiness of body, the width of the head, and the relative length of the tail vary greatly. Among our North American snakes, the most slender are the rare Arizona tree snake (*Oxybelis microphthalmus*), the common rough green snake (*Opheodrys aestivus*) and some of the racers such as the striped whip snake (*Coluber taeniatus taeniatus*). Some tropical tree snakes are even more elongate. Our most stout-bodied snake is probably the water moccasin, and most of the pit vipers are relatively stocky in form and short-tailed. Most snakes have a flattened belly, but burrowing snakes may be quite cylindrical.

The relative size and breadth of the head varies, and it is customary to note whether it is wider than the neck or not distinct from the neck. In the blind snakes and many other burrowing forms the head is no wider than the body (or than the "neck"). At the opposite extreme are the rattlesnakes and other pit vipers, with the head greatly widened to make room for the enlarged poison glands.

The eye is well developed in all North American snakes except the blind snakes. It moves beneath a clear scale which appears to represent the lower eyelid of lizards, since numerous lizards are known in which there is a clear windowlike scale in the center of the lower eyelid, while in others the "window" is enlarged and the eyelid permanently raised. The eyes of snakes vary greatly in size. They are extremely small in some burrowing snakes, and so large as to modify the shape of the skull in others. In the blind snakes, which represent extreme modification for burrowing, the eyes lie beneath scales of the head, through which they are visible as pigmented spots. The pupil is round in the majority of our snakes, vertical and catlike in others. It is even horizontal in some Old World tropical forms.

The length of the snout anterior to the eyes may afford distinctive characters. The angle between the upper surface of the snout and its sides may be sharp or rounded; it is referred to as the *canthus rostralis.* The sides of the snout are termed the lores or the *loreal region.* The *loreal pit* is a sensory organ in this part of the head found only in the pit vipers. Elongation of the snout is associated with elongation of the scales covering it, while shortening, narrowing, or widening of the head are likewise reflected in changes in the head plates.

The mouth of most snakes extends far back beyond the eyes, to permit of wide opening for the swallowing of large food (see p. 51). Most snakes have a longitudinal groove, the *mental groove,* beneath the chin, bordered by enlarged scales, to permit the expansion of the skin when the jaws are spread.

The tail is ordinarily about a fourth of the total length, but may amount to a third or even two-fifths as in the rough green snake, or may be only about an eighth of the total in some short-tailed colubrid snakes. In the blind snakes the tail is extremely short, scarcely more than twice as long as broad; it is short also in our two types of boas and in the pit vipers. It may end in an enlarged spinelike scale, and some such structure no doubt gave rise to the remarkable rattle of the rattlesnakes. The tail of the true sea snakes is flattened and oarlike, and a small evolutionary step in this direction is to be seen in the flat-tailed water snake of the brackish waters along the Florida coast (*Natrix sipedon compressicauda*).

SEX CHARACTERS

The tail is usually somewhat longer in males than in females of the same species. The fact that the hemipenes (the paired organs for copulation) are retracted into the base of the tail gives it a distinctly stouter shape than that of the female. There are secondary male sexual characters in some snakes in the form of tubercles on the chin shields (diamond-backed water snake) and tubercles on the scales above the anus on each side (the ring-necked snakes). These tubercles are difficult to distinguish in keeled-scaled snakes, but may be found by attentive examination in water snakes and garter snakes as an accessory lump or node on the keel. These characters are entirely absent in many forms.

SCALE CHARACTERS

The evolution of the scaly covering of snakes has produced conspicuous differences between groups and between species. It is these "scale characters," together with characteristic color patterns, that are most used in the definition of the species of snakes. Again with the exception of the blind snakes, all our snakes have *ventral plates* or *"ventrals"* on the undersurface of the body, which extend across from side to side. The *subcaudal* plates, or simply *caudals,* beneath the tail, may be transverse like the ventrals, and are then said to be *single;* more usually they are in two rows. The ventrals and caudals of snakes correspond (with some variation) to the number of vertebrae. It is customary to count their number, beginning beneath the chin with the first one distinctly wider than long, and excluding the *anal plate,* which may be *divided* or *single,* that covers the anal cleft. The first caudal, when they are in two rows, is the first one that meets one of the opposite side. It is customary to count them on only one side, and to include the terminal single scale. The ventrals extend entirely across the belly in most of our snakes, but are much reduced in size in the boas *Charina* and *Lichanura,* and are not different from the smaller dorsal scales in the blind snakes (*Leptotyphlops*). In many snakes the ventrals extend onto the sides of the body, with a more or less abrupt angle where they turn upward; the ventrals are then said to be *angularly bent.* In some tropical tree snakes a sharp keel is present at the angulation of the ventrals, and in some even on the caudals.

The dorsal scales are usually longer than they are wide, arranged in straight longitudinal rows and in diagonal rows across the body, and in the vast majority of snakes are in an odd number of longitudinal rows. The number of rows often varies on different parts of the body, reflecting the amount of tapering. Counted a head length behind the head, at mid-body, and a short distance anterior to the anus, the

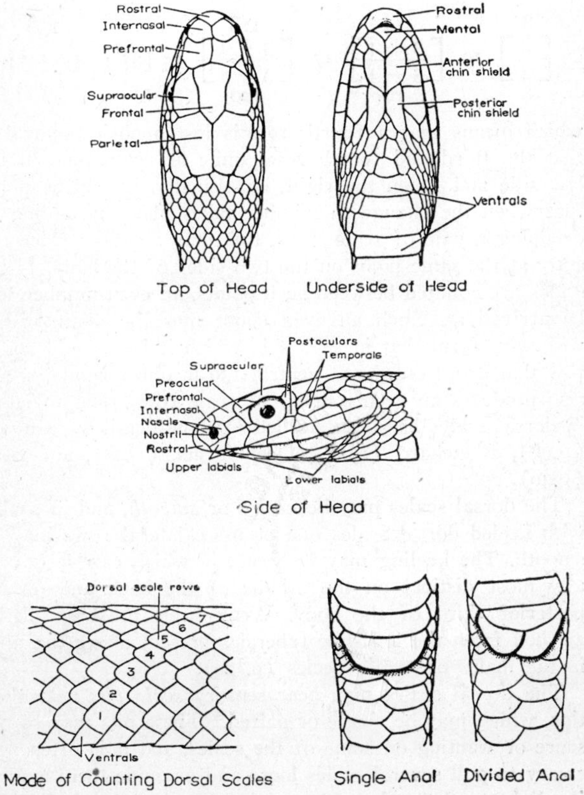

Fig. 1. Scale characters of snakes, with names of head scales.

6593

sucessive numbers give the *dorsal scale formula.* Thus a whip snake may have the scale formula 21-17-13, and such a simple statement suffices for all ordinary study. If examined in more detail, the complete dorsal scale formula would state every change in number of scale rows, and would note where (in terms of ventrals) the change takes place and *which row* is dropped or added. Thus a complete formula expanded from the above is:

$$21 \overset{8}{\underset{8}{\left[\frac{4}{4}\right]}} \ 19 \overset{14}{\underset{12}{\left[\frac{3+4}{3+4}\right]}} \ 17 \overset{118}{\underset{120}{\left[\frac{3+4}{3+4}\right]}} \ 15 \underset{130}{[8]} \ 14 \overset{150}{\underset{150}{[7+7]}} \ 13$$

which means that a fourth row is lost opposite ventral 8, that the third and fourth rows unite at ventral 14 on the left side and 12 on the right, etc. Finally, it may be noted that when the change in number takes place by adding or dropping a pair of scale rows, this may not take place exactly at the same point on the two sides of the body. If the scales are counted between such points, an even number will be arrived at. Such an even count must be distinguished with care from that in snakes in which it is the mid-dorsal row that drops out, as at ventral 130 in our formula, which also produces an even number of scale rows. The variation in dorsal scales has been studied in some detail by Ruthven (1908), Blanchard (1921), Ortenburger (1928), and Stull (1940).

The dorsal scales may be *keeled* or *smooth,* and in snakes with keeled dorsal scales one or more lateral rows may be smooth. The keeling may be weak, in which case it is usually most distinct on the middle of the back and on the posterior third of the body. Weak keels must be distinguished from the keel-like tubercles present above the anus in the males of some species (p. 26).

The dorsal scales may bear sensory *scale pits* near their tips, which may be single or paired.* These pits may be obscure or wanting on some of the scales, and it is often necessary to pull several scales loose and examine them against the light to determine the presence or absence of the pits.

* More numerous in some exotic forms

The scales covering the head are almost always enlarged and different from those on the rest of the body, and are referred to as the *head shields,* or plates of the head. There is a very uniform normal arrangement of these shields among snakes not modified for special habits. There are nine shields on the upper surface of the head: the paired *internasals, prefrontals, supraoculars,* and *parietals,* and the central *frontal* (Fig. 1). A *rostral* at the tip of the snout and a series of *upper labials* border the lip above, and a *mental* and a series of *lower labials* border it below. The *nasal plate,* either single, partly divided, or divided (into an anterior and posterior portion), encloses the nostril. This is followed (on the loreal region) by one or more *loreal plates* (or *loreals*), inserted between the nasal and the preoculars. The *preoculars* border the eye between the labials and the supraocular, and vary in number from one to three or more, as do the *postoculars,* which border the eye posteriorly. The *temporals* are the shields between the parietals above, the postoculars anteriorly, and the upper labials below. They are usually counted from front to back, stating the number in each vertical row—thus 1-2, or 2-2, or 2-2-3.

Since these shields may vary on the two sides of the head, it is customary to indicate this fact by writing the condition of the left side as a numerator and that on the right as a denominator. Thus, temporals $1 - \frac{2}{3}$ or 1 — 2/3 indicates that there is a single temporal in the first row on each side, while in the second row there are two on the left side and three on the right. The same notation is used for other variation between right and left side—thus "upper labials 7/8" means that there are seven on the left and eight on the right side.

The *chin shields* are elongate scales bordering the mental groove, and in contact anteriorly with the lower labials, usually an anterior and a posterior pair. Posteriorly *gular* scales are inserted between the lower labials and the anterior ventrals.

It is interesting to note the modifications of the head shields, especially of the snout, associated with burrowing habits (see *Heterodon, Lichanura, Leptotyphlops*), and with any change in shape of the head. Thus the elongate snout of *Oxybelis* has greatly elongate but otherwise unmodified scales. Widening of the head, on the other hand, as in the rattlesnakes, seems to involve breaking up of the head shields, which may be completely scalelike, usually with the exception of the supraoculars and certain other plates.

It is customary to prepare tables of scale counts of any series of specimens of snakes, as an indispensable basis for systematic studies (Fig. 7). A detailed description will, of course, state many other characteristics and relations between the various head scales besides those that can be put down as entries in a tabulation.

COLOR AND COLOR PATTERN

The species of snakes are often very well distinguished by their color patterns or colors, or both. Within the whole group there is an extraordinary diversity of both coloration and pattern. There are black, brown, gray, and green snakes in nearly solid colors, while more usually there is a pattern of darker markings on a lighter ground color, and the pattern may include brilliant yellows and reds. This pattern may consist of transverse bands or rings, of spots, or blotches, or of longitudinal stripes, and with almost every combination of the three. Pattern characters have been used wherever possible in defining species in this book, and the following terms, which are employed repeatedly, must be carefully distinguished (see Fig. 2):

Uniform ....a solid color, without any markings.
Stripe ....a narrow line of color running *lengthwise.*
Band ....a wider (more than 2 scale rows) line of color running lengthwise.
Blotch ....a large rounded or squarish marking, usually with a narrow dark border.
Spot ....a small rounded marking, usually without a border.
Crossband ....a half-ring of color extending across the sides and back, *but not across the belly.*

Ring ....a band of color completely encircling the body, therefore differing from a crossband in that it continues across the belly.

The colors of snakes are produced by a multitude of minute bodies, called chromatophores, in the scales. The chromatophores are of two very different kinds. One kind, typified by the so-called "melanophores," is colored because each of the bodies contains pigment. The melanophores are chiefly responsible for the blacks and browns of the pattern. The other kind of chromatophore, called "guanophores," produces color effects by optical diffraction. These bodies have no pigment, but contain small crystals that break up light rays in the same way that a prism does. The guanophores are the chief source of the yellows and whites seen in the

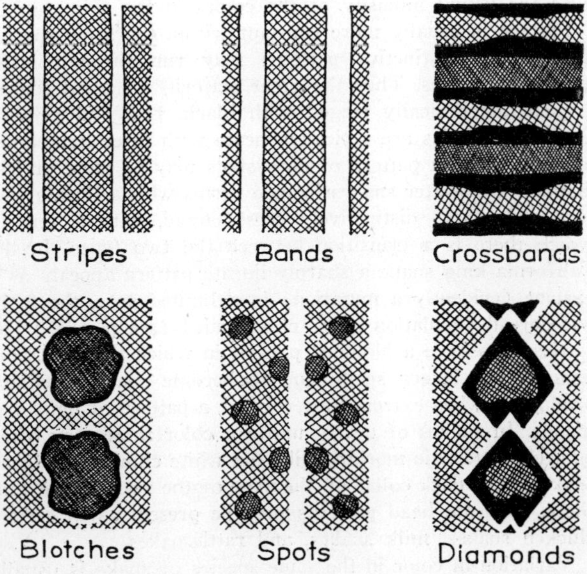

Fig. 2. Explanation of terms used in describing patterns of snakes.

ground colors of many snakes, and for the white tips of the scales found in many species. No studies have been made, but it is probable that the bright red found in coral snakes and other snakes is produced, as it is in other animals, by a third kind of chromatophore, the "allophores."

Snakes are unable to change color as many lizards can. Recent experiments by Hermann Rahn have revealed, however, that prairie rattlesnakes become very pale if their pituitary glands are removed, but assume their normal color again if an extract of the pituitary gland is injected into them. Since the pituitary gland governs color change in lizards, it seems that the situation is not fundamentally very different in lizards and snakes.

A snake is always comparatively very brilliant immediately after shedding its skin. This is because of the transparency of the new layer of cuticle and has nothing to do with the actual intensity of the colors in the skin.

Pattern is usually more constant within the same species than color. Distinctive patterns may run through large groups of snakes. Thus the great majority of coral snakes are characteristically ringed with black, red, and yellow; the garter snakes are typically lineate with three light lines, between which a pattern of dark spots may be more or less distinct. The water snakes include forms with a lineate pattern and others distinctively cross-barred, with a few in which there is a transition between the two types. In the California king snake a sharply lineate pattern appears as a variant (evidently a mutation) in a limited area, the more widespread population being crossbanded (see p. 180). The rattlesnakes have a blotched pattern in which the light borders of the larger spots tend to become sharply defined, producing, when extremely developed, a pattern of light diamonds. In snakes of nearly uniform color there may often be a characteristic marking, like the white chin of the black snake or the dark collar on the nape of the rear-fanged tantillas. Intricate head patterns may be present as in certain chicken snakes, milk snakes, and rattlesnakes.

Variation in color in the same species of snake is usually a matter of increase or decrease in the dark pigment of the ground color, obscuring the normal dark pattern or leaving it more distinct. Darkening of the coloration reaches an extreme as melanism, which may be more or less prevalent, and may tend to be especially frequent in a limited geographic area, as is the case with the common garter snakes of Ontario. Albinism, while rare, is well known in snakes and has been recorded for many species. It is characterized by absence of dark pigment throughout the specimen, the red blood vessels showing through the white skin, the eyes pink, and the normal dark pattern (in snakes that have one) showing vestigially in faint yellow. Yellow and red mutations (xanthism and erythrism) are also known. A yellowish brown and a bluish green phase are known as rare variants in the smooth green snake, and are doubtless due to the absence of one or the other of several types of chromatophores that combine to produce the normal green color.

Very few snakes exhibit conspicuous differences in coloration between the sexes. Juvenile patterns are almost invariably more sharply defined, with both the ground color and the color of the darker pattern more brilliant. The young of the common northeastern milk snake, whose adult pattern is brown and black or gray, is so red as often to be referred to as a "coral snake." The usual course of change from juvenile to adult pattern consists in a darkening of the ground color with resulting increasing obscurity of the pattern. Such a change is clearly seen in the water moccasin in which the young are almost as brightly marked as the copperhead, while the dark adults have the pattern extremely obscure, and may be quite black. One of the most remarkable changes of this nature in North American snakes is that from the spotted juvenile of the black snake or blue racer to the uniform black or greenish-gray of the adult. Other solid-colored snakes, like our green snakes, may exhibit scarcely any change of color with growth.

The relation of the coloration of the species of snakes to their surroundings may be quite evident or it may be obscure. In general, snakes of the desert tend to be pale, often resembling their background quite accurately. Snakes of humid forest regions tend to be dark. Tree snakes are usually green, resembling the foliage, but may be brown or variously spotted, perhaps resembling bark or vines. Terrestrial snakes of forested regions may have a blotched or barred pattern sometimes extremely like the background of dead leaves and sticks on which they lie. Even when they are apparently brightly colored, like the copperhead, such colorations may be surprisingly effective as concealment. Resemblance to the background appears to be definitely advantageous to the snake concerned, either by way of concealment from enemies or as a useful camouflage while lying in wait for prey. The dark markings on the sides of the head in many snakes apparently serve as camouflage to conceal the eye.

Klauber has pointed out that the snakes in the southern California area may be divided into "active," "moderate," and "slow" forms, and that the color patterns of the species are definitely correlated with the degree of activity. All the active species (racers, garter snakes, and patch-nosed snakes) are either unicolor or striped. Nearly all of the moderately active forms are ringed or blotched (king snakes, bull snakes, faded snake, etc.), while most of the slow snakes are blotched (rattlesnakes, leaf-nosed snake). In commenting further on the pattern of active snakes this author states that "the effect of color continuity and its value in escape can be best observed by attempting to follow with the eye such a snake as the striped whip snake traveling amongst brush or rocks. Try as you will to follow the head, your eye will become anchored to what appears to be a stationary section of the body, in a striking contrast of black with the two bright yellow stripes. But this stationary section is in reality a flowing body; curiously, without apparent longitudinal motion, it seems to diminish in width, the tail flashes by and it has vanished, before the eye can be advanced to another section."

The brilliantly colored snakes like the coral snakes and coral king snakes are for the most part burrowers, or are at least secretive in their habits. Protective resemblance can scarcely explain their color patterns, and is clearly not the entire explanation of the diverse color and patterns of snakes in general. It may well be that some distinctive color patterns are due to obscure factors in the evolution of snakes, and may in fact be quite useless to the snake.

The color of the skin between the scales may be quite independent of the pattern, and different from that of the scales, appearing only when the skin is stretched; or, this skin pattern may be directly associated with the pattern and coloration of the scales. Many snakes of tropical regions spread or inflate the neck, exhibiting bright colors or markings which are concealed in the normal condition. This feature of coloration is exhibited by our hog-nosed snakes, in which the pattern of the neck becomes much more conspicuous when it is spread in their characteristic warning behavior (p. 117).

Changes of coloration in the course of evolution may be indicated in series of related forms. The reader is referred to such series as the milk snakes (p. 185) and king snakes (p. 166) for examples, and to the literature, especially Blanchard's paper on the king snakes and Gloyd's on the rattlesnakes, for speculations as to the evolutionary history of such series.

THE POISON APPARATUS AND TREATMENT OF SNAKE BITE

The effects from the bite of a poisonous snake are so remarkable that it is not surprising that the venomousness of a few has given rise to a widespread fear of all snakes. The snakes of the United States and Canada actually include only seventeen species in any way dangerous to man, and a number of these are so rare or secretive that there is no record of a human being being bitten by them. It is not as widely understood as it should be that the venom and venom-injecting apparatus of snakes are primarily *for the capture of their food.* Their use for defense against larger animals is entirely secondary.

The genuinely poisonous snakes are dangerous to man in almost direct proportion to their size. The large eastern and western diamond-backed rattlesnakes and their more western relatives are among the most dangerous snakes of the world. We are extraordinarily fortunate that these creatures usually give their warning rattle when approached, and that they are not likely to strike in any case until actually molested. The copperhead and water moccasin, which are so well known in the eastern and southern states, are somewhat more feared than the rattlesnakes, on account of their failure to give any warning; but these species are also slow to strike. The poisonous coral snake is so inoffensive that it is often taken by the hand under the impression that so handsome a creature must be harmless; but the extreme potency of its venom makes such handling highly dangerous.

It would be extremely satisfactory if one could give some simple rule whereby poisonous snakes could be distinguished at a glance from the harmless ones, but there is none. The poison-conducting fangs, long and folding in the pit vipers and short and fixed in the coral snakes, are an infallible means of distinguishing the dangerously venomous forms; but these are best looked for in the dead snake. The head is triangular in shape in the pit vipers due to its enlargement for the poison glands; but there are numerous harmless water snakes and various others in which the head is so well set off from the neck that this simple rule fails. Fortunately the recognition of rattlesnakes is made simple by the rattle. This leaves only the copperheads and the water moccasin and the two kinds of coral snakes. Everyone who spends much time in hunting or fishing or camping in the regions where these snakes occur should learn to recognize them at sight. This is simple in the case of the coral snakes and the copperheads, which have a characteristic pattern. The adult water moccasin is nearly without pattern; it should be recognizable from its curiously shaped head and of course from its habit of facing one when approached with its mouth widely opened, the white interior of which gives it the name "cottonmouth." The juvenile water moccasin has a pattern not very different from that of the copperhead.

The living types of snakes exhibit various stages of the development of a poison apparatus. Even in the non-poisonous water snakes experiments seem to show that the saliva, when injected into small animals, has some poisonous qualities. This makes it easier to understand the fact that grooved teeth and the alteration of a part of the salivary glands (the parotid) for venom production have apparently been developed independently in various groups of snakes.

The rear-fanged or "opisthoglyph" * snakes have one or more enlarged teeth at the rear of the upper jaw, each with a groove on the front face of the tooth. There are numerous such snakes in tropical regions, while we have only the genera *Coniophanes, Tantilla, Leptodeira, Trimorphodon,* and *Oxybelis* within the United States.

The front-fanged or "proteroglyph" snakes include the cobras of the Old World and the mambas of Africa, with various other forms and numerous distinct types in Australia. In North America this group of snakes is represented only by the very poisonous coral snakes of the genera *Micrurus* and *Micruroides.* In these snakes the head is not at all wider than the body, and the venom glands must be small;

---

* Opisthoglyph means rear-grooved in Greek.

but the venom is extremely potent as is shown by the high proportion of deaths in the few recorded cases of bite from them. In these snakes the poison-conducting fang is at the front end of the upper jaw, and it is greatly improved from the grooved condition by the closing of the groove in front.

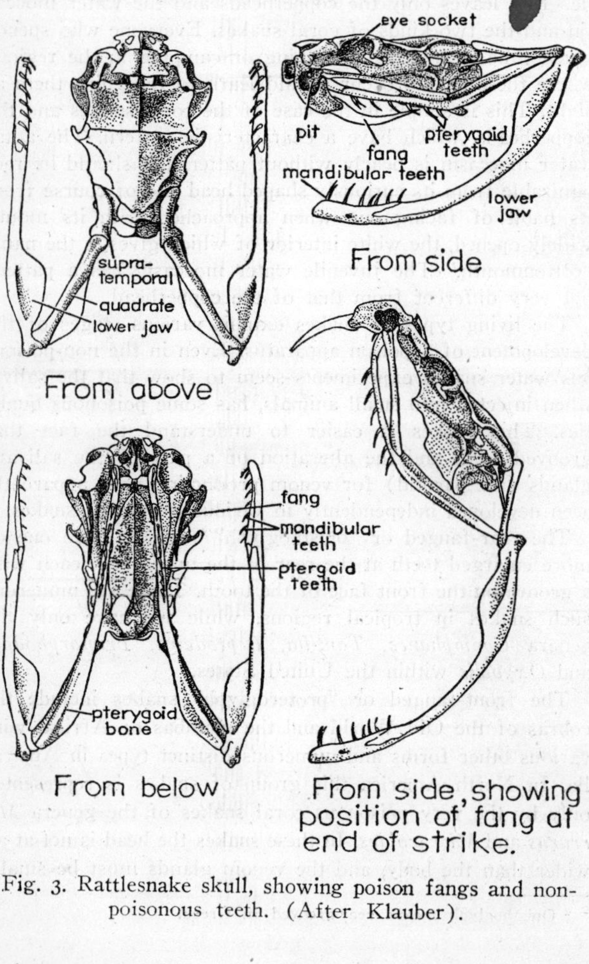

Fig. 3. Rattlesnake skull, showing poison fangs and non-poisonous teeth. (After Klauber).

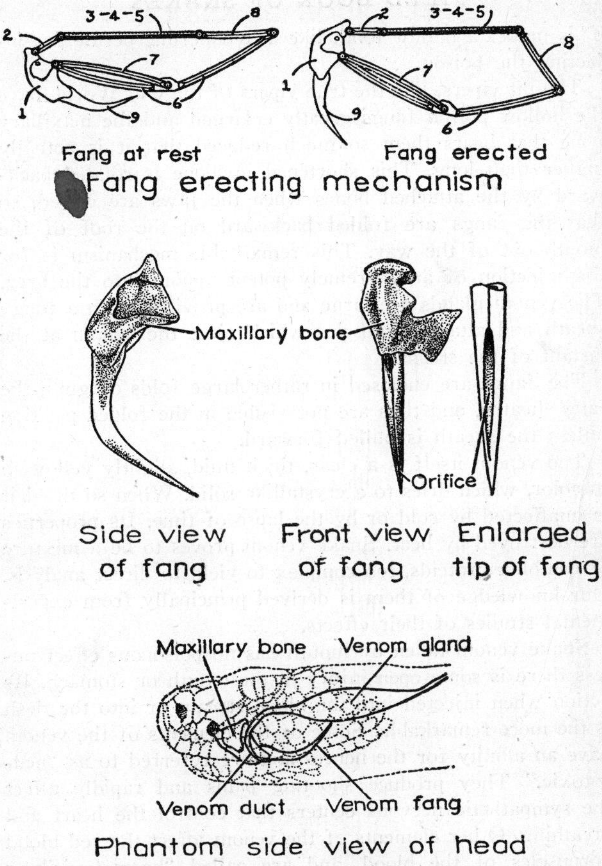

Fig. 4. Poison apparatus of rattlesnake. (*Above*) Fang-tilting mechanism, diagrammed. 1, maxillary bone. 2, prefrontal. 3, 4, 5, frontal, parietal, and supratemporal bones. 6, pterygoid. 7, ectopterygoid. 8, quadrate. 9, fang. The quadrate pushes the pterygoid and ectopterygoid forward; these, pushing against the base of the maxillary bone (with a short leverage), rotate the fang through nearly a 90° angle. (*Middle*) Details of fang. (*Below*) Phantom side view of head, showing position of venom gland and duct in relation to the fang. (After Klauber).

This makes a hollow tooth like a hypodermic needle for injecting the poison.

The pit vipers, like the true vipers of the Old World, have the hollow poison fangs greatly enlarged and the maxillary bone that bears them so much reduced that it is actually higher than long. This shortened jawbone is rotated backward by the attached bones when the jaws are closed, so that the fangs are folded backward on the roof of the mouth out of the way. This remarkable mechanism is for the injection of an extremely potent venom into the prey. The venom glands are large and are provided with a tough sheath and attached muscles which eject the venom at the instant of the strike.

The fangs are enclosed in rather large folds of gum, the fang sheaths, and thus are not visible in the folded position unless the sheath is pulled forward.

The venom itself is a clear, thick fluid, slightly yellowish in color, which dries to a crystallike solid. When so dried it is unaffected by cold or by the lapse of time. Its properties are destroyed by heat. Snake venom proves to be a mixture of complex proteids, too complex to yield to direct analysis. Our knowledge of them is derived principally from experimental studies of their effects.

Snake venom taken by mouth has no poisonous effect unless there is some open injury in the mouth or stomach. Its action when injected into the blood stream or into the flesh is the more remarkable. Some of the elements of the venom have an affinity for the nerves and are referred to as "neurotoxic." They produce shooting pains and rapidly affect the sympathetic nervous centers that control the heart and breathing. Other elements of the venom affect the red blood corpuscles of the blood, and are called "haemotoxic" or "haemorhaghic." Still others appear to affect the walls of the capillary vessels, dissolve them, and permit the blood to escape into the tissues. It is this rapidly blackening blood that produces the most startling of the symptoms of snake bite from our pit vipers, the great swelling and discoloration of the parts near the bite.

One of the most remarkable effects of snake venom is to call forth the production by the victim's blood of an antivenin that counteracts it. If a horse be injected with gradually increasing doses of venom, it becomes entirely immune to a dose of venom many times as great as would have killed it at first. The antivenin is contained in the serum of the blood, and it is an effective antidote for man and other animals if injected into the blood stream of the victim of snake bite. A suitable amount of blood is drawn off from an immunized horse, centrifuged to remove the blood corpuscles, concentrated, and preserved in sealed glass tubes. As prepared for use, these tubes may be provided with a built-in hypodermic apparatus for the injection of the antivenin.

The high hopes raised by the apparently magical effect of antivenin under experimental conditions and in some cases of accidental snake bite have not been entirely sustained by further investigation. Perhaps the principal difficulty lies in the extremely specific nature of the venoms and of the antivenins that counteract them. Thus antivenin prepared by the use of rattlesnake venom does not perfectly neutralize the venom of a copperhead, nor even that of another species of rattlesnake, and has little or no effect on coral-snake venom. It is impossible for an ordinary person to carry several tubes of different kinds of antivenin (which would cost several dollars each), and many persons would not recognize the kind of snake that had bitten them. The antivenin manufactured for North American snakes is accordingly made as a mixture, a so-called "polyvalent" serum, to counteract the effect of the bite of the rattlesnakes and of that of the copperhead and water moccasin.

The treatment of snake bite has been cursed for ages by a host of popular remedies ranging from pure witchcraft to the serious attempt to neutralize the poison with burning gunpowder or some strong disinfecting agent such as permanganate of potash. It is somewhat horrifying to learn that the injection of permanganate solution in the vicinity of the bite, which was long recommended by the medical profession, is no more effective than the application of half of a freshly killed chicken, and is in fact more positively harmful. Modern experimentation has fortunately developed a first-aid procedure which is genuinely effective.

The first aid now shown to be most effective consists simply in cutting open the spot bitten and the application of continued suction. Suction by mouth would be better than none; suction by means of the small rubber bulb in suction kits available on the market for this purpose proves to be astonishingly effective.*

The first-aid procedure now recommended results from experiments and experience in treatment of snake bite by Dr. Dudley Jackson, of the Robert B. Green Hospital, at San Antonio, Texas. Dr. H. K. Gloyd ** suggests the following:

1. Do not run or do anything that will speed up circulation; do not use whisky or other forms of alcohol internally.

2. Apply a tourniquet between the bite and the heart. Do not tie it too tight. Soft rubber tubing, such as that furnished with the various snake-bite kits, makes the best tourniquet, but a shoe string, handkerchief, or necktie will do.

3. Sterilize the skin over the area of the bite and with a sharp knife or razor blade, also sterilized, make cross cuts over each fang mark at least a quarter of an inch deep. Any standard antiseptic, such as iodine or mercurochrome, may be used for sterilization. If an antiseptic is not available, use the flame of a match.

4. Apply suction to the incision. If the small rubber bulbs supplied with kits for this purpose are not available, the mouth may be used. There is no danger if there are no cuts or sores in the mouth or on the lips. The venom must get into the blood stream to cause harm.

   A sheet of thin rubber through which to suck is the best and simplest first aid equipment.

5. Continue the suction, loosening the tourniquet every ten minutes for a few seconds. As swelling progresses the

---

* These are the B-D Snake Bite Outfit No. 2006, Becton-Dickinson and Co., Rutherford, N. J.; the Dudley Kit, made by the Flack-Hendrick Co. of San Antonio, Texas; and the Venex Snake Bite Outfit, made by the E. D. Bullard Co., Chicago.

** Gloyd, H. K. 1938. *Bull. Jackson Park Br. Chicago Medical Soc.* Vol. 15, No. 7, pp. 3-11, and No. 8, pp. 13-17.

tourniquet should be moved and kept just above it, and just tight enough to retard, but not obstruct, the flow of blood in the veins. Great harm may result if it is too tight. It should be loose enough to allow a finger to be slipped under it easily.

6. Get to a doctor or hospital as quickly as possible. Meanwhile continue suction.
7. If antivenin is available, after about an hour of suction, inject five ampouls (50 cc) directly into the bite and the surrounding areas. An amount smaller than this, according to Dr. Jackson, is of no practical value.

   On account of the serum reaction suffered by many persons, antivenin should be given only by a physician, except in cases of extreme emergency.
8. If antivenin has been given as above, wait one hour before resuming suction; otherwise continue the active suction treatment.

   By this time you should have reached a physician. If not, continue suction for at least 15 hours.

We have slightly modified Dr. Gloyd's suggestions. It should be strongly emphasized that a snake-bitten person should be taken to a physician or hospital at once, if possible. Only a physician is qualified to meet emergencies that may arise during treatment.

HABITS AND BEHAVIOR

A snake is one of the most highly specialized of all backboned animals. Nearly every structure of its body, even including its internal organs, is more or less different from the corresponding structures of other animals. It is remarkable that every one of these adaptations may be traced directly to a single cause—the fact that snakes have lost their legs, in the course of the evolution of their elongate body form—no matter how remotely the structure in question may be related to locomotion. Nearly all snakes have only one lung, for example, because a legless creature must have a long and slender body if it is to move with speed and efficiency, and this does not leave space for two lungs lying side by side. For the same reason the heart is pulled out into a long organ that looks little like the heart of other animals, and the gall bladder is located far behind the liver instead of being embedded in it in the usual way. The unique architecture of the skull, which enables a snake to engulf an animal greatly exceeding the diameter of its own head, may be attributed in part to the same cause. Without any means of holding an animal down a snake cannot tear its prey apart. Therefore, unless it is to content itself with such relatively minute food as insects, a snake must be capable of swallowing fair-sized prey entire.

Since the loss of their legs has influenced the structure and behavior of snakes so profoundly, it is only natural that students of snakes should have tried to determine how they came to lose them. Fossils do not help, since all known fossil snakes are as specialized in this respect as the ones living today. There are two chief theories, each supported to some extent by technical details in the structure of snakes. One theory is that snakes originally lived in the high grass of savannah regions, where legs would have been a hindrance to gliding swiftly and easily through the close-packed vegetation. The original snakes would then have been something like such elongate limbless lizards as the glass snakes, which move about actively on the surface of the ground. Such limbless but still terrestrial lizards have developed independently in various parts of the world, and they naturally exhibit snakelike characteristics. The second theory, which is based on the fact that many burrowing animals tend to lose their legs, is that the ancestors of snakes lived underground. The eyes of burrowing animals also degenerate, and Dr. Gordon L. Walls, who has studied the eyes of lizards and snakes in great detail, finds that a snake's eyes are quite different from those of lizards and other animals. He believes, consequently, that the eyes of snakes were redeveloped from degenerate vestiges after snakes returned to a life above ground.

HABITAT

Such snakes as the banded sand snake (*Chilomeniscus*) and the horned rattlesnake are not found anywhere except in deserts. Other snakes, like the blind snakes (*Leptotyphlops*), live underground like earthworms, and rarely come to the surface unless drowned out by rains or floods. In the tropics some kinds of snakes spend their entire lives in trees, apparently never descending to the ground. The structure and behavior of all these snakes are greatly altered to adapt them to their respective environments.

Such examples are extreme cases of habitat restriction. Most of our snakes are much less particular as to where they live, and many seem to range promiscuously over a variety of environments. Nevertheless, careful study would probably show that every kind of snake has some sort of habitat preference, dictated by soil and vegetation conditions, temperature, moisture, feeding habits, or still more obscure psychic or physiological factors within the snake itself. Remarkably little is known of the habitat preferences of even our commonest snakes, and because such studies cannot be made on preserved snakes in a museum or captive snakes in a zoo they offer an excellent opportunity for the intelligent amateur to contribute to our fund of knowledge.

An example of the kind of factor that may be responsible for the general distribution of snakes is afforded by a study recently made by the senior author. Botanists have long known that a tongue or "peninsula" of the western prairies extends eastward across northern Illinois, Indiana, Michigan, Ohio, and into western Pennsylvania and New York. Civilization has greatly altered the character of this area, but careful study shows that the distribution of such snakes as the fox snake, Kirtland's water snake, Butler's garter snake, and the eastern massasauga coincide almost exactly with its boundaries, although no one knows exactly why they do not spread out into the surrounding regions.

LOCOMOTION

A red racer is able to cover ground at an astonishing rate, its speed and grace being almost incredible for an animal that has no legs. Other snakes can outclimb the monkeys, outswim the fishes, or outburrow the earthworms. The mechanical adjustments that enable snakes to perform these feats are among the most remarkable in nature. They have been studied in great detail by the late Dr. Walter Mosauer, but cannot be discussed here except to point out that the backbone gains its great flexibility from the great number of vertebrae (up to 200 and more) of which it is composed, and that the muscles that bend it (several pairs to each vertebra) may be long stringlike affairs extending over a dozen or more joints.

Much nonsense has been written about the speed of snakes, and stories about snakes outrunning men are false. Because of its slender form a racer looks as if it were traveling faster that it really is. Moreover, a snake is rarely encountered where there are no shrubs or bushes, and there is no question that an agile snake could *outdodge* a man under such circumstances. Dr. Mosauer tested the speeds of various snakes by placing them in the center of a measured circle and timing them with a stop watch. The following table summarizes his results.

Species	Number of trials	Prowling speed miles per hour	Maximum speed miles per hour
Lichanura r. roseofusca	7	.09	.22
Lampropeltis multicincta	12	.17	.72
Pituophis spp.	36	.13	1.18
Salvadora h. hexalepis	12	.22	1.43
Crotalus cerastes	41	.31	2.04
Coluber f. frenatus	39	.29	3.60

Dr. Mosauer found that there are three main types of locomotion in snakes. The one used by most snakes he calls the "horizontal undulatory" type—what would, with less accuracy, be called simply "wriggling" by most people. The body is thrown into a series of gentle curves (sideways, not up-and-down as many people believe), and then seems to flow smoothly along these curves like a stream of water flowing along a narrow, winding bed. Actually each of the curves is pushing against irregularities in the ground, grass stems, or other points of contact, thus thrusting the snake forward. That this is actually the case may be demonstrated by allowing a snake to crawl in fine sand and then examining its track; a little pile of sand back of each curve shows where the push was exerted. A spectacular proof is provided by placing the snake on a piece of smooth glass. It will thrash about helplessly, making little or no progress, but if a staggered row of pegs is fastened to the glass it is able to crawl through them with ease.

A second type of locomotion is often used by relatively clumsy, heavy-bodied snakes such as rattlesnakes. If one of these snakes is allowed to crawl in sand it leaves a straight track, as if a piece of heavy rope had been dragged along. Careful examination of the crawling snake reveals that it is moving by alternate movement of the skin on the body and of the body within its tube of skin. Little waves can be seen traveling over the body as the skin is pulled forward, then anchored by pressing the edges of the belly plates against irregularities in the ground. Dr. Mosauer called this the "caterpillar" type of locomotion.

The third type of locomotion is "sidewinding," and is used only by the sidewinder (*Crotalus cerastes*) among our North American snakes. This extraordinary method of crawling, which is described on p. 300, is a special adaptation for crawling on the loose sand of the desert, which is the home of the sidewinder. A fourth type of locomotion, not emphasized by Mosauer, consists of thrusting the head and fore part of the body forward, anchoring it, and then hauling the rear part of the body forward.

Any snake can swim if placed in water, and all snakes, whether natural swimmers or not, swim by the "horizontal undulatory" type of movement. The sea snakes, which rarely come out of the water, have their swimming ability greatly increased by having the tail vertically flattened into an oarlike structure. A suggestion of this flattening is found in some of our water snakes (*Natrix*). Flat tails are very common in aquatic animals, occurring for example in musk-rats, otters, many lizards, and even in the ridiculously small tail of the hippopotamus!

Because their bodies are long and flexible, any snake is able to climb, and any kind of snake is likely to be found in bushes or trees at one time or another. This is true even of the heavy-bodied rattlesnakes. Snakes that spend much time in climbing have developed special techniques. The black snake and blue racer are able to crawl along the tops of bushes nearly as fast as they can on the ground, merely by distributing their weight over the twigs. Bull snakes and rat snakes can climb vertical tree trunks by pressing little folds of their bellies into crevices in the bark, and some tropical snakes even have a special ridge along each side of the belly to assist in this. There are no true tree snakes in the United States, although the rough green snake and the Arizona vine snake are very similar to some of the tropical tree snakes. In the tropics, tree snakes are of two different kinds. One kind has the body extremely long and slender, and stiff like a piece of wire so that the snake can reach across from one branch to another. The other kind has a short, heavy body, but the tail is "prehensile," i.e., it is a strong fingerlike structure that can wrap tightly around a branch and support the entire weight of the snake.

Burrowing snakes have only their heads to assist them, but many different kinds of snakes are skillful burrowers, some, like the blind snakes, even living like earthworms in the ground. No one has made a careful study of burrowing in snakes, but preliminary studies by the junior author show that the method used, and the modification of the head that goes with it, depends on whether the snake lives in sand, mud, or soil. All burrowers have the bones of the skull more or less consolidated to withstand the pressure to which the head is subjected. Sand burrowers, like the banded burrowing snake, the leaf-nosed snakes, and the hog-nosed snakes, use their heads as augurs or shovels, and all these snakes have the head more or less modified to increase its efficiency (see Figs. 66, 36, and 25). Mud burrowers, like the mud snake and the rainbow snake, have conical heads and glassy-smooth scales. No one knows how they use their heads in burrowing. Bull snakes have very pointed noses, which aids them in digging into pocket gopher burrows.

Certain snakes have been seen to use a loop of the neck to scrape out small hollows in sand. This method of burrowing could hardly be very efficient, and no one knows why or how generally snakes use it. It is said that bull snakes use this method to scoop out the ground loosened by their noses, when they excavate pocket gopher burrows.

FOOD AND FEEDING

All snakes live exclusively on animal food; leaves or grass blades occasionally found in the stomach have been swallowed accidentally while the snake was engulfing its prey. The size of the food is roughly proportional to the size of the snake, the smaller species feeding on insects, spiders, slugs and other small creatures, while the larger forms subsist chiefly on fishes, frogs, lizards, birds, and small mammals.

To some extent the type of food eaten by a particular kind of snake is determined by the kind of environment in which the snake lives. Water snakes live largely on fishes, frogs, tadpoles, and crayfish because these animals are abundant where water snakes live, while desert snakes eat chiefly lizards and small mammals.

It was formerly thought that most snakes are very particular about what they eat, restricting their diets to one kind of animal. Recently several important studies based on analysis of the contents of hundreds of stomachs,* together with accumulated exact information, have revealed that most snakes eat a considerable variety of food. A few snakes, like the Florida swamp snake and the queen snake, both of which rarely eat anything but crayfish, and the red-bellied snake, which seems to eat slugs almost exclusively, are exceptions.

Snakes find their food by foraging for it, spotting prey by means of their eyes. Odor also plays a part in recognizing food. A few years ago a Swiss zoo keeper wrote of a European water snake that vigorously tried to swallow a part of its own body that was scented with fish, and there are many records of rat snakes having swallowed china nest eggs. Laboratory experiments have shown that hungry DeKay's snakes will follow a trail made by rubbing earthworm "extract" along the floor of a cage.

Snakes can live for months without eating, but their appetites when food is abundant are prodigious. There are many records of captive snakes eating mice or frogs, one after the other, almost as long as they were provided. Klauber fed 30 tree frogs to a moderate-sized two-striped garter snake, which it ate as rapidly as they were handed in. Occasionally garter snakes are found in nature that are so stuffed with earthworms that they look like sausages and are barely able to move.

Prey is subdued in one of four ways: by merely seizing it in the mouth and swallowing it directly; by holding it down with a coil of the body; by constricting it; or by means of venom. Constriction, which is employed only by certain snakes (the bull snakes, for example), is well known but often misunderstood. Prey is not literally crushed, as many people think. Instead the heart action is stopped by

---

* Notably Uhler, Cottam, and Clarke, 1939, *Trans. Fourth Amer. Wildlife Conference,* pp. 605-622 (snakes of the George Washington National Forest, Virginia), and Fitch, 1941, *Calif. Fish and Game,* Vol. 27, No. 2, pp. 1-32 (California garter snakes).

the powerful squeezing of the snake, and the animal is thus quickly killed. It should also be emphasized that venomous snakes use their poison apparatus primarily for securing food, rather than for defending themselves.

Swallowing the prey is an extremely complicated operation that is not thoroughly understood. A complex chain of bones that fastens the lower jaw to the skull may be moved out sideways, which greatly increases the size of the mouth opening. This, together with the fact that the throat is very elastic, makes it possible for a snake to swallow an object several times the size of its own head. Actually, in swallowing, the snake slowly draws itself forward over its prey, instead of swallowing it by means of the tongue as human beings do. The two halves of the upper jaw and the two halves of the lower jaw may be moved independently, and by moving each of these four elements forward independently and in rotation, and anchoring each by means of the needle-sharp teeth, the snake slowly crawls over its prey. This operation is extremely slow if the prey is much larger than the snake. Sometimes more than an hour elapses before the last of the prey disappears into the snake's mouth. At the other extreme, a garter snake eating an earthworm draws it in quickly, chiefly by contracting the muscles in its throat. The effect is somewhat similar to a small boy sucking in a piece of spaghetti.

A snake cannot live long without water. It drinks like a horse, thrusting its nose in and sucking up water by means of rhythmic contractions of its throat.

BREEDING HABITS

Snakes usually gather in considerable numbers to hibernate over winter. Mating takes place in the spring, before the members of the colony have scattered for the summer. There are isolated records of snakes mating in the fall, but fall matings are not typical for any species. Exact mating dates, where they are known, are given under the discussions of individual species.

Like most other animals, snakes engage in a "courtship" behavior before mating. Courtship has been observed for a very few species only, and careful descriptions, or better still, motion picture records, of this behavior offer a wide-open field to the amateur. Courtship behavior is very characteristic for any given species, and there are at least two basically different types among the snakes of the United States. In garter snakes and water snakes the male rubs his chin along the back of the female until he reaches the neck region, the female remaining entirely passive. The chin of the male in these snakes is provided with minute sensory organs (visible to the naked eye in the diamond-backed water snake, Fig. 70), and the rubbing apparently serves to stimulate him. The racers engage in a sort of courtship "dance," in which both sexes participate.

There have been many attempts to determine the gestation periods for various species of snakes. It is now known, however, that a female will continue to lay fertile eggs for several years after being isolated from males, so that there is probably no relation between the time of mating and the time of egg-laying or giving birth.

Some of our snakes lay eggs, while others give birth to living young. Among American snakes, the species bearing living young outnumber those laying eggs. Details as to the egg-laying or live-bearing habits are given under each species.

Snakes that bear their young alive produce them in late summer and early fall (late July to early October). Until recently it was thought that live-bearing snakes merely retained the eggs in the oviduct, but it is now known that at least in some snakes (and perhaps only to a limited extent) the embryos are nourished by the mother somewhat as they are in mammals. The number of young in a brood varies enormously, even between different individuals of the same species. Small snakes generally have fewer young than larger snakes do, the little DeKay's snake sometimes having only two or three at a time. Garter snakes and water snakes are very prolific. There is a record of a common garter snake that produced 78 young, and of a common water snake that had 76.

The female usually refuses food for several days preceding parturition. Just before the young are born she becomes restless, although she lies quietly while the young are emerging, elevating her tail and extruding them one at a time. The entire process may consume from a few minutes to more than an hour. When large numbers of young are produced they usually arrive in series of about a half dozen, with a rest period of several minutes between each group. Each snake is enclosed in a thin transparent membrane at birth, which it ruptures, and then sallies forth, ready to shift for itself from the start. The mother takes no interest in her young after they are born.

Egg-laying species deposit their eggs in a variety of situations, usually deserting them to hatch of themselves. Decaying vegetation, rotting logs, manure piles, and holes in embankments are the sites usually chosen. The actual process of nest building has rarely been witnessed under natural conditions. In some species, notably the ring-necked snakes, a number of females often lay at the same site, so that large numbers of eggs may be found together.

There is much variation in the number of eggs laid by a species, and also considerable variation in the size of the eggs in a clutch. The eggs (Plate 7) are elongate, white in color when laid, and covered with a tough leathery shell. The eggs of some snakes adhere tightly to one another, while those of other snakes are free. The eggs are surprisingly large in small species, those of the little smooth green snake measuring an inch in length while those of the bull snake are only a little more than two inches long.

Eggs are laid during June and July, sometimes even into early August. The incubation period depends on the stage of development of the embryo at laying and on the temperature at which the eggs are kept. Consequently there is no definite period of incubation for any species. Eggs have been known to hatch within four days after they were laid, while at the other extreme more than three months were required. In general, hatching takes place during August and September. The young snakes, of course, are able to fend for themselves from the start.

GROWTH AND LONGEVITY

Snakes differ from most other animals in that they do not stop growing when they become adult. Instead their rate of growth merely slows down and they continue to grow at a gradually diminishing rate, apparently as long as they live. For this reason the "maximum length" of a large species may exceed the "average adult length" by several feet. Both of these measurements are given for each species, in so far as they are known, on the following pages. There are occasional reliable reports of snakes that so greatly exceed the normal limits of their species that they should probably be regarded as freakish giants. It is not known whether such giants are very old individuals that have grown slowly for many years, or whether they are caused by abnormal functioning of the ductless glands, as human giants are.

The most obvious way of determining how fast a snake grows would be to measure a captive individual at regular intervals. Unfortunately this simple method yields very misleading results because the growth rate of snakes is affected by temperature, food, and other factors that would be quite different under natural conditions. In most parts of the United States snakes hibernate over winter, and growth is greatly retarded or stops entirely during this period. Blanchard allowed only five growing months for snakes in northern Michigan, for example.

The average growth rate for any species may be determined accurately by collecting large numbers of specimens during any given month, and then measuring the length of each one. When these measurements are assembled it is found that the length of those snakes not yet full grown tend to fall into several "size groups," and each size group represents snakes of a certain age. The chief difficulty of this method is the large number of specimens required (hundreds, if the results are to be accurate), and for this reason the growth rate is known for very few of our snakes. Klauber has studied growth in the Pacific rattlesnake (*Crotalus v. oreganus*), and Blanchard in the red-bellied snake (*Storeria occipitomaculata*). Their results on these two representative American snakes may be summarized as follows:

	Length at birth	*At 1 yr.*	*At 2 yrs.*	*Av. adult length*	*Maximum known length*
Crotalus	10¾″	21″	31½″	36-45″	54″
Storeria	3⅜″	7¾″		9¾″	13″

These figures show that snakes grow much more rapidly than is usually supposed. Both of these species more than double their length during their first year of life, and information on snakes from other parts of the world indicates that this is true of snakes in general. The rattlesnake becomes sexually mature during its third year, the red-bellied snake during its second.

How long will a snake live? This question is even harder to answer than are questions as to growth rate. Our only information is based on records of captive individuals, and these figures may vary widely from the normal life span under natural conditions. In 1925, Major S. S. Flower published a summary of all the known records (chiefly from the London Zoo) of snakes that had survived ten years or longer in captivity. The following list, taken from his paper, gives the *longest* (not average) period that various snakes have lived in captivity.

Boa constrictor	23	years
European viper	22	"
Reticulated python	21	"
Water moccasin	21	"
Pilot blacksnake	14	"
Cobra	13	"
Rattlesnake	13	"
Garter snake	11	"

Flower concluded that any snake will probably die of old age soon after twenty years. Some kinds of snakes, of course, would succumb to old age much sooner.

SKIN SHEDDING

One of the most characteristic features of snakes is that at intervals they literally "crawl out of their skins," leaving the cast skin behind as a ghostlike replica of themselves.

Such semitransparent skins are often found by those who visit places frequented by snakes. Klauber reported finding a dozen recently shed skins around a single boulder, where a group of snakes had apparently had a skin-shedding rendezvous. Such a find is most unusual; ordinarily cast skins are found singly.

Careful examination of one of these skins reveals that every minute detail of the outer surface of the snake is faithfully preserved, even to the transparent circular windows that cover the eyes. The skin that covered each scale looks like a tiny lens, surrounded by a raised network of thinner skin that represents the folds that lay between the scales. Often it is possible to identify the species to which the skin belonged.

Robert M. Stabler kept a careful record of the frequency with which a group of twenty-one captive snakes shed. His records (*Copeia,* 1939:227) show that during the warm six months (late spring, summer, and early fall) when they were active these snakes molted at quite regular intervals of one and a half months, irrespective of the species.

Molting in snakes consists of shedding the outermost layer of skin (the cuticle), which of course has been replaced by a new layer of cuticle that develops from below. Ten days or so before it sheds, the snake's eyes become milky and opaque, looking as if they were filled with smoke. The snake is blind at this time. The colors on the body are also much dulled, so that the snake has a drab and dirty appearance. About a week before molting the eyes become clear again.

The old layer of skin first begins to loosen about the head, and by rubbing its head against stones, shrubbery, or other objects the snake works the skin back, turning it inside out as it goes. By a combination of wavelike muscular contractions and by rubbing its body against surrounding objects, the snake gradually strips the skin back over its body, turning it inside out as it peels off. The shed skin is intact except for the mouth and anal openings. The process is much as if a stocking were grasped at the top and carelessly stripped off by turning it wrong side out. Since the dead cuticle is not elastic, it is interesting to note that a snake would be unable to perform this feat of shedding its skin in one piece were it not for the fact that the folds that extend down between the scales, by flattening out as the skin peels off, increase the diameter of the skin, much as a pleated skirt may be increased in size by unfolding the pleats.

Skin shedding is closely related to the formation of the rattle in rattlesnakes, since the substance of which the rattle is composed is merely a modified area of the cuticle of the tail. A new segment is added to the rattle each time the skin is shed. (For an excellent discussion of the function, structure, and formation of the rattle, see L. M. Klauber, 1940, Occ. Papers San Diego Soc. Nat. Hist., No. 6).

DEFENSIVE AND WARNING BEHAVIOR

Nearly any snake will try to escape a pursuer if given half a chance, although rattlesnakes often stop and assume a defensive coil while a person is still some distance away, perhaps because their large size, heavy bodies, and slow movements make flight difficult.

When snakes are cornered or seized, however, they usually defend themselves in a variety of ways, and definite types of defensive behavior are sometimes very characteristic of certain kinds of snakes. Some snakes, like the little smooth green snake, are so mild-tempered that they may be picked up and handled without any sign of resentment.

Most snakes, like other animals, do not hesitate to bite in self defense, and biting is by far the most general way snakes have of defending themselves. Biting becomes a very formidable means of defense if the snake is armed with a poison apparatus, but the vast majority of snakes do not possess this lethal weapon. In all harmless snakes the teeth are numerous and needle-sharp, and produce only a group of tiny punctures. These punctures bleed very profusely, apparently partly because the snake's saliva retards or prevents coagulation of the blood, and consequently the wound is likely to look much more dangerous than it really is. Only a few of our snakes, such as the larger water snakes of the South, are likely to inflict a wound that is more than a trivial scratch.

Snakes have a second very common and widely distributed way of defending themselves—pouring out the secretion of the anal scent glands. This secretion, which has a penetrating musky or occasionally sweetish odor and is colorless, whitish, or yellowish in color, is produced by a special pair of glands located in the base of the tail. It is often supposed to be feces because it passes out through the vent, but it has nothing to do with the digestive system. This evil-smelling liquid, which is smeared about liberally by the thrashings of the snake, should be quite effective in discouraging an animal that had seized the snake with the intention of eating it. There is much variation in the readiness with which this defense mechanism is employed. Garter snakes and water snakes rarely fail to use it, while many other snakes seemingly never do although their scent glands are just as well developed.

Some snakes rear up and strike at an intruder, and large snakes such as pine snakes or bull snakes may put on a spectacular display. Each strike is often accompanied by a hiss, which in the case of hog-nosed snakes or bull snakes may be so loud that it sounds like escaping steam.

Many snakes, instead of rearing up in order to look threatening, keep their bodies on the ground but flatten themselves out as much as possible. This makes the snake look much bigger than it really is, and at the same time makes the pattern more conspicuous by revealing the skin between the scales. Such flattening reaches an extreme in Kirtland's water snake, where almost the whole body may be flattened out until it looks no thicker than a knife blade. The hog-nosed snakes do this only with the fore part of the body.

The reverse of flattening consists of inflating the body with air until it is as large as possible. In some tropical snakes there are special thin-walled air sacs connected with the wind pipe, and in these snakes only the fore part of the body is inflated. Inflation may be seen to best advantage in the hog-nosed snakes among American snakes. In these snakes the whole lung is distended with air, so that the snake looks like a toy balloon. The air is then exhaled with a loud and prolonged hiss.

The most famous warning behavior of snakes is the rattling of rattlesnakes. This unique and remarkably effective behavior is much easier to understand when it is known that a great many kinds of snakes vibrate their tails exactly like rattlesnakes when they are nervous. This habit is very characteristic of the king snakes and the rat snakes, for example. If the snake is among dry leaves it produces a sound very similar to the buzz of a rattlesnake.

There are several unique types of defensive behavior employed by certain snakes. Dr. Raymond B. Cowles found that a rattlesnake placed in a cage with a king snake (which does not hesitate to eat rattlesnakes) defended itself by pushing at the king snake with a loop of its body, much as a person might thrust someone away with his elbow. The rattler responded in the same way to the presence of a skunk, and recently a massasauga in the laboratories of Field Museum exhibited exactly the same behavior when confronted with a king snake. The rubber boa, if annoyed, often rolls itself into a compact ball with its head in the center, and blue racers, whip snakes, and even garter snakes have been seen to hide their heads under their coils if they are repeatedly annoyed. The ring-necked snakes (*Diadophis*) have the underside of the tail colored red, and these snakes often curl the tail up in a spiral, revealing its brilliantly colored lower surface, when they are disturbed.

Probably the most remarkable defensive behavior of all is the extraordinary death feint of the hog-nosed snakes (Plate 1). This behavior is described in detail on p. 117.

SENSES

Of the five senses (sight, hearing, smell, taste, and touch), only sight and smell seem to be well developed in snakes. It is often hard to tell whether a snake is seeing or hearing or tasting, but by means of cleverly devised experiments we know something at least about the senses of these animals.

Vision seems to be very acute in snakes, but probably they can see only for relatively short distances. A snake's eye is very similar to the eye of other animals, except that there are no eyelids; this is why snakes have their characteristic unwinking stare, and means of course that they even sleep with their eyes open. The lens can be focused sharply on objects at various distances (an important feature in an animal that stalks its prey), and Dr. Gordon L. Walls discovered that the lens in snakes that prowl by day is yellow, which eye doctors have long known makes vision sharper by filtering out the ultra-violet rays. Snakes that are active by day have round pupils, while those that forage chiefly at night have pupils that are vertical and catlike. Compare the eye of a whip snake (Fig. 29) with that of a rattlesnake (Fig. 101).

Snakes are totally deaf, so that the old expression "deaf as an adder" has a foundation in fact. It is hard to tell whether or not a snake is hearing a sound, but several persons have taken advantage of the extreme nervousness of certain snakes to prove that they could not hear. F. B. Manning selected a group of particularly nervous rattlesnakes, so sensitive that the appearance of even a finger from behind the blind concealing him from the snakes would cause some of them to rattle, and found that they were indifferent to a loud noise made within a few inches of their heads. Colonel Wall covered the eyes of some nervous cobras with adhesive tape, and found that they then paid no attention to such sounds as the blowing of a bugle or beating on a large empty tin can, although the scraping of a chair or a footfall (which would transmit vibrations through the floor) caused them to rear immediately. It is of course possible that snakes can hear sounds above the limits of human audibility, but this apparently has never been tested.

We have seen that smell is an important factor in aiding snakes to follow their prey. Rattlesnakes, after striking a rabbit or a mouse, lie quietly while the doomed victim staggers away. Some moments later the rattler picks up the trail left by the animal, following it like a hound until he finds his waiting meal. Experiments have shown that smell is also important in helping snakes to recognize other members of their own kind, and to recognize the sex of other individuals.

Anyone who has watched a live snake knows that snakes continually flick their tongues in and out. This is partly an aid in smelling. The delicate tips of the tongue pick up minute particles and transfer them to two tiny cavities in the front of the roof of the mouth. These pits, which are lined with delicate sensory cells and are known as the "Jacobson's organ," are a special derivative of the smelling area of the nose and are not developed in man and other mammals. The tongue itself cannot smell, of course, but merely carries the particles to the Jacobson's organ.

All snakes are covered with horny scales, and consequently the skin is much less sensitive to touch than ours is. It was pointed out above that many male snakes have special sensory structures on their chins, and many other male snakes have similar structures on the sides of the body near the base of the tail, which assist them at the time of mating. The most important sensory structure in snakes, however, is the delicate tongue, which is not a "stinger" as is often supposed, but a very sensitive organ of touch. When a snake flicks its tongue in and out the two fine tips are touched lightly to the ground, and the snake thus keeps itself informed as to the nature of the ground over which it is crawling.

Snakes apparently have no sense of taste, which is scarcely surprising since taste would be of little use to an animal that swallows its prey whole, without any chewing. The sense of taste is located in the tongue in other animals, and as we have seen, a snake's tongue is greatly modified to serve other functions. Taste buds seem to be entirely lacking.

The facial pit situated on either side of the face in rattlesnakes and their relatives (see Fig. 9) is a special sense organ used in detecting delicate heat waves, and experiments have shown that the pits aid these snakes in directing the strike. They are described in more detail on p. 281. A row of somewhat similar pits (called labial pits) is found along the edge of the upper lip in many tropical boas.

COLLECTION, PRESERVATION, AND THE STUDY OF SNAKES

HOW TO LOOK FOR SNAKES

Snakes may be extremely difficult to find, even when considerable numbers are known to be present, and this is true even of the tropical forests which in popular imagination are thought to be alive with serpents. Museum collectors on their first trip to a tropical region always comment on the scarcity of snakes. In our temperate region the numbers of the larger species are now greatly reduced throughout the cultivated sections of the country, and there is much local variation in the abundance of the smaller and more secretive species that remain. A few snakes, like the common garter snake in the East and the plains garter snake in the Middle West, are abundant everywhere, even in suburban backyards and vacant city lots. In general, the capture of the larger snakes, except for water snakes, is a matter of chance, while the smaller forms are best found by searching beneath logs and stones. The abundance of the common forms is remarkably seasonal. After seeing numerous specimens in the spring, one scarcely finds a snake through the summer.

Natural cover, such as is provided by loose stones or by rotting logs, is so scarce in more settled regions that snakes can most easily be obtained by providing a substitute. Squares of linoleum, roofing, tin, or better still of boards supported by one-inch cleats, set out in vacant lots in suburban regions seem to collect snakes as if by magic; and this simple device makes it possible to observe snakes instead of collecting specimens.

Snakes are often found on roads at night, as is especially evident from the mangled remains found in daytime driving. Mr. L. M. Klauber, of San Diego, California, has developed the technique of collecting snakes by cruising suitable roads ("black top" pavement is best) at night at slow speed. He finds that many specimens are not seen at all at higher speeds and in the time consumed in stopping and running back, many specimens will have escaped. At slower speeds one sees every object on the road (including the "stick snake," the "banana peel lizard" and, most deceptive of all, the "fan belt snake") and can stop and investigate it. Any effective collecting by this means demands a system of locality records based on the speedometer readings. A specimen found "dead on road" is referred to by Klauber as a "DOR," and this useful term may well be adopted into the language as "dor." On a little-used road, at the height of the spring season of abundance, one may find great numbers of snakes by this means, and species thought to be extremely rare have been collected in great numbers. It is essential that such snake hunting be confined to little used roads, for driving at ten miles an hour on a trunk highway is highly dangerous, and against the law in many states.

In the plains region of the Middle West much useful data, along with occasional preservable specimens, may be accumulated during daytime touring at normal driving speed if the time consumed by frequent stops to pick up or identify specimens can be spared. A day from the log of a trip made by the authors from Chicago to Boulder, Colorado, is given below as an example of the way in which data may be recorded. The numbers are speedometer readings, by means of which the exact localities of specimens can be determined from road maps.

Aug. 10, 1941. Weather fair and very warm. Leave Homewood, Illinois, 1:00 P.M. Across Illinois and eastern fifth of Iowa on U. S. 34. No reptiles seen. (Average driving speed 50 m.p.h.).

Aug. 11. Weather fair and very warm. Across Iowa on U. S. 34.

Coluber c. flaviventris, DOR at eastern edge of Albia, Monroe County, Iowa. Typical Iowa farming country. (Entire specimen saved).

38083—*Lampropeltis calligaster* DOR. Cornfield one side

of road, pasture on other, snake on cornfield side. (Specimen saved).

38093—Chariton.

38124—*Lampropeltis calligaster* ♂ DOR. Cornfield-pasture, snake on cornfield side. Ventrals 200, Caudals 49, dorsal blotches 45 + 13.

38129—*Lampropeltis g. holbrooki* ♂ DOR. Open pasture both sides, 1/8 mile above creek. V 211, C 51, belly posteriorly more than half black.

38144—Afton.

38146—*Pituophis s. sayi,* yg. adult DOR. Markings black on neck, reddish-brown to center of body, darker posteriorly.

38175—Corning.

38181—*Pituophis s. sayi* DOR. Open pasture both sides. 1:00 P.M., but specimen fresh! (saved).

38201—*Thamnophis radix* ♀, DOR. Alfalfa-farmyard. V. 151. Dorsal stripe orange anteriorly, yellow posteriorly; spots at ends of ventrals small and rather isolated.

38206—Red Oak.

38217—*Pituophis s. sayi,* DOR immediately west of Emerson. Hayfield-pasture. Specimen not saved.

Pitouphis s. sayi, DOR just west of preceding specimen. Cornfield-hayfield. Not saved.

38233—*Elaphe?* DOR (very flat), Cornfield-pasture. Head, section at midbody, and tail saved.

38245—Iowa-Nebraska state line, Missouri River.

HOW TO CATCH SNAKES

It is possible to catch most snakes by hand, but a suitable snake stick is essential for handling poisonous forms. The most practical kind is a three- or four-foot staff of broomstick size with a quarter-inch iron rod bent at a right angle at the end. A stick with a leather strap or thong and provided with guides so that a loop can be pulled up at the end is often used for handling poisonous snakes (Fig. 5). For all smaller snakes harmless or poisonous, a most convenient collecting instrument is the placental forceps of the medical profession.

A most essential item of equipment to the snake collector is a set of cloth bags of assorted sizes with tapes or strings sewed on at the open end so that they can be securely tied. Sugar, salt, and flour sacks, if carefully inspected for holes, serve excellently for this purpose.

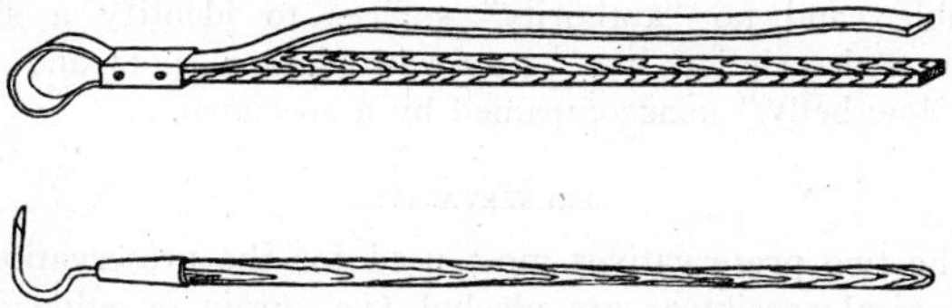

Fig. 5. "Snake sticks" for handling snakes. (*Above*) Stick with leather loop, which is passed over the snake's head. (*Below*) Stick with iron hook, by means of which poisonous snakes may be held down or lifted.

In collecting specimens for museum preservation, especially poisonous snakes or water snakes that are likely to escape into deep water, a .22 caliber pistol is most useful, shooting shot cartridges. A pistol with a ten-inch barrel and with the barrel smooth bored is excellent and one with a six- or eight-inch barrel provided with an aluminum extension barrel is ideal.

PRESERVATION OF SPECIMENS

It is often desirable to preserve a snake for future examination and study or for permanent preservation as a museum specimen. The ordinary methods of taxidermy applied to snake skins are quite unsatisfactory, and it has long been the practice of the larger museums to prepare models of snakes intended for exhibition in wax, plaster, or celluloid. Smaller museums, school museums, and private collectors may exhibit specimens preserved in alcohol or formalin, and specimens so preserved form the reference or study collections maintained in large museums independent of their exhibition series. Studies on the relations and distribution of the species of snakes are based on such research or reference collections, and are carried on in most of the larger museums of natural history and in many colleges and universities. If it is desired to have a specimen identified by an authority at such an institution, a well-preserved specimen will be a welcome exchange for the trouble; and no "authority" suffices to identify a snake from a description like "gray with darker spots and with a yellow belly," unaccompanied by a specimen.

PRESERVATIVES

The two preservatives most used for the preservation of zoological specimens are alcohol (i.e., grain or ethyl alcohol), and formalin. The high cost of grain alcohol, unless denatured, places it out of the reach of most private collectors, who are thus driven to the use of formalin. The solution most recommended is made by mixing 1 part of formalin (full strength, as purchased at the drugstore) with 9 equal parts of water. Alcohol is essential for permanent preservation, and all formalin specimens are transferred to alcohol in museum collections. Formalin specimens should be soaked in water for several days before transferring to alcohol.

Museum collectors usually kill their specimens by drowning them in the preserving fluid, keeping them beneath the surface in a cloth sack; or by injecting a little preservative in the region of the heart with a large hypodermic syringe.

It has recently been found that snakes are quite promptly killed if placed in a tight jar with a layer of the common moth repellent "dichloricide" on the bottom.

PRESERVATION

After killing, it is essential that the specimen be well injected with the preservative if a syringe is available, or that the body wall (the belly) *be slit for the entry of the preservative* into the body cavity, with a further slit in the tail. The slits should be longer than the spaces between them. The next step is to place the specimen, coiled neatly and belly up, in a bottle or tin container. The specimen to be preserved should not be crowded or pressed against others, and there must be a good amount of the preserving fluid in proportion to the volume of the specimen. It is well to press specimens that have been slit to remove air bubbles and assure the free entry of the preservative. Glass mayonnaise jars are convenient containers for small specimens. For larger snakes, the gallon size friction top cans or pails, in which syrup is often sold, are most satisfactory for preservation while in camp or away from home, while assorted sizes of the glass "mayonnaise jars" (up to a gallon) are most useful at home for a permanent collection. Glass-topped fruit jars, especially the wide-mouthed type, are also satisfactory for permanent storage, (but do not come in gallon size). Snakes too large for the gallon tin or jar offer a difficult problem for the collector. The first suggestion is to remove the viscera of such larger specimens. If still too large for the containers available, the best solution lies in skinning out the body, leaving the head and tail entire and connected to the skin, rolling the whole loosely, and preserving. Such rolled skins require examination during the first day in the preservative to see that it reaches all of the surface; a tightly rolled skin may decay even in strong preservative. Finally the head alone is worth preserving, especially if the scale counts (see p. 74) are made and the sex is carefully determined before discarding the body.

Specimens placed in the preservative become hard and rigid within 24 hours, and if they do not, further opening of the specimen and removal to fresh formalin is necessary. The principal difficulty in preservation in general arises with specimens that have been dead for some time before the process of preservation begins; a stronger solution may be necessary to save such a specimen, or it should be discarded except for the head. Snakes with a lump of food in the body should have this removed, either by carefully forcing it forward and out of the mouth by "palping" with the finger and thumb (which can easily be done when the snake is alive), or through a slit if the specimen is dead. Such food remains often form a focus of decay that is difficult to arrest; if possible, such stomach contents should be preserved separately and labeled to correspond with the snake from which they come.

LABELING

Labeling of specimens for any permanent collection is necessary and by no means simple. Individual tags of waterproof paper may be purchased from the Dennison Manufacturing Company, Chicago ("fibre waterproof tags"). These tags do not become soft in liquid; it is best to write on them with Higgins Eternal Ink. It is customary to tie a knot in the thread that attaches the label at about 3/8 of an inch from the label. The minimum information required is the locality, date, and collector's name. If a catalogue is kept, the tag may be numbered and a corresponding entry made in the catalogue book. This should include further information about the place and mode of capture, the behavior of the specimen, etc.

SHIPMENT

Once well preserved, specimens may be forwarded to a museum with no other liquid than that of damp rags or newspaper in which they are packed, thus making the container much lighter to transport.

It should be noted that the sending of live snakes through the mails is prohibited, whether they be poisonous or not. Live snakes may be shipped by express, in any well-made wooden box. They should always be placed in cloth sacks (like sugar or flour sacks) within the box, since active species will injure themselves seriously by rubbing their noses in attempts to escape. It is important that any shipment of poisonous snakes be plainly marked "Poisonous Snakes."

Gloyd, Howard K., 1938, Methods of preserving and labeling amphibians and reptiles for scientific study. *Turtox News,* Vol. 16, pp. 19-53, 66-67.

SUGGESTIONS FOR THE STUDY OF SNAKES

Many young people come to a museum curator or other authority with questions about snakes which they assume can be answered offhand or from a book. While this may be possible, these people do not realize that our knowledge of snakes, as of most other creatures, is far from complete, and that it is being actively increased and corrected by enthusiastic students of nature. To such active students, the opportunity to make new observations and to correct and increase the existing body of information seems vastly more interesting and important than the mere learning of what has been set down in print.

There is an obvious psychological pitfall for children who are attracted to the study of snakes. The fear and excitement aroused in many persons by snakes makes it easy to use them merely to secure attention. Such "exhibitionism" is a natural element in most human beings, and may be useful if it is a springboard to expanding and broader interests. If the desire for attention remains the mainspring of an interest in snakes, the would-be student will develop only a modicum of information and will use this as a kind of patter on all occasions when he can find a listener. The centering of his interest on himself closes the door to a genuine interest in his subject, focussed on what needs to be learned instead of on what has been learned. Once this has been developed, time for study is too precious to be wasted in talk.

OBSERVATIONS ON CAPTIVE SNAKES

Snakes are often kept alive in a "terrarium," and the interest of such snake keeping can be greatly multiplied by a program and record of observation as has been suggested by Clifford H. Pope (1937, *Snakes Alive,* p. 150). We may modify his suggestions as follows:

I. A record of each snake, kept as a catalogue of specimens. This should include the scientific name, sex, collector of the specimen, and the time and place of capture.

II. Observation.

1. Monthly record of length and weight (weight taken before feeding).
2. Notes on feeding, with date, amount, and nature of

food taken; and readiness of acceptance or refusal of food. Water may be offered at regular intervals and record made of the amount taken.

3. Notes on the passage of excrement, especially its nature (solid or liquid, color, content of hair or scales) and the interval between feeding and passage of excrement.
4. Notes on shedding of skin, with dates.
5. Notes on reproduction; description of any courtship or mating; details about laying or hatching of eggs, or birth of young.
6. Notes on disposition and intelligence, describing any changes noted and especially any conditioning to the taking of food and any recognition of prey; recognition of the keeper; behavior toward an enemy (especially a snake-eating king snake, for example).

Only trained students with expensive laboratory facilities can undertake experiments with snake venom. The amateur student should keep a record of any cases of snake bite occurring in his vicinity, with names, dates, and as much "case history" as possible.

Careful record of the popularly current superstitions and fables about snakes is of interest as folklore.

FIELD OBSERVATION OF SNAKES

Observation of snakes in the field should be a natural outgrowth of any interest in the subject. The only essential equipment is a notebook, which should be permanent and which should be faithfully kept. A study of the journal *Copeia* will provide a great variety of suggestions for observation as will an examination of the gaps under the various headings under individual species in the present book, in which the word "unknown" appears all too often. The use of snake shelters made of boards or squares of roofing suggests a whole series of questions, such as the distances to which snakes wander; their recurrence in successive years; the location of their hibernating places; their numbers, and especially fluctuation of their numbers; their food; and their breeding habits, both as to courtship and mating and their production of eggs or young.

Recently taken food, usually evident as a considerable bulge in the snake's body, can be examined without injury to the snake by "palping" with the thumb and fingers, pressing the snake's body at a point just behind the food, and following it up as it moves forward until it is disgorged.

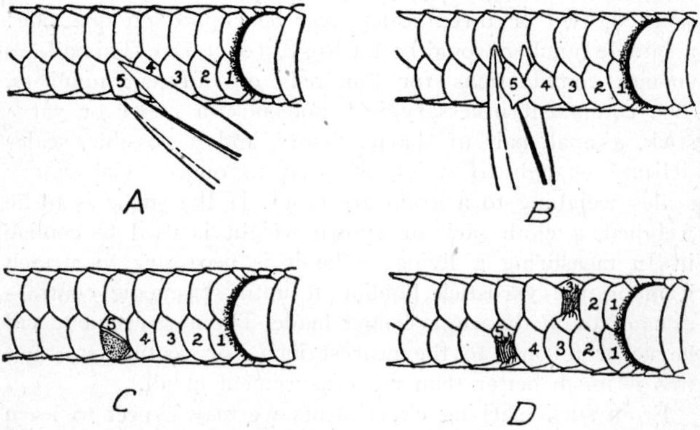

Fig. 6. How to mark living snakes for future recognition by scarring scales on underside of tail. A. Points of scissors in position to clip scale No. 5. B. The scale nearly cut off. C. Fresh scar after clipping scale. D. Old scars on snake marked "5-3." (Modified from Blanchard).

A method of marking individual snakes consists in clipping two or more scales beneath the tail with a sharp scissors and recording the number of such scales as counted from the anal cleft. (See Blanchard, F. N., and Finster, Ethel B., A method of marking living snakes for future recognition with a discussion of some problems and results, *Ecology,* Vol. 14, pp. 334-347, 7 figs.). The snake must be held firmly, lower side up and tail pointing away from the holder. The left side of the snake is then at the operator's left and the right at his right. With a sharp-pointed scissors, held firmly against the scale, nearly the whole scale can be cut away. It is essential that the cut be deep enough to take most of the true skin beneath the scale (down to the muscle layer) or no permanent scar will be formed; the cut will rarely draw blood, but no harm is done if a little blood is lost. Count backward from the anal cleft to the scale desired, say the fourth, on the left side, clip it, and then clip a scale on the right that represents a new number, say the sixth. The catalogue number of this snake will then be L4-R6 (or simply 4-6). If large numbers of snakes are marked, two or three scales may be clipped on one side; a sample number would be L4-R6, 8, (or 4-6,8). This allows enough combinations for hundreds of different numbers. The equipment necessary is a notebook, a meter or yardstick, a small pair of sharp scissors, and if possible, scales delicate enough to weigh at least to ounces (laboratory scales weighing to a gram are best). If the snake is to be weighed, a cloth sack of known weight is used to confine it. In measuring a living snake it is necessary to stretch it along the yardstick holding it until spasmodic contractions of the body are no longer made. The measurement will be accurate only to the nearest inch (or centimeter), but this is much better than no measurement at all.

From such marking experiments we may expect to learn about the rate of growth under natural conditions; the length of life; the extent of the home territory of individual snakes; and something about their capacity for "homing." Thus far, this method of marking has been applied in only a few localities, and returns of marked snakes after any considerable interval are astonishingly few. It is especially applicable, however, to backyard study with board shelters, and offers an immediate suggestion to any boy or girl who wishes to engage in the study of the habits of snakes, and to more advanced students as well.

SYSTEMATIC STUDIES OF SNAKES

The study of snakes in the past has been mainly an effort to define the species and subspecies by means of museum specimens. These are studied for the information they afford on the variation of the external characters described above in the chapter on external characters, and provide *locality records* which define the geographic distribution of the forms in question. Identification of such specimens is ordinarily made by means of "keys" such as that at the beginning of the systematic section of this book, and the use of such a key makes it necessary to learn the terms defined. The key itself must then be read with attention to *both* alternatives under each number, and with the specimen at hand; each half of the numbered sections asks a question which must be answered from the specimen, and this answer leads either to the genus (as in our key to the genera) or to that of the species or subspecies, as in more detailed keys.

Examination of the teeth of snakes, which has not been emphasized in our keys, becomes a necessity if exotic species are to be studies; the teeth of a large snake can be counted with the naked eye and without removing the jaw. For smaller specimens a hand lens is necessary and a binocular microscope is better. The jaw of a specimen can be clipped out by means of a cuticle scissors; the teeth are then quite concealed in the gum, but become evident if the jaw is dried. If the gum tissues are teased away with a needle some loose teeth are quite certain to be lost, but with attentive examination of the bone their place of attachment can be seen. The characters to be recorded are: grooving of the posterior teeth; enlargement of certain teeth; gaps in the tooth row (frequent before the grooved fangs in groove-fanged snakes); and the number and relative length of the teeth.

Aside from the use of scale counts of snakes for the identification of specimens, such data is accumulated for the more detailed study of the species. When it is realized that the limits of variation are known only for a minority of the species and that there are still many kinds of snakes in the United States known from only a few specimens, it is evident that much more such information needs to be accumulated. The accompanying figure shows all that is known of the variation in scale characters of the Arizona coral snake, *Micruroides euryxanthus.* Large numbers of scale counts of the common garter snakes were necessary before

NAME *Micruroides euryxanthus Kennicott*

Museum	Number	LOCALITY	When Collected	COLLECTOR	Sex	Scale Rows	Ventrals	Caudals	Supralabials	Infralabials	Oculars	Temporals	Black Rings	Total Length	Tail Length	Tail Divided by Total Length
C.A.S.	35324	Arizona: Tucson	1912	Brown	♂	17-15-13	222	28	7	7	1-2	1-2	10+2	355	28	
U.Ariz.	a	" Metcalf	1917	—	♂	17-15-13	220	27	—	—	—	—	11+2	421	32	
"	b	" Tucson	—	—	♂	17-15-13	228	30	7	7	1-2	1-2	10+2	423	36	
"	c	" "	—	—	♂	17-15-13	220	28	7	7	1-2	1-2	10+2	454	37	
"	d	" near Tucson	—	—	♂	17-15-13	224	28	7	7	1-2	1-2	12+2	—	—	
"	e	" " "	—	—	♂	18-15-13	223	28	7	7	1-2	1-2	11+2	—	—	
A.M.N.H.	3910	" Rosemont	—	J.J. Thornber	♂	17-15-13	224	26	7	7	1-2	1-2	11+2	—	—	
C.M.	2030	"Texas"	1899	C. Daggett	♂	17-15-13	222	25	7	7	1-2	1-2	10+2	357	27	
F.M.N.H.	2918	Arizona: Tucson	1918	J.G. Sinclair	♀	17-15-15	240	24	7	7	1-2	1-2	14+2	337	21	
U.Ariz.	f	" "	—	—	♀	17-15-15	236	23	7	7	1-2	1-2	13+2	364	23	
C.A.S.	33837	" "	1905	Brown	♀	—	240	22	7	7	1-2	1-2	12+2	—	—	
"	35326	" "	—	J.R. Slevin	♀	17-15-14	229	25	7	-	1-2	1-2	9+1	275	20	
"	33845	" Rosemont	—	Brown	♀	17-16-15	231	27	7	-	1-2	1-2	11+2	445	33	
A.N.S.P.	17932	" near Tucson	1910	H.A. Pilsbry	♀	- 15-13	232	26	—	—	—	—	10+2	—	—	
C.M.	2055	Arizona —	—	G.A. Wilson	♀	17-15-13	241	—	7	7	1-2	1-2	—	—	—	
A.M.N.H.	20592	" Sta. Cruz Village	1916	Lutz & Rehn	♀	17-15-15	230	25	7	7	1-2	1-2	11+2	450	31	
"	26014	" Pima Co.	—	A.I. Ortenburger	♀	17-15-15	237	24	7	7	1-2	1-2	12+2	—	—	
"	3909	Sonora: La Chispas	1902	O.F. Pfordte	♀	17-16-13	228	23	7	7	1-2	1-2	11+1	330	20	

Fig. 7. Example of an actual scale-count sheet, used in studying variation of scale characters in snakes.

it could be discerned that the number of ventral plates in this group is higher in males than in females, the reverse of the usual condition. When sufficient series of specimens are available, their characters can be subjected to *statistical analysis* in renewed and more accurate studies of populations and of geographic variation (see Klauber, A statistical study of the rattlesnakes. Occ. Papers San Diego Soc. Nat. Hist. 1936-1940).

The identification of snakes from foreign countries and especially from the tropics is still difficult because summarizing works and keys to genera and species are still wanting or inadequate. The snakes of tropical regions are in fact only beginning to be adequately described, and numerous "new species" still remain to be discovered or defined. Exotic specimens should be submitted to a specialist at a museum, or if possible, taken to the museum and identified with his aid.

Detailed knowledge of the distribution of animals in many states has been built up by means of local and county lists. There is room for much study of this kind, and carefully drawn up local lists afford a framework into which much miscellaneous observation can be incorporated. Every amateur should own the publications in his field of interest of his own state (and of the adjacent states also). The list of such state publications on snakes at the back of the present book, by the extraordinary unevenness of date and of merit of the various titles, is a challenge to local naturalists.

A glance at the maps in the present book, or at those in more technical works, will show that the outlines of the geographic range of most species of snakes are only very imperfectly known. The studies of L. M. Klauber have produced unusually accurate maps of the ranges of the snakes of southern California, and the distribution of the rattlesnakes, which attract general interest everywhere, has been rather accurately mapped by Klauber and H. K. Gloyd. Maps of distribution in general, however, are a challenge to the local naturalist to improve them. Such maps often define excellent problems for study, as in the accompanying map of the range of the smooth green snake, in which the populations in the Black Hills and in the Rockies appear

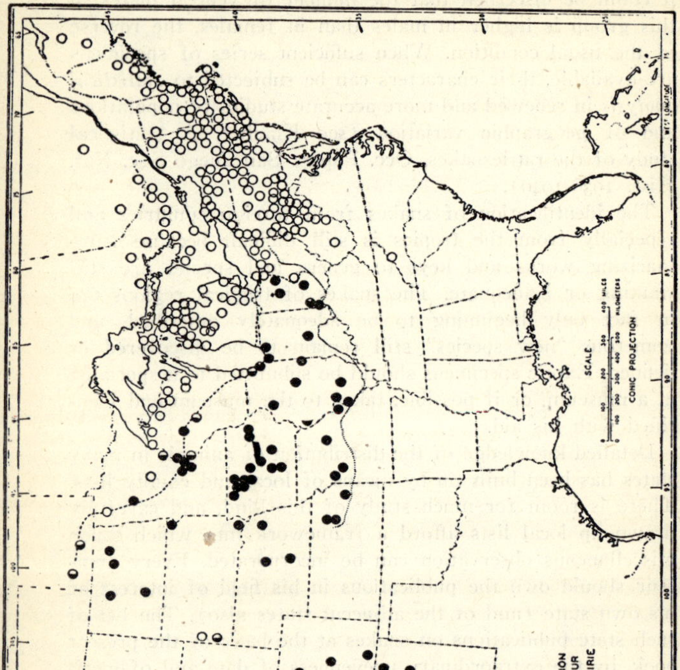

Fig. 8. Example of distribution map made by plotting locality records from museum specimens.

to be isolated from the main population in the Middle West, while the eastward projection of the western form of the green snake affords important evidence bearing on the explanation of distributions (see the senior author's paper, Herpetological evidence for the postglacial eastward extension of the steppe in North America, *Ecology,* Vol. 19, pp. 396-407 9 figs.). This map, showing distribution of a species by means of a spot for each locality record, illustrates a method of studying geographic distribution.

Finally, the best introduction to the serious study of snakes, as of other groups of reptiles and amphibians, is the study of the two journals *Copeia* and *Herpetologica.* These include numerous notes of the kind that may result from amateur observation and afford obvious suggestions for further studies. For information regarding *Copeia,* address the Secretary of the American Society of Ichthyologists and Herpetologists, at the Carnegie Museum, Pittsburgh, Pa. *Herpetologica* may be purchased from the editors, address Mr. Walter L. Necker, % Dept. of Zoology, Field Museum of Natural History, Chicago.

The present work is based on the studies of others, and is provided with references to their publications in various scientific journals in addition to *Copeia* and *Herpetologica.* Many such journals will be available in public libraries only in rather large cities, and in college and university libraries. Most smaller public libraries, however, can borrow from the larger libraries; and the serious student should not hesitate to look up such original sources by borrowing through his local library. He should also correspond with the nearest available zoologist, beginning with his local high school teacher, who may be able to help him directly, or to put him in touch with a near-by college professor, with his state university, or with a museum.

SYSTEMATIC ACCOUNT OF THE SNAKES OF THE UNITED STATES AND CANADA

KEY TO THE GENERA OF THE SNAKES OF THE UNITED STATES AND CANADA

HOW TO IDENTIFY A SNAKE

If you do not know the *genus* of a snake to be identified (that is, whether it is a water snake, a garter snake, a rat snake, etc.), it is first necessary to determine this from the following key to the genera. If the key is followed carefully, you will learn the group to which your snake belongs. In the key the name of the genus is followed by a page reference and on that page you will find the snakes of that genus discussed and illustrated. If there is only one species in the genus your identification will be finished, but if there are several you will need to proceed further, either by comparing your snake with the descriptions given or, where there are many forms in the genus (as in the king snakes, for example), by continuing to trace it in a key to the species. It is of course necessary to start back at 1 a in the key to the species.

Perhaps your snake will not agree with any of the descriptions or illustrations given. This usually means that you have made a mistake somewhere in tracing it through the key to the genera, and it is advisable to "run" it through the key again more carefully. Occasionally an abnormal specimen will not "key out" no matter how carefully it is traced; such a specimen should be sent to an expert if an identification is wanted.

HOW TO USE A KEY

A key is likely to look complicated and formidable if you have never used one, but actually it is a simple device based on a series of alternative choices. In our keys you will notice that each entry starts with a number and a letter, and that each number is repeated, once followed by "a" and again followed by "b." These indicate the two choices between which you must decide, and your snake *must* agree with either a or b.

To use the key, look first at the belly of your snake. Are the scales on the belly small like those of the back (1 a), or are they widened into straplike plates (1 b)? If they are widened into plates (and in nearly all snakes they are), the 3 at the end of the dotted line means "go to 3 a." Then look at the side of your snake's face and choose between 3 a and 3 b. Is there a deep pit between the eye and the nostril, as indicated by the arrow in Fig. 9? (Do not be confused by a black spot or a crease between the scales.) If there is no pit (3 a) proceed to 4, but if there is a pit (3 b) turn at once to 53 and go on from there. Eventually you will come to an entry that has the name of a genus and a page reference at the right-hand end of the line. This is the genus in which your snake belongs, and on the page referred to you will find descriptions and illustrations, or another key by which you can determine the species.

Keys look much less discouraging after they have been used once or twice than they do the first time.

KEY TO THE GENERA *

1 a. No ventral plates, scales of underside like those of the back 2
1 b. Ventral plates present (enlarged transverse scales on belly, see Fig. 1, p. 27) 3

2 a. Wormlike snakes with eyes concealed beneath scales, tail extremely short .. *Leptotyphlops*, p. 92
2 b. Sea snakes, with eyes distinct and a flattened oar-like tail .... *Pelamydrus*, p. 278

* Adapted from Perkins, C. B., "A Key to the snakes of the United States." *Bull. Zool. Soc. San Diego*, No. 16, 1940.

3 a. No loreal pit (on side of face between eye and nostril) (Fig. 9) 4

3 b. Loreal pit present (Fig. 9) 54

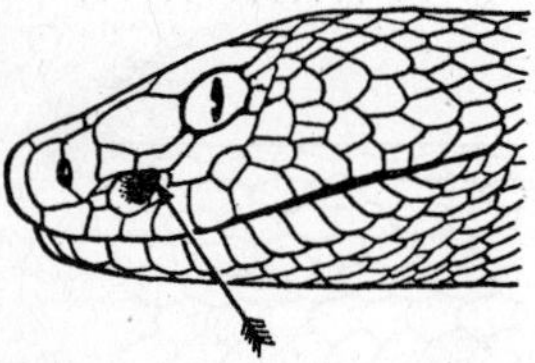

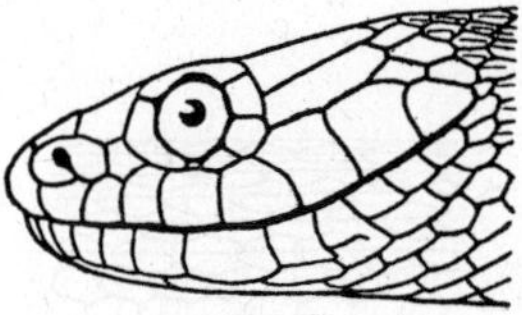

Fig. 9. Loreal pit present. Loreal pit absent.

4 a. No elongate paired chin shields between lower labials (Fig. 10) 5

4 b. Two pairs of well-defined chin shields between lower labials (rarely only one pair) (Fig. 10) . 6

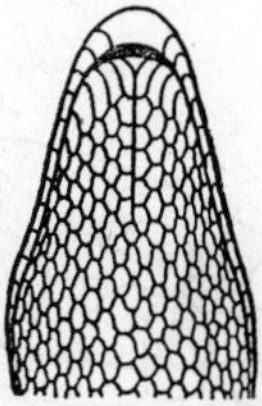

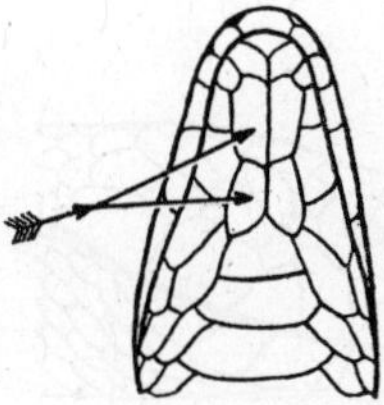

Fig. 10. Chin shields absent. Chin shields present.

5 a. Scales of top of head all small ... *Lichanura,* p. 96

5 b. Scales of top of head enlarged ..... *Charina,* p. 98

6 a. A single internasal shield 7

6 b. Two internasals 9

7 a. Scales distinctly keeled, upper labials 5, lower labials 6 .... *Haldea,* p. 231

7 b. Scales smooth except on tail, where faint or moderately developed keels are present; upper labials 7 or 8, lower labials 8 to 10 8

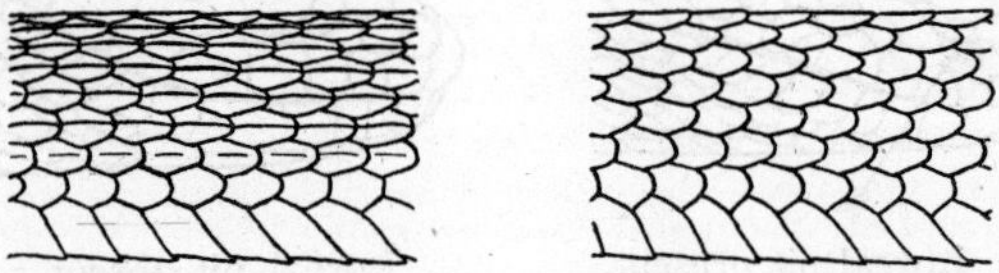

Fig. 11. Keeled scales. Smooth scales.

8 a. No preocular, loreal shield reaching the eye (Fig. 12); ventrals more than 160 ..... *Farancia,* p. 105

8 b. Preocular present, separating loreal from eye (Fig. 12) .... *Liodytes,* p. 234

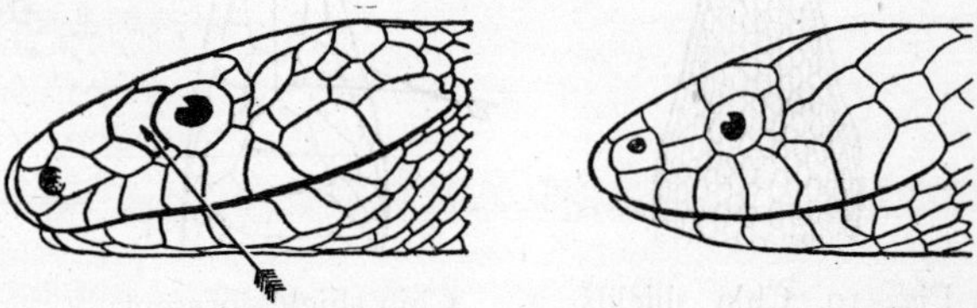

Fig. 12. Preocular present. Preocular absent.

9 a. Dorsal scales keeled, sometimes only faintly on the uppermost scale rows and on the posterior part of the body 10

9 b. Dorsal scales smooth 23

10 a. Anal plate divided (Fig. 13) 11

10 b. Anal plate entire (Fig. 13) 19

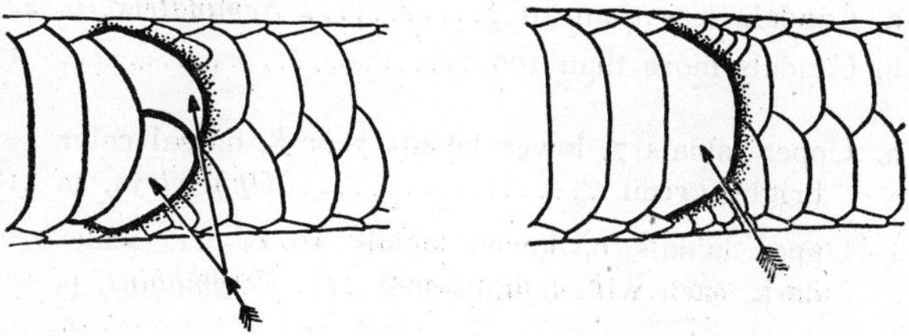

Fig. 13. Anal plate divided. Anal plate entire (or single).

11 a. Rostral turned up and keeled above. *Heterodon*, p. 115

11 b. Rostral normal 12

12 a. No loreal, the preocular in contact with the posterior part of the nasal (Fig. 14) .. *Storeria*, p. 227

12 b. Loreal present (Fig. 14) 13

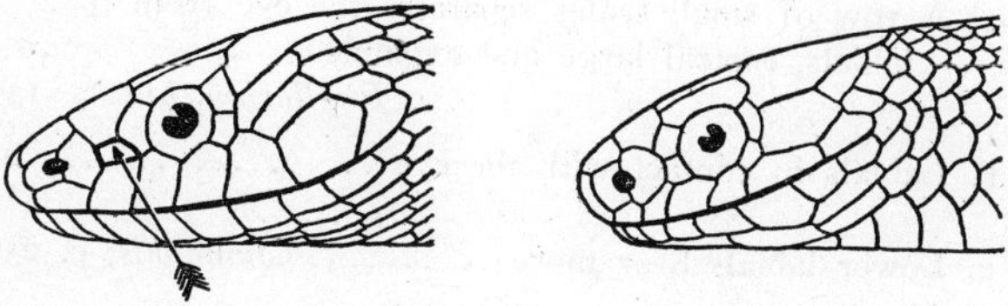

Fig. 14. Loreal present. Loreal absent.

13 a. No preoculars, the loreal in contact with the eye 14

13 b. Preoculars present, 1 or 2, separating loreal from eye 15

14 a. Upper labials 5 or 6 .... *Haldea*, p. 231

14 b. Upper labials 7 (scales only faintly keeled) ...... *Abastor*, p. 104

15 a. Scale rows 17 * 16

15 b. Scale rows more than 17 * 18

16 a. Caudals less than 50 .... *Seminatrix,* p. 225

16 b. Caudals more than 100 17

17 a. Upper labials 7, lower labials 7 or 8, dorsal color bright green .... *Opheodrys,* p. 118

17 b. Upper labials 9, lower labials 10 or 11, scales dark, each with a light spot .... *Drymobius,* p. 131

18 a. Dorsal scales strongly keeled; postoculars 2 or 3 (if only 2 the dorsal scales are usually in less than 23 rows) .... *Natrix,* p. 205

18 b. Dorsal scales weakly keeled, scale rows 25 to 33, 2 postoculars .... *Elaphe,* p. 142

19 a. Scale rows in 29 or more rows, prefrontals usually 4 .... *Pituophis,* p. 158

19 b. Scale rows fewer than 29; two prefrontals 20

20 a. A row of small scales separates the eye from the labials, rostral large and expanded ...... *Phyllorhynchus,* p. 139

20 b. Labials in contact with the eye 21

21 a. Lower labials 8 or more .... *Thamnophis,* p. 236

21 b. Lower labials less than 8 22

22 a. Under side with a double row of black spots ...... *Tropidoclonion,* p. 257

22 b. No black spots on belly .... *Haldea,* p. 231

23 a. Anal plate not divided 24

23 b. Anal plate divided 31

---

* See Fig. 1 (p. 27) for method of counting scale rows.

24 a. Caudals in two rows (Fig. 15) 25
24 b. Caudals in a single row (a few may be divided) (Fig. 15) .... *Rhinocheilus*, p. 194

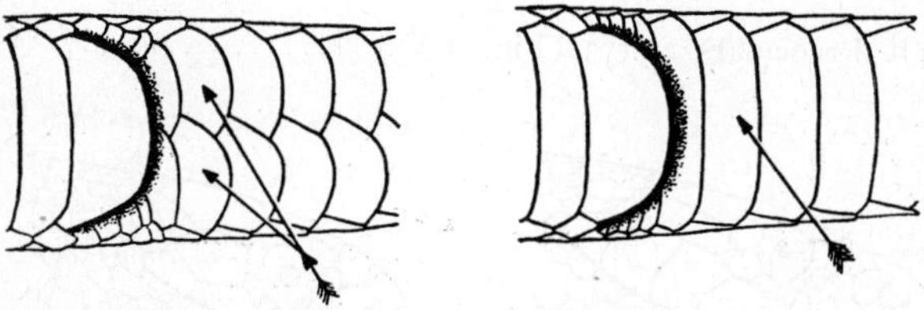

Fig. 15. Caudals in two rows. Caudals in single row.

25 a. Pupil of eye round 26
25 b. Pupil vertically elliptical 30

26 a. No loreal .... *Stilosoma*, p. 191
26 b. Loreal present 27

27 a. Ventral surface light without markings 28
27 b. Ventral surface with more or less dark markings 29

28 a. Upper labials 6, lower labials 8 .. *Cemophora*, p. 193
28 b. Upper labials 8, lower labials 12 or more ...... *Arizona*, p. 155

29 a. Scale rows 17, slightly oblique .. *Drymarchon*, p. 133
29 b. Scale rows more than 17 ...... *Lampropeltis*, p. 166

30 a. Scales between eye and labials ...... *Phyllorhynchus*, p. 139
30 b. No scales between eye and labials ...... *Trimorphodon*, p. 263

31 a. Scale rows less than 19 32
31 b. Scale rows more than 19 48

32 a. Loreal present 33
32 b. No loreal 43

33 a. Preoculars present (1 or more) 34

33 b. No preocular, loreal reaching the eye 42

34 a. A single preocular (Fig. 16) 35

34 b. Preoculars 2 or 3 (Fig. 16) 39

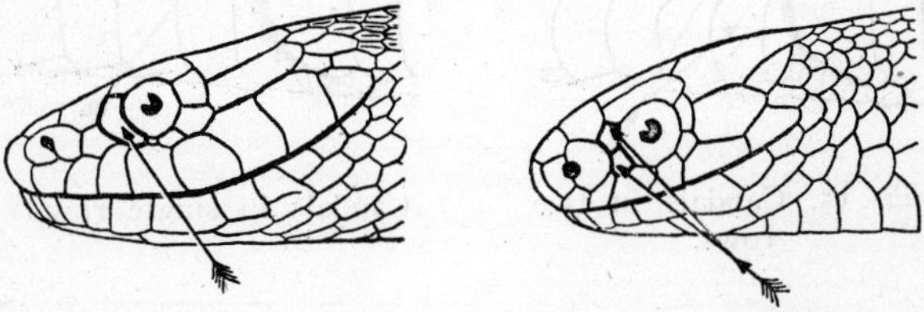

Fig. 16. Single preocular. Two preoculars.

35 a. Scale rows 17 36

35 b. Scale rows fewer than 17 37

36 a. Caudals more than 60; upper labials 7
...... *Rhadinaea,* p. 113

36 b. Caudals less than 60; upper labials usually 8
...... *Seminatrix,* p. 225

37 a. Posterior chin shields about as long as the anterior; caudals more than 65; color bright green above .... *Opheodrys,* p. 118

37 b. Posterior chin shields much shorter than the anterior pair; caudals less than 65 38

38 a. Each ventral with a black anterior border; nasal divided beneath the nostril .... *Contia,* p. 196

38 b. Ventrals uniformly light, or dark where the body is encircled by black rings; nostril in an undivided nasal plate .... *Sonora,* p. 197

39 a. Rostral enlarged, with free lateral edges ...... *Salvadora*, p. 135

39 b. Rostral normal 40

40 a. Anterior temporals 2 or 3; a small lower preocular wedged between labials .... *Coluber*, p. 121

40 b. Anterior temporal single; no small lower preocular 41

41 a. Nasal plate undivided, dorsal color green ...... *Opheodrys*, p. 118

41 b. Nasal plate divided, back not green, usually a ring of the bright ventral color on the neck ...... *Diadophis*, p. 108

42 a. Nasal plate undivided, upper labials 5, dorsal scales in 13 rows .... *Carphophis*, p. 102

42 b. Nasal plate divided, upper labials 6, dorsal scales in 15 or 17 rows .... *Haldea*, p. 231

43 a. Scale rows more than 13 44

43 b. Scales in 13 rows .... *Chilomeniscus*, p. 204

44 a. Scales in 15 rows, rostral normal 45

44 b. Scales in 17 rows, rostral pointed 47

45 a. Color pattern of red, yellow, and black rings 46

45 b. Color pattern without rings .... *Tantilla*, p. 268

46 a. Ring on neck black .... *Micrurus*, p. 274

46 b. Chin shields a single pair, the anterior ones replaced by the enlarged first lower labials; ring on neck red .... *Micruroides*, p. 276

47 a. Entire head elongate, nose especially long and sharp .... *Oxybelis*, p. 266

47 b. Rostral scale pointed, the point turned up in front ...... *Ficimia*, p. 202

48 a. Preoculars wanting, loreal reaching eye 49

48 b. Preoculars present 50

49 a. A dorsal pattern of red longitudinal stripes ...... *Abastor*, p. 104

49 b. Back without pattern, belly boldly red and black ...... *Farancia*, p. 105

50 a. Pupil of eye round 51

50 b. Pupil vertically elliptical 52

51 a. Scale rows 25 to 33 .... *Elaphe*, p. 142

51 b. Scale rows 19 .... *Coniophanes*, p. 265

52 a. Loreals 2 or more, postoculars 3 or 4, anterior temporals 2 or 3 .... *Trimorphodon*, p. 263

52 b. Loreal single, postoculars 2, anterior temporal single 53

53 a. Dorsal pattern of 22-26 large blotches, without alternating smaller spots on the side ...... *Leptodeira*, p. 261

53 b. Dorsal pattern of small spots with alternating small dark spots on the sides ... *Hypsiglena*, p. 259

54 a. No rattle on end of tail .... *Agkistrodon*, p. 283

54 b. Tail provided with a rattle 55

55 a. Top of head with the normal 9 enlarged shields ...... *Sistrurus*, p. 287

55 b. Top of head with the head shields much broken up .... *Crotalus*, p. 290

THE BLIND SNAKES

Family LEPTOTYPHLOPIDAE

These snakes are strikingly similar to earthworms in appearance, color, and even in habits, and hence are often called worm snakes. The members of another group of snakes (*Carphophis*) have long been referred to as the "worm snakes," however, and this illustrates one of the grave defects of popular names—totally different animals in different parts of the country are often known by the same name, so that no one can be positive as to which animal is referred to.

The term blind snakes really includes two families of snakes, the Typhlopidae and the Leptotyphlopidae, which are remarkably alike in external appearance and remarkably distinct in skull characters. Only the Leptotyphlopidae occur within the limits of the United States proper, but the small typhlopid, *Typhlops braminus,* which may be called the "flower-pot snake" from its frequent transport with growing plants, has been introduced into the Hawaiian Islands. Our worm snakes are entirely confined to the Southwest, from Kansas and Texas to California.

The blind snakes of the family Leptotyphlopidae are all small, entirely blind, or at least with the eyes covered over by the scales of the head and visible only as small dark spots. These snakes are shown to be primitive forms, remotely allied to the boas and pythons, by the fact that there are internal vestiges of the pelvis. They are sharply set off from all other snakes in our fauna by the fact that they have no enlarged ventral scales. Living specimens are semitransparent, with a pinkish or purplish cast. They become opaque in preservative, and color differences between the back and the belly, and between different species, may then become apparent.

THE SLENDER BLIND SNAKES
(Leptotyphlops)
Plate 8

The arrangement of the head shields in the blind snakes of the genus *Leptotyphlops* is strikingly different from that of all other snakes in our area, and appears to be correlated with the solidification of the skull, the reduced size of the mouth, and the loss of the enlarged ventral scales in ad-

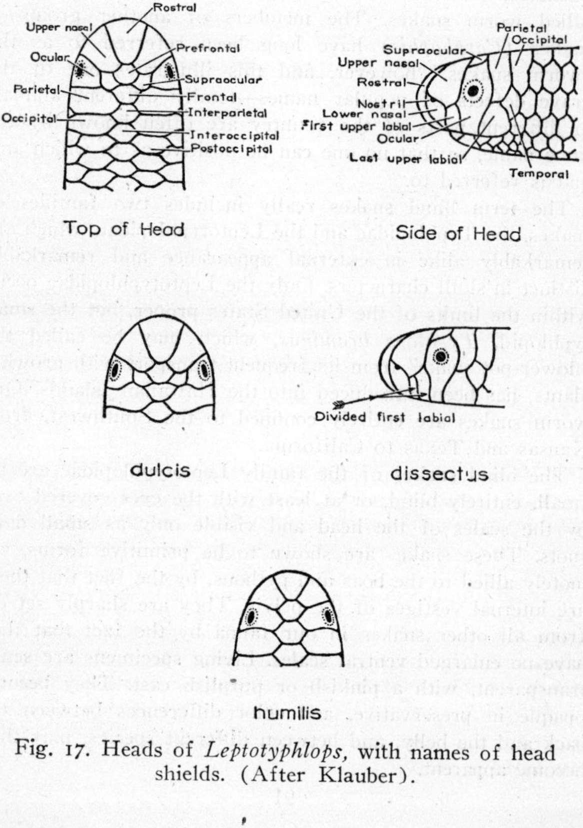

Fig. 17. Heads of *Leptotyphlops,* with names of head shields. (After Klauber).

justment to burrowing habits. Our species fall into two well-defined groups, in one of which there are three small scales between the oculars (the large scales covering the eye spots), while in the other there is only a single scale. The former group includes *Leptotyphlops dulcis* and its subspecies. The latter has frequently been given generic rank as *Siagonodon;* it includes only *Leptotyphlops humilis* and its subspecies.

KEY TO THE BLIND SNAKES OF THE UNITED STATES

1 a. Supraoculars present (Fig. 17, center) 2

1 b. No supraoculars (Fig. 17, bottom) 3

2 a. A single supralabial between the enlarged ocular and the nasal shields ..... *Leptotyphlops dulcis dulcis*

2 b. Two supralabials between the ocular and nasal shields .... *Leptotyphlops dulcis dissectus*

3 a. Ten scale rows around the tail ...... *Leptotyphlops humilis segregus*

3 b. Twelve scale rows around the tail 4

4 a. Fourth mid-dorsal scale often divided longitudinally; fifth dorsal much wider than sixth; dorsal scales number more than 288 ...... *Leptotyphlops humilis utahensis*

4 b. Fourth mid-dorsal scale undivided; fifth little if at all wider than sixth 5

5 a. Five lightly pigmented rows of dorsal scales; dorsal scales usually 285 or more ...... *Leptotyphlops humilis cahuilae*

5 b. Seven or more heavily pigmented dorsal scales; dorsal scales less than 285 ...... *Leptotyphlops humilis humilis*

Texas Blind Snake.—*Leptotyphlops dulcis dulcis* Baird and Girard. Characterized by the presence of three small scales between the large oculars; a single labial scale between the ocular and the nasal on each side. The coloration is pale brown, the upper seven scale rows being brown or light brown.

Range.—Central Oklahoma and the Panhandle south through central Texas to northern Tamaulipas and central Nuevo León, Mexico.

New Mexican Blind Snake.—*Leptotyphlops dulcis dissectus* Cope. Three small scales between the oculars, as in *dulcis dulcis* and with a similar coloration, distinguished by having the anterior supralabial divided vertically into two.

Range.—Southern Kansas through Oklahoma, southwest through western Texas and southern New Mexico to southeastern Arizona and adjacent parts of Mexico.

Brown Blind Snake.—*Leptotyphlops humilis humilis* Baird and Girard. The seven upper rows of scales are chocolate brown, and scales of the next row on each side may also be dark spotted. A single scale between the large oculars. The dorsal scales from head to tip of tail average 273.

Range.—Southwestern California and southeastern Arizona, southward into Lower California and to the Mexican Plateau.

Desert Blind Snake.—*Leptotyphlops humilis cahuilae* Klauber. Five uppermost scale rows light in color, average dorsal scales 289.

Range.—Desert areas from eastern San Diego County, California, to Nevada and western Arizona.

Klauber's Blind Snake.—*Leptotyphlops humilis segregus* Klauber. Like the brown blind snake in coloration; the seven uppermost scale rows brown, the scales with slightly lighter borders. Distinguished from other subspecies of *humilis* by having ten rows of scales around the tail instead of twelve.

Range.—Western Texas and adjacent part of Mexico.

Utah Blind Snake.—*Leptotyphlops humilis utahensis* Tanner. Seven mid-dorsal scale rows darker; dorsal scale count high (289-308); fourth mid-dorsal scale often divided longitudinally, and fifth much wider than sixth.

Range.—Known only from Washington County, southwestern Utah.

The blind snakes live beneath the surface of the ground, and as with other subterranean creatures little is known of their habits. They inhabit deserts or semi-arid areas, but prefer moist spots when available and rocks and boulders seem to be essential. Their habitat is described by Klauber as "rocky and sandy deserts, chaparral-covered foothills, boulder-strewn mountain sides, and the more arid southwestern corner of the Mississippi Basin prairies." They are often discovered in the course of excavations for foundations, pipe lines, post holes, etc.

Klauber has discovered that blind snakes come to the surface at night, where they wander about during the early evening hours, becoming scarce after 8:30 P.M. It is possible that they may be similarly active during the early morning. In crawling on the surface they flick the tongue continually like other snakes, and use the spine on the tip of the stubby tail as an aid to motion.

Blind snakes are entirely inoffensive, and do not even attempt to bite when handled. Their burrowing powers are astonishing, and an individual found under a rock in loose or sandy soil must be seized quickly or it will escape. Burrowing is accomplished by means of the head, coupled with peristaltic movements of the body.

Size.—The subspecies of *Leptotyphlops humilis* exceed the other American blind snakes in average size. The largest specimen known (a desert blind snake from Yuma, Arizona) measures thirteen inches in length and a specimen less than ten inches long has been recorded with eggs in the body.

Food.—No detailed studies have been made.

Breeding Habits.—Egg-laying, but otherwise unknown. The eggs are long and slender and average about four in number. Many tropical species of the same group lay their eggs in termite nests.

Klauber, L. M., 1940, The Worm Snakes of the Genus *Leptotyphlops* in the United States and northern Mexico. *Trans. San Diego Soc. Nat. Hist.*, Vol. 9, pp. 87-162, il. (technical descriptions and general natural history).

THE BOAS

Family BOIDAE

The boas are mainly tropical snakes. Only three of approximately 100 known forms reach the United States, and of these three only the rubber snake (*Charina*) is found beyond the extreme southwestern corner of the country.

Boas are popularly believed to be gigantic snakes. Actually most of them are very moderate sized, and many would even be classed as small. Members of this family are primitive, as is shown for example by the fact that they have two well-developed lungs, while in higher snakes one lung is reduced to a tiny vestige or is absent altogether. Still more striking is the presence of vestiges of the hind legs, which usually appear as small spurs near the vent. These spurs are largest in male specimens.

Boas feed largely on warm-blooded prey, which they usually kill by constriction. Nearly all the members of this family bring forth living young, and in this respect they differ from their nearest relatives, the Pythonidae, which lay eggs.

THE CALIFORNIA BOAS
(Lichanura)
Plate 8

These snakes are typical boas in general appearance, with heavy bodies, triangular heads, and short heavy tails. The top of the head is covered with small smooth scales, and the pupil of the eye is vertical. The California boas are restricted to southern California, adjacent southwestern Arizona and northern Mexico, and Lower California, and due to their limited distribution and secretive habits the life history of none of them is known in detail. The "spurs" are present in members of this genus, although they are sometimes difficult to find.

Scales smooth. Anal plate not divided.

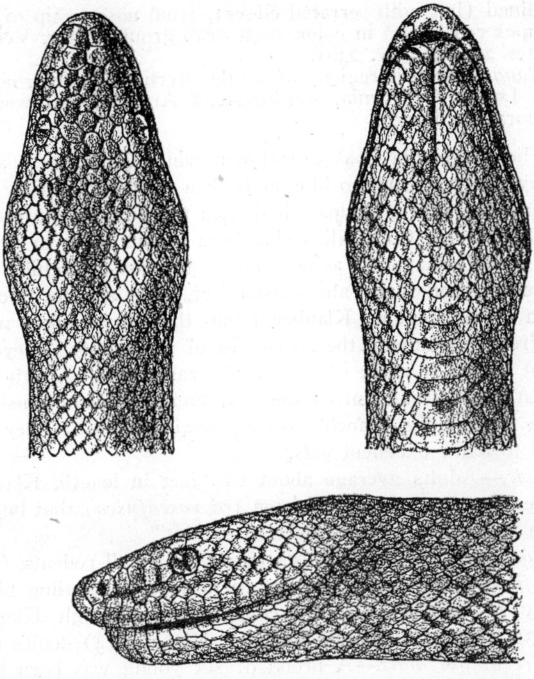

Fig. 18. California boa (*Lichanura r. roseofusca*).

California Boa.—*Lichanura roseofusca roseofusca* Cope. A pattern of three poorly defined and poorly contrasting zig-zag longitudinal stripes from nose to tip of tail, pink to dull brown (usually red brown) in color, on a bluish or gray ground color. The scales are smooth which, combined with the color, produces a metallic effect in life. In some individuals the pattern is broken up, more or less blended with the ground color, and occasionally even entirely obliterated.

Range.—Southwestern California and northern Lower California.

Desert Boa.—*Lichanura roseofusca gracia* Klauber. A pattern of three clearly defined longitudinal stripes, evenly outlined (but with serrated edges), from nose to tip of tail. Stripes red brown in color, on a drab ground color. Ventral scutes 220-236 (av. 230).

Range.—Desert regions of southeastern California, northern Lower California, southwestern Arizona, and western Sonora in Mexico.

The California boas are slow-moving, deliberate snakes. They never attempt to bite, and when disturbed usually roll themselves into a compact ball with the head in the center. In San Diego Co., California, these snakes seem to prefer the granite-chaparral association of the coast foothills, but have not been found above 4500 feet. They are not uncommon in this region; Klauber found that they ranked ninth in frequency among the 29 species of the county. They are most active at night or during the early evening, although often seen abroad during the day. Captives spend considerable time in the branches of any available bush. They are said to make excellent pets.

Size.—Adults average about two feet in length. Klauber states that the longest specimen (of *roseofusca*) that he has seen "measured slightly over three feet."

Food.—Apparently consists largely of small rodents. Captive individuals have been known to feed on nestling birds. Prey is usually killed by constriction, although Klauber (1931, Trans. San Diego Soc. Nat. Hist., 6:314) denies this.

Breeding Habits.—A brood of six young was born to a captive California boa on Nov. 16. They measured about 12 inches in length.

Klauber, L. M., 1931, A new Subspecies of the California Boa, with notes on the Genus *Lichanura. Trans. San Diego Soc. Nat. Hist.*, Vol. 6, pp. 305-318, il.

RUBBER SNAKE
(*Charina bottae* Blainville)
Plate 8

A small heavy-bodied snake, with body higher than wide. Head not distinct from the neck, and a very short and extremely blunt tail. Eye small, with a vertical pupil. Top of head covered with irregular large plates; dorsal body scales small and smooth; tail with undivided plates below. Color uniform grayish, yellowish, or greenish brown, without pattern. Belly yellowish white. Anal "spurs" present.

Scales smooth. Anal plate single.

Range.—Humid districts of California south to San Bernardino Mountains; Nevada, Idaho, Oregon, and Washington, east to Montana, Wyoming, and Utah.

The rubber snake is partial to a damp environment, and according to Van Denburgh is usually found in or near coniferous woods. It is primarily a burrowing snake, and in adaptation to this habit the bones of the skull are more or less solidly united and the last vertebrae of the tail are fused together to form an irregular, solid mass. Its common name comes from its peculiar "rubbery" appearance in life.

Charina is an unusually inoffensive snake, never trying to

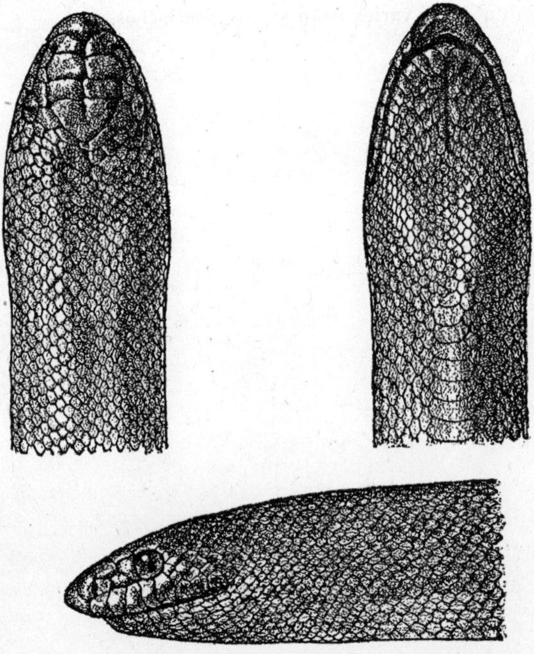

Fig. 19. Rubber snake (*Charina bottae*).

defend itself by biting. When annoyed it is apt to roll itself into a compact ball, and hence is sometimes called the "ball snake." Like many stubby-tailed snakes, it often raises its tail and moves it about like an exploring head while keeping its real head motionless and inconspicuous.

Size.—Adults average about 18 inches. The longest known specimen measured two feet (Van Denburgh).

Food.—The bulk of the diet apparently consists of small mammals, though there are several records of lizards having been eaten. Mammals, at least, are killed by constriction.

Breeding Habits.—Tanner and Tanner (1939, Great Basin Nat., 1: 28-30) report that Utah specimens usually give birth to young in September, the number varying from 1 to 8. The usual number of young appears to be 3 or 4. The length at birth varies from six to nine inches.

THE HARMLESS SNAKES

Family **COLUBRIDAE**

The family Colubridae embraces the vast majority of the snakes of the world, and almost 75 per cent of all North American snakes are included in it. Thus it is not surprising that most of the commonest snakes, such as garter snakes, water snakes, and racers, are colubrids. The family scarcely needs to be defined here, since they are the typical "snakes" that most people think of when they hear the word. (See Key, p. 82.)

As might be expected, the colubrids vary enormously among themselves. In size they range from the huge indigo snake, which may reach a length of eight feet, to the tiny worm snakes, which average only nine inches. They have invaded a variety of habitats, and numerous structural adaptations are associated with particular types of behavior. Some, like the hog-nosed snakes, the mud snakes, and the leaf-nosed snakes, are modified for burrowing. The rough green snake (*Opheodrys aestivus*) resembles the extremely slender tropical vine snakes in adaptation to climbing, by elongation of the body. The whipsnakes and racers are slender but extremely powerful and active cursorial creatures. The flat-tailed water snake even has the tail modified (though only slightly) into an oarlike structure for aquatic life.

Feeding habits are equally varied. Many forms (e.g., the bull snakes) are restricted to a warm-blooded diet, and this prey is usually killed by constriction. Other species subsist entirely on cold-blooded vertebrates, like frogs or salamanders or fishes, and these snakes do not constrict, while the king snakes, so-called from their snake-eating habits, are powerful constrictors. Their size alone would force the smallest species to feed on insects and worms. The mud snake apparently feeds almost exclusively on amphibians, chiefly salamanders, while garter snakes, by contrast, will eat anything within reason. Captive garter snakes can even be taught to eat hamburger out of a dish!

THE WORM SNAKES
(*Carphophis*)
Plate 10

The genus *Carphophis* contains a single species, *amoena*, which is divided into three very similar integrading subspecies. These three forms are so similar in all known characters that identification is best made on the basis of the locality from which a specimen came. The technical characters on which each subspecies is based are given below, but it must be emphasized that these hold only in a majority of specimens.

Scales smooth. Anal plate divided.

Eastern Worm Snake.—*Carphophis amoena amoena* Say. Color above generally brown, belly bright pink; light color of belly extending onto first or second row of dorsal scales; commonly two temporal scutes behind the first. Internasals and prefrontals usually separate.

Range.—Connecticut to New York, south to Central Florida, and west into the Appalachian Mountains.

Central Worm Snake.—*Carphophis amoena helenae* Kennicott. Color above generally brown; pink color of belly extending usually onto the first or second rows of dorsal scales; commonly two temporal scutes behind the first. Internasals and prefrontals usually united into two large shields.

Range.—Central Illinois south to Mississippi, east to northwestern Alabama, the Tennessee Valley to eastern Tennessee, West Virginia and eastern Ohio.

Western Worm Snake.—*Carphophis amoena vermis* Kennicott. Color above generally gray or black; pink color of belly extending usually onto the third row of dorsal scales; commonly a single temporal scute behind the first.

Range.—Southeastern Nebraska and central Missouri through eastern Oklahoma, Arkansas, Louisiana, Kansas, and Texas.

The worm snakes, as their common name implies, are small and wormlike in appearance. They are secretive creatures, partial to moist forested situations, and are generally found beneath stones or logs or beneath the loose bark of rotting logs. Like many small and secretive snakes, they are inclined to be spotty in their distribution, occurring in abundance in some localities while in others they are absent entirely.

In keeping with their semi-burrowing habits, worm snakes have small heads with little or no constriction at the neck, small eyes, smooth glassy scales, and a short and sharply pointed tail. They do not attempt to bite when handled, but the sharp tail tip is pressed into the hand while the head makes exploratory burrowing movements.

Conant states that milk snakes were often found in the vicinity of worm snake colonies in Ohio, and suggests that they may be important enemies of *Carphophis*. This suggestion is reinforced by the fact that one of his milk snakes disgorged a worm snake after its capture.

Size.—Adults average about 9 inches in length. Conant

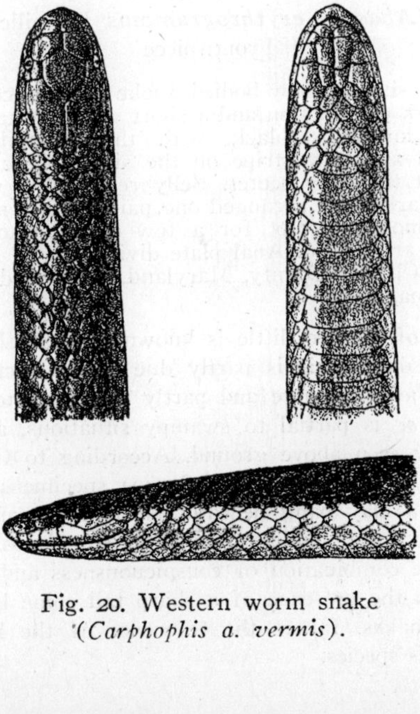

Fig. 20. Western worm snake (*Carphophis a. vermis*).

records a specimen of *C. a. helenae* from Ohio that measured 12¾ inches; Anderson (1942, B. Chi. Acad. Sci., 6: 209) records a Missouri specimen of *vermis* 14¾ inches in length.

Food.—The diet apparently consists entirely or almost entirely of earthworms. Blanchard states that a captive refused a small frog, although it fed voraciously on earthworms.

Breeding Habits.—Blanchard (1926, Pap. Mich. Acad. Sci., 5:373) reported four clutches laid in captivity by *C. a. helenae;* two eggs were deposited in three cases, while the fourth female laid five. The eggs were very elongate, varying from 17 to 27.5 mm. in length at laying, and from 7.5 to 9 mm. in width. The eggs were laid during the first and second weeks of July and hatched about the middle of September. The young were about 4 inches in length at hatching.

RAINBOW SNAKE

(*Abastor erythrogrammus* Latreille)

Frontispiece

A large, shiny, heavy-bodied snake with a conical head without neck constriction and a short, abruptly tapering tail. Ground color bluish-black, with three longitudinal red stripes and a yellow stripe on the sides where the dorsal scales meet the belly scutes. Belly red, with a double row of round dark spots arranged one pair to each scute.

Scales smooth, except for a few on the back near the tail, which are keeled. Anal plate divided.

Range.—Charles County, Maryland, southward to Florida and Alabama.

In spite of its size, little is known of the habits of this snake. No doubt this is partly due to the fact that it is burrowing and secretive and partly to its limited distribution. *Abastor* is partial to swampy situations, and is only occasionally seen above ground. According to Cope (1900, Rept. U. S. Nat. Mus. for 1898:740) specimens have been dug from a clay bank beneath ten feet of sand. This is one of the most brilliantly colored of North American snakes. The combination of conspicuousness and rarity, together with the presence of a sharp tail spine like that of the mud snakes, favors the reference of the hoop snake story to this species.

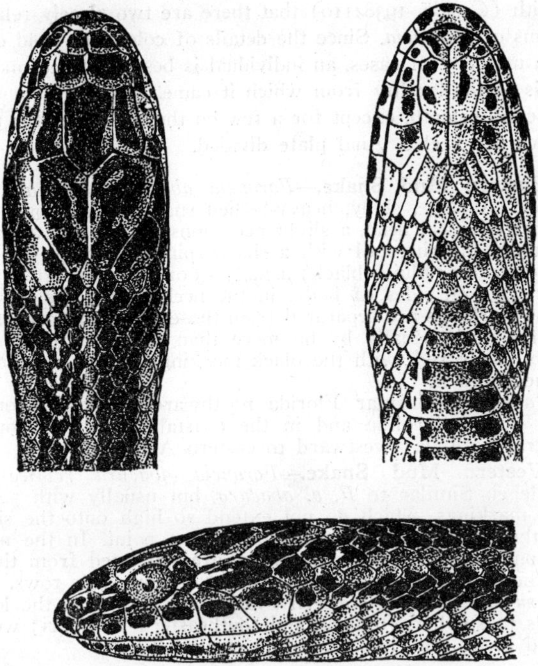

Fig. 21. Rainbow snake (*Abastor erythrogrammus*).

Size.—Adults average nearly four feet in length.

Food.—Unknown.

Breeding Habits.—According to Conant and Bridges 22 to 43 eggs are laid, and the young average about 9¼ inches in length at hatching.

MUD SNAKES
(*Farancia*)
Plate 9

The mud snakes differ from the rainbow snakes in having a single internasal plate. It has recently been shown by

Smith (*Copeia,* 1938:110) that there are two closely related forms of *Farancia.* Since the details of coloration hold only in a majority of cases, an individual is best identified on the basis of the locality from which it came.

Scales smooth, except for a few on the back near the tail, which are keeled. Anal plate divided.

Eastern Mud Snake.—*Farancia abacura abacura* Holbrook. A large, shiny, heavy-bodied snake with a long and rather elliptical head, a slight neck constriction, and a short, abruptly tapering tail with a sharp spine at its tip. Ground color black or bluish-black; usually 53 or more triangular red markings on sides of body, in the neck region the tips of these markings are separated from those on the opposite side of the neck usually by no more than three or four scale rows. Belly red, with the black markings of the sides continued onto it.

Range.—Peninsular Florida northward through Georgia and South Carolina and in the coastal regions to south-central Virginia; westward to eastern Alabama.

Western Mud Snake.—*Farancia abacura reinwardtii* Schlegel. Similar to *F. a. abacura,* but usually with 52 or less markings, which do not extend so high onto the sides of the body, and not terminating in a point. In the neck region the tips of these markings are separated from those on the opposite side usually by eight or nine scale rows.

Range.—Extreme western Florida northward in the lowlands to southern Indiana and southeastern Missouri; westward along the Gulf coast into eastern Texas.

The mud snake, often known as the horn snake or "stinging snake" because of the hornlike spine on its tail, is an inhabitant of the swampy lowlands of the south. It is a burrower like the rainbow snake, and is consequently secretive in its habits. It is greatly feared by many because of the supposed deadly nature of the "horn," which is often pushed into the flesh of the hand or arm if the snake is handled. The true use of this spine is unknown, although it probably functions during burrowing. It has often been suggested that it aids in holding prey during feeding, but this has been denied by Meade (*Copeia,* 1940:165) after careful observation.

The "stinging snake" story appears to be a simple form of the hoop snake story; the latter may in some localities be transferred to this snake.

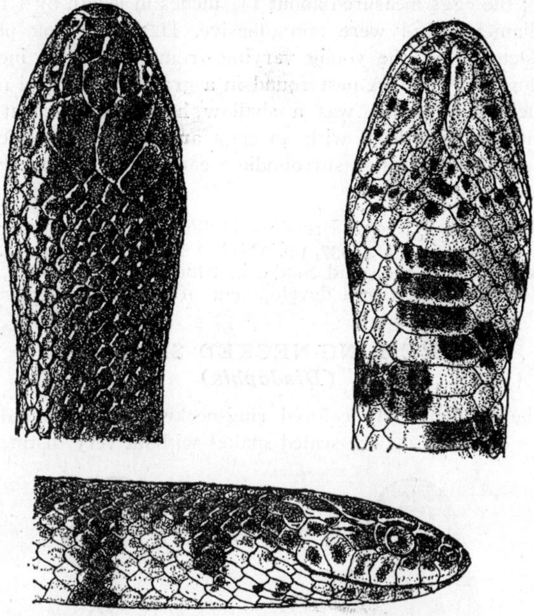

Fig. 22. Western mud snake (*Farancia a. reinwardtii*).

Size.—Adults average about four feet in length. The maximum length is given by Smith as 5 ft. 9 in.

Food.—Van Hyning (Copeia, 1932:37) examined 25 stomachs of this species. Of the 9 that contained food, the mud eel (*Siren lacertina*) was present in 7, and this salamander made up 56% of the bulk of the diet. Other salamanders were present in two stomachs, frogs in one, and fish in one. G. P. Meade, on the other hand, found that captive specimens would feed only on the congo eel (*Amphiuma*), another eel-shaped salamander.

Breeding Habits.—According to Conant and Bridges the number of eggs in a clutch varies from 22 to 104. Meade reported that a mating took place in captivity on July 11. The same female laid 28 eggs during the second week of

July; the eggs measured about 1¾ inches in length by 1 inch in diameter, and were non-adhesive. Hatching took place on October 30, the young varying from 6¼ to 9½ inches in length at birth. A nest found in a graveyard mound near Gainesville, Florida, was a shallow horizontal excavation, about 4 inches deep, with 40 eggs arranged in three concentric layers in the surrounding earth. The female was coiled in the hole.

Meade, G. P., 1937, Breeding Habits of *Farancia abacura* in Captivity. *Copeia,* 1937, pp. 12-15, 1 fig.; **Goldstein, R. C.**, 1941, Notes on the Mud Snake in Florida. *Copeia,* 1941, pp. 49-50, 1 fig. (nest and development of eggs).

THE RING-NECKED SNAKES
(*Diadophis*)

The harmoniously colored ring-necked snakes include a series of small smooth-scaled snakes without very distinctive

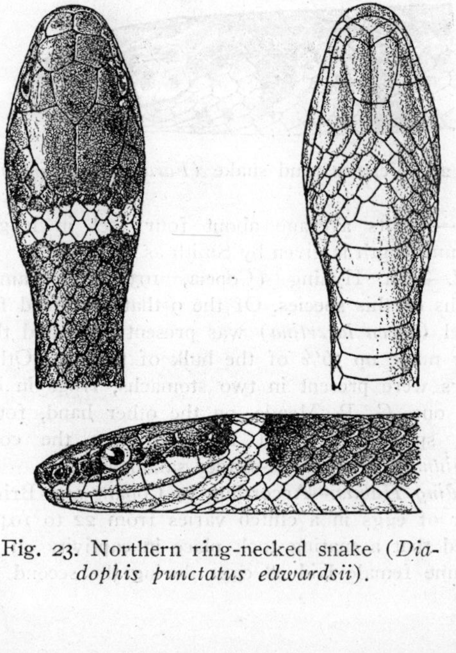

Fig. 23. Northern ring-necked snake (*Diadophis punctatus edwardsii*).

modifications of any kind. Adult males exhibit the secondary sex character of tubercles on the scales above the anus. The ring of the bright ventral color on the neck forms a very satisfactory recognition character.

Scales smooth. Anal plate divided.

KEY TO SPECIES OF *DIADOPHIS*

1 a. Color of ventral plates of anterior part of body covering one or more of lowermost rows of dorsal scales 2

1 b. Color of ventral plates of anterior part of body not reaching lowermost row of dorsal scales
...... Eastern ring-necked snakes (*D. punctatus*)

2 a. More than 206 ventral plates in males or more than 220 in females
......Southwestern ring-necked snakes (*D. regalis*)

2 b. Fewer than 206 ventral plates in males or fewer than 220 in females
........Western ring-necked snakes (*D. amabilis*)

WESTERN RING-NECKED SNAKES

(*Diadophis amabilis*)

Plate 10

The western ring-necked snakes are confined to the west coast region. Six closely related subspecies are known, and so far as known these are very similar to one another in habits and behavior.

The color above in all western ring-necked snakes is a uniform olive, bluish or gray, with the yellowish neck ring standing out boldly. This somber hue of the back contrasts sharply with the brilliant yellow, orange or coral-red of the belly.

Pacific Ring-Necked Snake.—*Diadophis amabilis amabilis* Baird and Girard. Neck ring narrow (1 to 1½ scales wide), and often interrupted. Light coloration of belly usually extending onto the lower part of the second row of dorsal scales. Numerous small black spots scattered over the belly.

Range.—California, restricted to the regions about San Francisco and to the San Joaquin and Sacramento Valleys.

San Bernardino Ring-Necked Snake.—*Diadophis amabilis modestus* Duméril and Bocourt. This snake and *D. a. vandenburghi* differ from the other subspecies of *D. amabilis* in having the dorsal scale rows 17-15 instead of 15-15. The light coloration of the belly extends only onto the first row of dorsal scales. The belly is usually conspicuously spotted with black.

Range.—San Bernardino Mountains, Los Angeles County, and Santa Catalina Island, California.

Northwestern Ring-Necked Snake.—*Diadophis amabilis occidentalis* Blanchard. Neck ring wide (1½ to 3 scales in width), and not interrupted. Light coloration of belly covering from 1½ to 2 or more rows of scales, the two lowermost rows of dorsal scales flecked with black. The belly is rather conspicuously, although sparsely, marked with small black dots.

Range.—From Sonoma County, California, northward to Cowlitz and Whitman Counties, Washington and Boise County, Idaho.

Coral-Bellied Ring-Necked Snake.—*Diadophis amabilis pulchellus* Baird and Girard. Similar to *D. a. occidentalis*, but with the two lowermost rows of dorsal scales unicolor (not flecked with black), and with the belly almost or quite unspotted.

Range.—Western slopes of the Sierra Nevada south, perhaps to Tejon Pass in California, and north to southern Oregon.

Southern California Ring-Necked Snake.—*Diadophis amabilis similis* Blanchard. Neck ring about 1½ scales wide, and only rarely interrupted. Light coloration of belly covering two-thirds or less of the first row of dorsal scales.

Range.—From southwestern San Bernardino County, California, south into the San Pedro Martir range in Lower California.

Van Denburgh's Ring-Necked Snake.—*Diadophis amabilis vandenburghi* Blanchard. Dorsal scale rows 17-15 instead of 15-15. Neck ring moderately wide (1½ to 2½ scales in width), and not interrupted. Light coloration of belly covering from 1½ to 2 of the lowermost rows of dorsal scales. Belly usually only lightly spotted with black.

Range.—Ventura to Santa Cruz Counties, California.

The western ring-necked snakes, sometimes called "red-bellied snakes," are found throughout the west coast region except in the desert area and the hot interior valleys. They are secretive like their eastern relatives, and are usually found coiled under stones or logs in moist situations.

Size.—Adults average about 16 inches in length, with a maximum of about two feet.

Food.—Young tree frogs have been found in the stomachs of captured individuals. Captive specimens have been known to eat skinks.

Breeding Habits.—Four eggs were found in a large female *D. a. occidentalis* from Oregon (Fitch, 1936, Amer. Midl. Nat., 17:644). The breeding habits are otherwise unknown.

EASTERN RING-NECKED SNAKES
(*Diadophis punctatus*)
Plate 10

The eastern ring-necked snakes occupy the eastern part of the United States. They differ from their western relatives (*D. amabilis* and *D. regalis*) in having the reddish color of the belly confined to the ventral plates, and not reaching up onto the lowermost scales of the body.

The color above in these snakes is uniform gray, bluish slate or black. The lighter neck ring stands out in bold contrast.

Southern Ring-Necked Snake.—*Diadophis punctatus punctatus* Linnaeus. The yellow neck ring is usually broken at the midline. Belly yellow or orange, and marked with a series of large half-circular black spots down the center.

Range.—Southeastern states northward to northern North Carolina from sea-level to about 2500 feet, possibly higher in the mountains of South Carolina and Georgia.

Prairie Ring-Necked Snake.—*Diadophis punctatus arnyi* Kennicott. Yellow neck ring not broken at the midline. Belly yellow, marked with black spots scattered or in pairs.

Range.—Iowa, Missouri and northwestern Arkansas to South Dakota, Oklahoma and Texas.

Northern Ring-Necked Snake.—*Diadophis punctatus edwardsii* Merrem. Yellow or orange-yellow neck ring, one to three scales wide, rarely broken at the midline. Belly yellow or orange, usually unspotted but sometimes with a row of small imperfectly developed black spots down the center.

Range.—The northern peninsula of Michigan, Wisconsin, eastward to Nova Scotia; the northeastern United States; and southward through the Appalachians to the Carolinas.

Mississippi Ring-Necked Snake.—*Diadophis punctatus stictogenys* Cope. Similar to the northern ring-necked snake, but with belly conspicuously spotted with black, the spots showing a tendency to fuse into a single row or irregularly massed.

Range.—Southern Illinois through the lower Mississippi Valley to the Gulf.

The eastern ring-necked snakes are partial to moist woodland situations. They are secretive, but not burrowing, and are usually found beneath stones, boards, or other debris. They are often found beneath the bark of decaying logs and stumps or in hollow logs. Several individuals may be found together.

Freshly captured snakes rarely attempt to bite, but most of them promptly pour out the evil-smelling anal secretion.

Size.—Adults average about a foot in length, with a maximum of 18 to 20 inches.

Food.—The food of these snakes is quite varied and the size of their prey is limited only by the capacity of the snake. Small snakes of other species, small toads, small salamanders, earthworms, and various insects have been recorded.

Breeding Habits.—Blanchard has made extensive studies of the breeding habits of the northern ring-necked snake in Michigan. Eggs are laid in late June or early July in damp rotten logs, and a dozen or more females may use the same nest, so that 50 or more eggs may occur in a single nest. A single female may lay from 1 to 7 eggs, with an average number of about 3. The eggs are white and elongate, averaging about two inches in length by ¼ in. in diameter. Hatching takes place in late August and through September, the young averaging about 5 inches (124 mm.) at birth.

Blanchard, F. N., 1930, Further Studies on the Eggs and Young of the Eastern Ring-Neck Snake, *Diadophis punctatus edwardsii*. *Bull. Antivenin Inst. Amer.*, vol. 4, pp. 4-10, 7 figs.—1937, Eggs and Natural Nests of the Eastern Ring-Neck Snake, *Diadophis punctatus edwardsii*. *Pap. Mich. Acad. Sci.*, vol. 22, pp. 521-532, il.

SOUTHWESTERN RING-NECKED SNAKES
(*Diadophis regalis*)

Two closely related forms in the desert areas of the southwest are the largest of the ring-necked snakes. They agree with the forms of *D. amabilis* in that the reddish color of the belly extends up onto the lowermost scales of the body, but differ from them in having a greater number of ventral scales (more than 206 in males, or 220 in females).

Southwestern Ring-Necked Snake.—*Diadophis regalis regalis* Baird and Girard. The neck ring is usually absent, or is much reduced. The upper surface of the body is colored a uniform greenish or grayish brown, the belly and lowermost row of body scales yellowish to bright red.

Range.—Southern Utah, southeastern Arizona, to central Texas and the state of Vera Cruz, Mexico.

Arizona Ring-Necked Snake.—*Diadophis regalis arizonae* Blanchard. A light-colored neck ring, 2 to 4 scales in width, present. Coloration otherwise is similar to that of *D. r. regalis.*

Range.—Central Arizona to northern Sonora in Mexico.

Remarkably little is known of the habits of these snakes, which are sometimes called the "thimble snakes." They appear to be mountain forms not found in the desert areas.

Size.—Adults average about 2 ft. in length. The longest authentic record is 29 inches (Van Denburgh).

Food.—Van Denburgh reported a specimen containing a black-headed snake (*Tantilla*).

Breeding Habits.—Unknown.

YELLOW-LIPPED SNAKE
(*Rhadinaea flavilata* Cope)
Plate 9

A small, slender, smooth-scaled snake, the scales with a definite velvety iridescence. Uniformly colored, reddish-brown to golden-brown above, sometimes with a faint indication of a darker median stripe. A dark band from the eye to the corner of the mouth; upper lip yellow. Belly uniform yellow.

Scales smooth. Anal plate divided.

Range.—A narrow coastal strip from eastern North Carolina to Florida, and along the gulf coast to western Texas.

This small, secretive snake is usually considered rare, although Allen (*Copeia,* 1939:175) recently announced that it is abundant near Burbank, Florida. Individuals are found

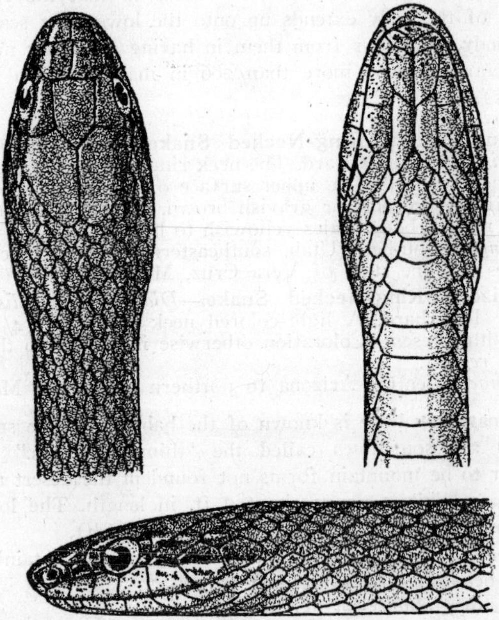

Fig. 24. Yellow-lipped snake (*Rhadinea flavilata*).

beneath logs, bark, or other debris. They seem to be partial to damp situations.

Size.—Adults average about a foot in length. Allen recorded a specimen that measured 15½ inches.

Food.—Captives have eaten small species of frogs, toads, and lizards. Remains of small frogs and lizards have been found in stomach contents.

Breeding Habits.—A captive female laid three eggs, which

measured 23 mm. in length and 8 mm. in diameter, on August 19; these hatched in September.

Malnate, E., 1939, A Study of the Yellow-Lipped Snake, *Rhadinaea flavilata* (Cope). *Zoologica,* vol. 24, pp. 359-366, il. (review of habits, behavior, etc.).

THE HOG-NOSED SNAKES
(Heterodon)
Plate 11

The hog-nosed snakes are characterized by their up-turned, shovel-like snouts. Almost equally diagnostic is their habit of spreading the head and fore part of the body, inflating the lung, and lunging threateningly when molested. All are rather stout bodied, conspicuously spotted snakes.

Scales keeled. Anal plate divided.

Common Hog-Nosed Snake.—*Heterodon contortrix contortrix* Linnaeus. This snake, together with the closely related Florida hog-nose, differs from the remaining hog-nosed snakes in having the prefrontals in contact. The internasals are separated by a small median scale, the azygous. The snout is less sharply up-turned than in the other two species, and the under side of the tail is also generally conspicuously lighter than the abdomen. There are 20 or more light cross bars on the body.

Range.—New Hampshire to central Florida, westward to Texas and Oklahoma and northward through the states of the Mississippi basin to Minnesota.

Florida Hog-Nosed Snake.—*Heterodon contortrix browni* Stejneger. Differs from all other hog-noses in that it usually lacks the small scale on the top of the nose that separates the internasals in the other species. There are fewer than 20 light cross-bars on the body.

Range.—Confined to southern Florida.

Western Hog-Nosed Snake.—*Heterodon nasicus nasicus* Baird and Girard. Snout very sharply upturned. There is a series of about 40 blotches down the middle of the back. The belly is largely black. Differs from *H. n. kennerlyi* in having 8 or more small scales on top of the snout.

Range.—Southwestern Iowa, Kansas and Nebraska west to Montana and south to northern Mexico.

Southwestern Hog-Nosed Snake.—*Heterodon nasicus kennerlyi* Kennicott. Similar to *H. n. nasicus,* but with fewer (2 to 6) small scales accessory to the azygous. The loreal is also single, and is usually much reduced.

Range.—Western Texas, southern New Mexico, southern Arizona, and northwestern Mexico.

Southern Hog-Nosed Snake.—*Heterodon simus* Linnaeus. Similar to *Heterodon contortrix,* but with the under side of the tail not conspicuously lighter than the belly. The snout is also more sharply upturned, and the coloration is usually paler.

Range.—North Carolina southward to central Florida, and northwest to Indiana.

Fig. 25. Three species of hog-nosed snakes. (*Top*) Common hog-nosed snake (*Heterodon c. contortrix*). (*Middle*) Western hog-nosed snake (*H. n. nasicus*). (*Bottom*) Southern hog-nosed snake (*H. simus*). Note great development of "shovel" in *nasicus* and *simus.*

The hog-nosed snakes, because of their alarming defensive behavior, are known by a greater variety of vernacular names than any other American snake. Among these are spread head, blow snake, puff adder, hissing viper, etc. The defensive behavior usually follows a stereotyped pattern. The snake holds its ground if cornered, flattening and

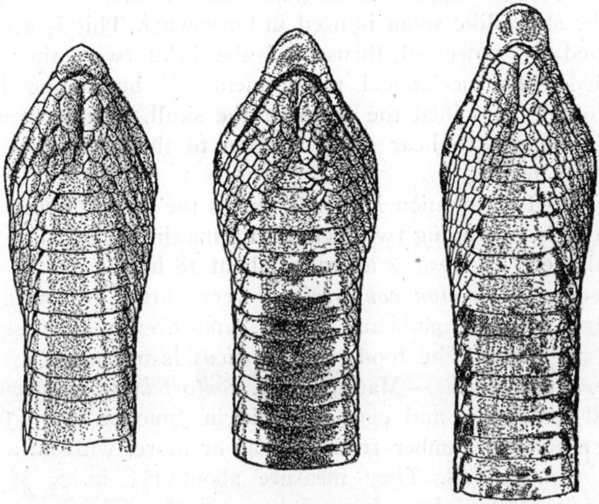

Fig. 26. Common, western, and southern hog-nosed snakes; heads from below, showing differences in size and shape of rostral shield.

spreading the head and fore part of the body to twice their normal width. Meantime the lung is slowly inflated with air, which is then expelled with a loud hiss. Occasional individuals will strike, with mouth either wide open or closed. If further annoyed, the mouth is opened and rubbed on the ground and the body is contorted as if the snake were in the final stages of a death agony; dirt and debris adhering to the inside of the mouth add realism to the procedure. The snake then rolls onto its back and lies perfectly still. If picked up it is limp and lifeless, and remains that way in spite of rough handling. It can easily be induced to betray itself, however, if placed on its belly, since it invariably promptly rolls onto its back! This unique and remarkable behavior is lost after a very short time in captivity. The western hog-nosed snake holds the mouth very widely opened in the active stage of its defensive behavior.

The eastern species are usually found in dry sandy situations, although *H. simus* is often found in dry woods. The western forms appear to be plains inhabitants.

The shovellike snout is used in burrowing. This is accomplished by powerful thrusts of the head, with the neck arched. The mechanical requirements of burrowing have profoundly modified the form of the skull. The burrowing habit appears to bear some relation to the preference for toads as food.

Size.—The common *H. contortrix* is the largest species of the genus, averaging two feet, with a maximum of three and a half feet. *H. nasicus* averages about 18 inches.

Food.—*Heterodon contortrix* is very partial to toads, although other amphibians, insects, and even an occasional bird are taken. The food of *H. nasicus* is unknown.

Breeding Habits.—Mating in *H. contortrix* takes place in April and May, and eggs are laid in June or early July. These vary in number from 8 to 40 or more, with an average of about 25. They measure about 1¼ in. x ⅞ in. Hatching takes place from July to September, the young measuring 6½ to 8 inches in length.

ROUGH GREEN SNAKE

(Opheodrys aestivus Linnaeus)

Plate 12

An extremely slender, long-tailed snake; uniform light green above, with a whitish, yellow-tinged belly. The scales are *prominently keeled*. Anal plate divided.

Range.—Connecticut to Florida and the Gulf states northward in the Mississippi basin to Kansas, Illinois, and Ohio. Reports from as far west as New Mexico require confirmation.

This snake is inclined to be arboreal, as its slender form indicates. Individuals are usually found in shrubs and low trees, where they are very hard to detect unless they are in

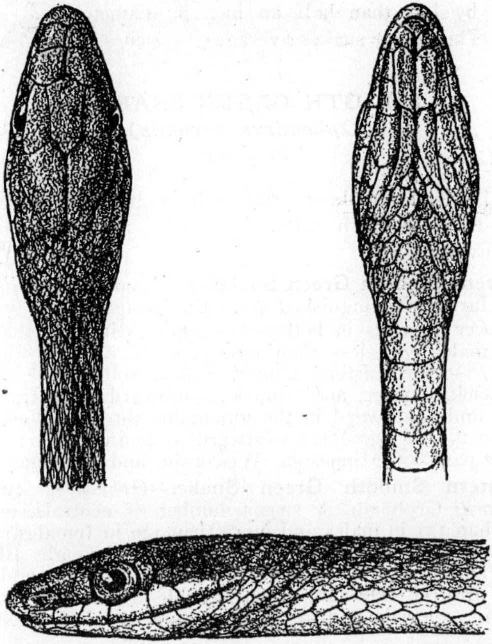

Fig. 27. Rough green snake (*Opheodrys aestivus*).

motion. They are usually mild-tempered, but occasionally will attempt to bite if molested.

Size.—Adults average about 28 inches, with a maximum of three and a half feet.

Food.—Feeds practically exclusively on insects. Van Hyning analyzed the contents of eight stomachs. Insects, chiefly caterpillars constituted 53% of the bulk; spiders made up 35% and one stomach contained a frog, which accounted for 12% of the total bulk of food.

Breeding Habits.—Eggs are laid in July and hatch in September. Four clutches numbered 4 to 9 eggs each, with an average of 6. The eggs are elongate, and have rather hard white shells. They measure slightly over an inch in length by less than half an inch in diameter (28 x 10.5 mm.). The young snakes average 7½ inches at hatching.

SMOOTH GREEN SNAKES
(Opheodrys vernalis)
Plate 12

Small, slender snakes; uniform light green above, with a yellow-tinged whitish belly. The scales are *smooth.* Anal plate divided.

Eastern Smooth Green Snake.—*Opheodrys vernalis vernalis* Harlan. Distinguished from the western form by having fewer ventrals in both sexes, males with less than 131 and females with less than 140.

Range. Northeastern United States, and adjacent New Brunswick, Quebec, and Ontario, southward to central New Jersey and southward in the mountains through West Virginia to North Carolina; westward to central Ohio; northeastern parts of Minnesota, Wisconsin, and Michigan.

Western Smooth Green Snake.—*Opheodrys vernalis blanchardi* Grobman. A larger number of ventrals, usually more than 131 in males and more than 140 in females.

Range.—Western Ohio and Indiana, through Illinois, Iowa, and northern Missouri to eastern Kansas and Nebraska and the Dakotas; a considerable area in northeastern Utah, in Colorado and in the mountains of New Mexico.

These pretty little snakes are much less arboreal than the rough green snake, although they often climb into low bushes. They are often referred to as the "grass snakes" and do in fact tend to be associated with meadows, clearings, and marshes. They are remarkably gentle and inoffensive, and individuals can seldom be induced to bite. The smooth green snakes often occur more commonly than is suspected, since their small size, secretive habits, and protective coloration render them inconspicuous

Size.—Adults average about 15 inches, with a maximum of two feet.

Food.—Apparently feeds exclusively on insects.

Breeding Habits.—Blanchard made a detailed study of the eggs and young of this species in Michigan. Eggs are laid in late July and August, and hatch in August and early September. Clutches vary from 3 to 11, with an average of

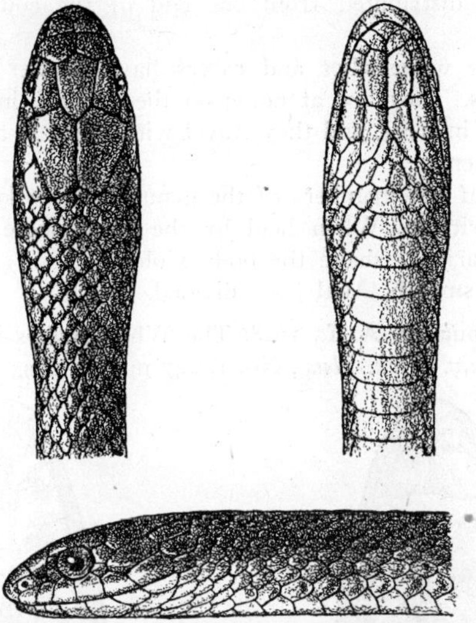

Fig. 28. Smooth green snake
(*Opheodrys v. vernalis*).

7. The eggs are elongate, measuring about an inch (19.5 to 30 mm. av. 20-30) in length by half an inch (8 to 18 mm., av. 10-15) in width. The young measure about 4½ inches (114 to 131 mm., extremes 101-166) in length at hatching.

Blanchard, F. N., 1933, Eggs and Young of the Smooth Green Snake, *Liopeltis vernalis* (Harlan). *Pap. Mich. Acad. Sci.*, vol. 17, pp. 493-508, il. **Grobman, A. E.**, 1941, A contribution to the knowledge of variation in *Opheodrys vernalis* (Harlan), with a description of a new subspecies. *Misc. Publ. Mus. Zool., Univ. Mich.*, No. 50, pp. 1-38, 2 figs.

THE WHIPSNAKES AND RACERS
(*Coluber*)

These are among the largest, most active, and most graceful of the snakes of the United States. As might be expected of creatures of their bold and active natures, the genus is distributed from one end of the country to the other.

All the whipsnakes and racers have slender bodies and long tails. They are at home on the ground, in shrubbery, and even in trees, and they travel with speed in any of these environments.

None of the members of the genus *Coluber* kills its prey by constriction. When held by the neck, these snakes almost invariably shake the body violently.

Scales smooth. Anal plate divided.

Ortenburger, A. I., 1928, The Whip Snakes and Racers. *Mem. Univ. Mich. Mus.*, No. 1, 247 pp., 64 figs., 36 pl.

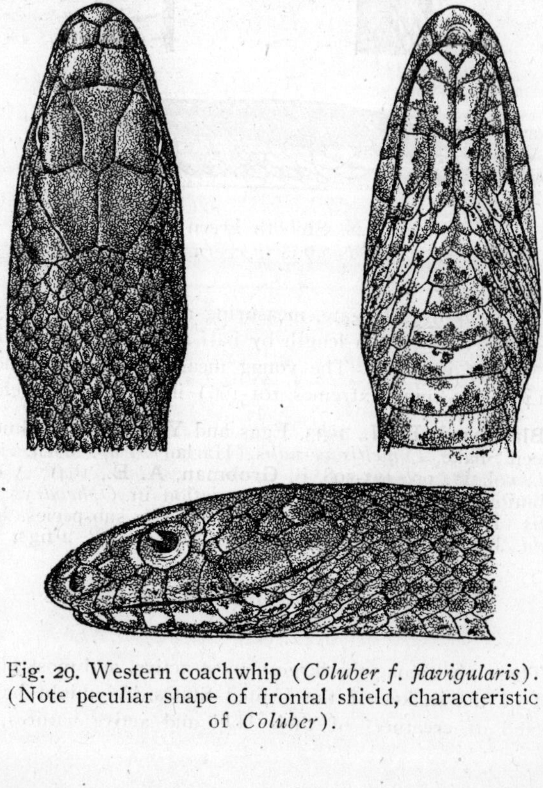

Fig. 29. Western coachwhip (*Coluber f. flavigularis*). (Note peculiar shape of frontal shield, characteristic of *Coluber*).

KEY TO SPECIES OF *COLUBER**

1 a. Scale rows at posterior end of body 15 (scale formula 17-15 or 15-15) 2

1 b. Scale rows at posterior end of body 13 or 11 (scale formula 17-13, 15-13, or 15-11) 5

2 a. Upper surface black or very dark gray; belly dark gray; caudals average 106. (Juveniles are blotched; under surface of jaw not marked with spots) 3

2 b. Upper surface not black or very dark gray; belly light bluish, greenish, or yellow; caudals usually less than 100 4

3 a. Some of the proximal spines of the hemipenes much enlarged into basal hooks** Florida blacksnake (*C. constrictor priapus*) p. 125

3 b. Proximal spines of hemipenes not enlarged into basal hooks**
......Common blacksnake
(*C. constrictor constrictor*) p. 125

4 a. 7 upper labials; caudals usually less than 85; color above blue-gray or bluish (Juveniles are blotched; under surface of lower jaw not marked with spots) .... Blue racer
(*C. constrictor flaviventris*) p. 125

4 b. Upper labials usually 8; caudals usually more than 85; color above olive-brown, greenish or blue-gray. (Juveniles are blotched; undersurface of lower jaw not marked with spots)
Western blue racer (*C. constrictor mormon*) p. 125

5 a. 15 scale rows 6

5 b. 17 scale rows 9

6 a. Head plates with light edges 8

6 b. Head unicolor 7

7 a. 2 to 4 dark and 2 light lateral stripes
....Green whipsnake (*C. taeniatus schotti*) p. 130

7 b. One or no light lateral stripe
Ruthven's whipsnake (*C. taeniatus ruthveni*) p. 129

---

* Adapted from Perkins, C. B., "A Key to the Snakes of the United States." *Bull. Zool. Soc. San Diego*, No. 16, 1940.

** If unable to use this internal character, separate these two subspecies by their ranges (see p. 125).

8 a. One or more light crossbands just behind head or on neck and body
... Ornate whipsnake (*C. taeniatus girardi*) p. 129

8 b. No light crossbands just behind head or on neck and body
...Striped whipsnake (*C. taeniatus taeniatus*) p. 129

9 a. Distinct longitudinal stripes present 10

9 b. No distinct longitudinal stripes 11

10 a. 2 or 3 light lateral stripes anteriorly, not continued to the tail
.......Sonoran whipsnake (*C. semilineatus*) p. 129

10 b. One light lateral stripe, continuing to the tail
...California striped whipsnake (*C. lateralis*) p. 127

11 a. Entire upper surface of body and tail black (Juvenile coloration unknown)
......Black whipsnake (*C. piceus*) p. 129

11 b. Entire upper surface not black 12

12 a. Black or dark brown crossbands across the neck or anterior fifth of body 14

12 b. No such black or dark brown crossbands 13

13 a. Head and fore part of body very dark brown or black, gradually becoming much lighter posteriorly
..Eastern coachwhip (*C. flagellum flagellum*) p. 127

13 b. Fore part of body not darker than posterior Western coachwhip (*C. flagellum flavigularis*) p. 127

14 a. A distinct horizontal white stripe, bordered by black through loreal. (Juveniles are blotched, under surface of lower jaw spotted)
......Red racer (*C. flagellum frenatus*) p. 127

14 b. No distinct horizontal white stripe through loreal 15

15 a. Dark brown crossbands on neck separated by 1 or 2 scales of lighter brown; most of last upper labial cream color
......Juvenile eastern coachwhip
(*C. flagellum flagellum*) p. 127

15 b. Dark brown crossbands on neck separated by 3 or more scales of lighter brown; all but anterior lower corner of last upper labial brown
......Juvenile western coachwhip
(*C. flagellum flavigularis*) p. 127

THE RACERS

Plates 4, 13

The racers form a small and compact group of forms that intergrade with one another where the edges of their ranges meet, so that individuals from these areas often show a mixture of the characters of two subspecies. The racers are not so slender as the whipsnakes, and differ from them in a number of minor anatomical details.

Blacksnake.—*Coluber constrictor constrictor* Linnaeus. A large, uniformly black snake, the scales with a definite satiny lustre. Belly dark to medium gray, without markings. Throat and chin white, the throat usually more or less blotched with dark gray posteriorly.

Range.—The whole of the eastern United States, except Florida, westward to central Indiana, thence southwest through southern Illinois and eastern parts of Missouri, Arkansas, and Texas.

Florida Blacksnake.—*Coluber constrictor priapus* Dunn and Wood. This recently described form is externally indistinguishable from the common blacksnake, but differs considerably from it in having the proximal spines of the hemipenes in the male much enlarged into basal hooks. Specimens are readily identified on the basis of their ranges, without resorting to this internal character.

Range.—Florida.

Blue Racer.—*Coluber constrictor flaviventris* Say. A large, bluish or greenish-blue snake, ranging to dark gray or olive-gray. Belly very light blue or greenish-gray or yellow, somewhat lighter on the throat and chin.

Range.—From the Rocky Mountains east through Texas, western Arkansas, Missouri, and Michigan, and northern parts of Illinois, Indiana, and Ohio.

Western Blue Racer.—*Coluber constrictor mormon* Baird and Girard. An olive-green, brown or yellowish-brown snake, changing on the sides of the body to blue or greenish. Belly yellow or yellow-green or blue-gray, lighter on chin and anterior part of throat.

Range.—From the Pacific Ocean east to Montana, south to extreme southern California, Idaho, Nevada, and Utah.

These snakes characteristically crawl with the head raised well above the ground. The racers are characteristically terrestrial snakes, but all three forms can climb through trees and bushes with ease and agility. They are the usual subjects of two popular superstitions: that they "charm" their prey, and that they "chase" people. Neither of these has any foundation in fact, although during the breeding season an occasional individual may advance toward an intruder. The fact that they run over the tops of bushes may be part of the origin of the hoop snake myth.

The racers often congregate in considerable numbers to hibernate. They usually pass the winter in limestone crevices or in the abandoned holes of woodchucks or other mammals. Blacksnakes and timber rattlesnakes often hibernate together.

The racers are remarkable for the difference in coloration between adults and young (Plate 4). Young individuals have a pattern of dorsal saddles or partial crossbands; these saddles number 50-65 in *constrictor,* 65-80 in *flaviventris,* and 70-85 in *mormon.* This pattern is gradually replaced by the uniform adult coloration when the snakes reach a length of about 24 inches.

Size.—Adult blacksnakes average about 4 feet in length; the maximum recorded length is 5 feet, 10½ inches (Atkinson). Blue racers average about 4 feet, with a maximum (Ortenburger) of 5 feet, 10 inches. The western blue racer is much smaller; the longest on record measured 4 feet, 3½ inches (Ortenburger).

Food.—The racers are indiscriminate feeders. A wide assortment of insects, frogs and toads, lizards, snakes, birds, bird's eggs, and small mammals has been recorded. Insects and small mammals, especially mice, make up the bulk of the diet. The prey is not killed by constriction.

Breeding Habits.—Mating has been observed on May 12 and laying takes place through June and early July. Up to 25 eggs are laid in a clutch. Five recorded clutches for the blacksnake give an average of 12, while four clutches for the blue racer average 17. The eggs are usually laid in decaying vegetable matter and hatch in August. They measure about 2 inches in length, and have a granular texture. The young are from 8 to 12 inches long at hatching.

THE WHIPSNAKES

Plates 13, 14

The whipsnakes are usually separated into two groups: the "flagellum" group (*flagellum* and its subspecies, and *piceus*), in which the pattern is one of crossbands anteriorly, or in which the snake is dark anteriorly and lighter posteriorly; and the "taeniatus" group (*taeniatus* and its subspecies; and *lateralis* and *semilineatus*), in which the pattern consists of longitudinal stripes.

Eastern Coachwhip.—*Coluber flagellum flagellum* Shaw. (Plate 13). A large slender snake with the head and fore part of the body dark brown or black, the color gradually becoming much lighter toward the tail. The color of the belly corresponds to that of the upper surface, being dark toward the head and much lighter toward the tail. The form and coloration of the scales on the tail give the snake the appearance of a braided whip, from which it derives its common name.

Range.—North Carolina to Florida, westward to Texas and central Kansas.

Western Coachwhip.—*Coluber flagellum flavigularis* Hallowell. Differs from the eastern coachwhip in that the ground color is not darker toward the head. The general color varies from light yellow-brown to dark brown, and there is often a faint indication of crossbanding. Belly cream-yellow to dirty brown, with a parallel series of brown blotches toward the head.

Range.—Western Kansas, southeastern Colorado south to central Mexico.

Red Racer.—*Coluber flagellum frenatus* Stejneger. (Plate 13). A light yellow-brown to red-brown or gray snake, the color becoming lighter toward the tail. From 2 to 10 or more distinct black crossbands on the top and sides of the neck, these bands usually abruptly becoming much lighter after the first three or five. Often the bands are fused, so that the neck appears black. Belly light cream color, heavily blotched with black or dark brown toward the head. There is always a distinct horizontal white stripe through the loreal.

Range.—Central and southern California, Lower California, Nevada, Utah, Arizona, western New Mexico, and Sonora to Sinaloa in Mexico.

California Striped Whipsnake.—*Coluber lateralis* Hallowell. (Plate 14). A dark brown or black snake with a single narrow yellow stripe on each side of the body, extending

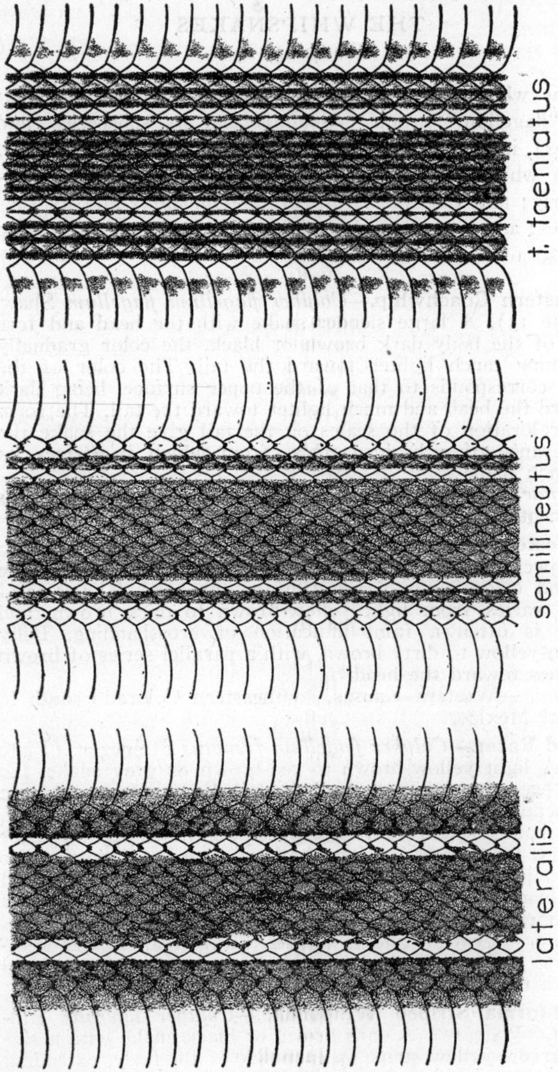

Fig. 30. Patterns of striped whipsnakes.

from the neck to the tail. The light stripes are narrowly margined with black on brown individuals. The upper and lower lips are cream-colored, and there are several cream spots on the sides of the head. Belly light yellow toward the head, gradually changing to pink toward the tail, with a parallel series of small dark gray spots on the anterior scutes. (Fig. 30).

Range.—California and Lower California.

Black Whipsnake.—*Coluber piceus* Cope. A large, stout whipsnake differing from all others in coloration. The color above is blue-black or brown-black for the entire length of the body and tail. The head may be entirely black, but usually is mottled with white on the sides. Belly coral red to cream color, with two parallel rows of large black blotches toward the head.

Range.—Southeastern Arizona, extreme southern California and Lower California.

Sonoran Whipsnake.—*Coluber semilineatus* Cope. Two or three cream-colored lateral stripes on the anterior part of the body, gradually fading out toward the tail and not extending onto the tail. The area between the stripes is darker than the unstriped middle of the back, so that the effect may be of three or four dark stripes on the sides. Belly usually immaculate cream in color; occasionally there is a single or double row of spots toward the head. (Fig. 30).

Range.—Southeastern Arizona, extreme southwestern New Mexico, and the adjacent territory of Mexico.

Striped Whipsnake.—*Coluber taeniatus taeniatus* Hallowell. Five narrow dark stripes against a cream-colored background on the sides of the body. The entire back is dark brown, except near the head where the edge of each scale is tipped with cream. The edges of the head plates are also cream-colored. Belly cream color anteriorly, shading to pink posteriorly; a brown lateral stripe on each side of the belly posteriorly. (Fig. 30).

Range.—Southeastern Oregon, southern Idaho and Utah, southward to Arizona and New Mexico, just entering Texas and California.

Ornate Whipsnake.—*Coluber taeniatus girardi* Stejneger and Barbour. (Plate 14). Differs from the striped whipsnake in having one or more (usually four) light-colored crossbands on the fore part of the body. The lateral stripes are also much darker and wider.

Range.—Central and western Texas southward to Zacatecas, Mexico.

Ruthven's Whipsnake.—*Coluber taeniatus ruthveni* Ortenburger. Coloration above olive-gray anteriorly, gradually changing to reddish-brown posteriorly. Lateral stripes are usually entirely absent or only faintly indicated. This whipsnake differs from all others in having the anterior edges of the dorsal scales cream-colored. Belly yellow, with numerous small gray dots tending to concentrate into two rows.

Range.—Southeastern Texas and Tamaulipas, Mexico.

Green Whipsnake.—*Coluber taeniatus schotti* Baird and Girard. General color above greenish gray or bluish gray, the anterior edge of the scales light cream color. There are two widely separated narrow light stripes on the side of the body, the lower stripe bordered by a black stripe above and the upper light stripe bordered by a black stripe both above and below. Belly cream-colored, with numerous small gray dots.

Range.—Southern Texas and northeastern Mexico.

The whipsnakes are characteristic of the arid southwest, only one form (the eastern coachwhip) occurring east of the Mississippi River. All are bold and active and hence are not limited to any definite habitat. Most of the species avoid extreme desert conditions, although the red racer and western racer apparently flourish in the creosote bush desert within their ranges. Ordinarily they are not found at high altitudes, but the striped whipsnake is a high-plateau form that has been found up to 6,700 feet. All whipsnakes are equally at home in bushes and trees and on the ground, except the black whipsnake, which declines to take to the bushes when pursued. They are able to move either through shrubbery or over the ground with astonishing rapidity. It appears that they may seem to move faster than they really do. Mosauer (Copeia, 1935:6) timed several individuals of the red racer and found that their top speed was only a fraction over 3.5 miles per hour.

These snakes are inclined to be nervous and savage, more so than the blacksnake or blue racers are. In attacking, the anterior part of the body is relaxed in a loose loop after the initial strike, and is suddenly straightened with a strong jerk. This results in tearing the flesh of the victim, instead of leaving clean punctures. Whipsnakes often vibrate their tails when annoyed.

Whipsnakes are often thought to be nocturnal from the large size of their eyes. Careful studies made by Klauber show that they are active almost exclusively during daylight.

A hibernating red racer was found by Kinney in early February, near Palmdale, California. It was coiled beneath the roots of a Joshua tree, at a depth of about a foot.

Size.—Adult whipsnakes average 3½ to 4 feet in length. The eastern coachwhip is by far the largest; a specimen recorded by Barbour measured 8 feet 2 inches, with an estimated 4 inches of its tail missing. There is no authentic record of any other whipsnake exceeding 6 feet. The California striped whipsnake is the smallest; the largest recorded individual measured only 4 feet 8 inches.

Food.—Prey is not constricted. Food records for various whipsnakes show that they feed on a wide variety of animals, ranging from insects up to birds and small mammals. The whip-tailed lizards (*Cnemidophorus*) appear oftener than any other animal, probably because they are most readily available. Rattlesnakes are sometimes eaten. Klauber timed a red racer seen to catch and swallow a white-footed mouse and found that the entire operation took 29 minutes.

Breeding Habits.—Mating has been observed in May and early April. Whipsnakes appear to lay fewer eggs than racers do, a clutch of 12 being the largest recorded. The average of six recorded clutches is 8. Eggs measure about 1⅝ inches in length by 1 inch in diameter (41 x 25 mm.). The surface of the eggs is granular, as in the racers. Gloyd (1937, *Bull. Chicago Acad. Sci.*, 5:118) described a nest of the red racer. It was located in the bank of a highway drainage ditch, 11 inches beneath the surface, and contained 8 eggs in a compact mass.

Strecker, J. K., 1927, Chapters from the Life-Histories of Texas Reptiles and Amphibians. *Contrib. Baylor Univ. Mus.*, No. 10, 14 pp.

SPECKLED GROUND SNAKE
(*Drymobius margaritiferus* Schlegel)

The speckled ground snake is a form characteristic of tropical Central America and Mexico. It barely enters the United States in the Brownsville area in extreme southern Texas, with a number of other invaders from the tropics. The genus *Drymobius* is related to the racers and to the patch-nosed snakes, from which it is readily distinguished by its keeled scales. Anal plate divided.

A moderate-sized, keeled-scaled snake, uniformly dark green, dark brown, or black above, each scale with a light spot. Belly yellowish, the base of each plate sometimes dark. Upper labials regularly 9, lower labials 10 or 11. Anal plate divided.

Range.—Southern Texas and along the eastern coast of Mexico to Central America and northwestern South America.

Only a few specimens of the speckled ground snake have been reported from north of the Rio Grande, and little is known about its habits. It is an active snake, like the whip-snakes and racers.

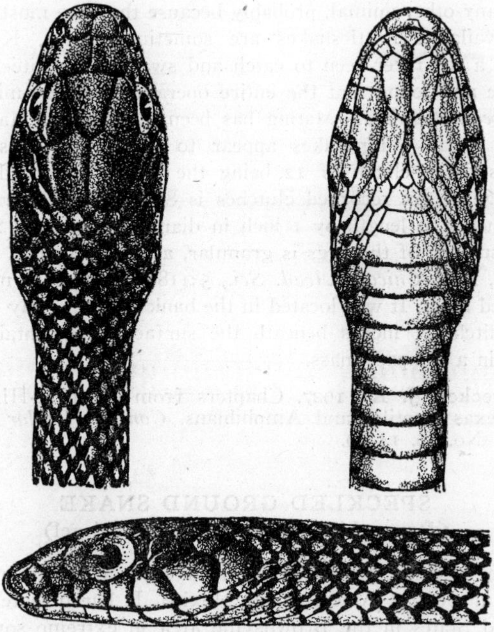

Fig. 31. Speckled ground snake (*Drymobius margaritiferus*).

Size.—Maximum length known 50 inches; evidently adult at about three feet.

Food.—Unknown.

Breeding Habits.—Nothing is known of the breeding habits. It is presumed that it is an egg-laying form.

THE INDIGO SNAKES

(Drymarchon)

Plate 14

The indigo snakes are tropical snakes that reach the extreme northern end of their distribution in the Gulf states. The two closely related forms found in the United States

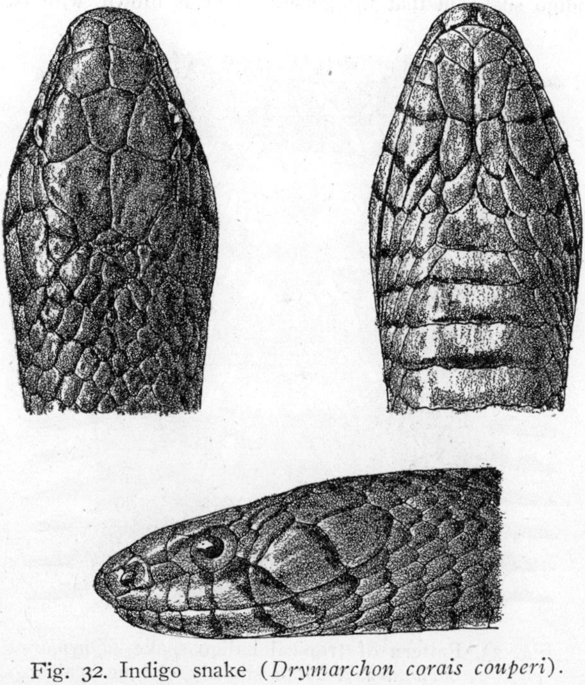

Fig. 32. Indigo snake (*Drymarchon corais couperi*).

are not easy to separate by their appearance, and a specimen is best identified on the basis of the locality from which it came.

Scales smooth. Anal plate single.

Indigo Snake.—*Drymarchon corais couperi* Holbrook. A large and rather heavy-bodied snake, uniform black or blue-black in color above and below. The chin, sides of head, and throat are orange-brown. Specimens from the western part of the range tend to be olive on the forward part of the body. The indigo snake has a highly polished, glassy appearance—never satiny as in the blacksnake.

Range.—South Carolina to Florida, westward to southern Louisiana.

Tropical Indigo Snake.—*Drymarchon corais melanurus* Duméril and Bibron. This snake differs from the common indigo snake in that the general color is brown, with only

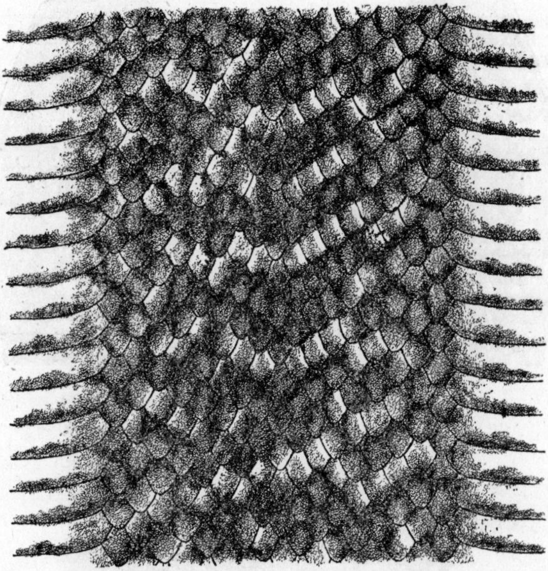

Fig. 33. Pattern of tropical indigo snake (*Drymarchon c. melanurus*). Note slightly oblique scales.

the posterior part of the body and the tail black. The upper labial behind the eye is usually in contact with the lower anterior temporal, while in the common indigo snake it is not.

Range.—Extreme southwestern Texas to northwestern South America.

These spectacular snakes are among the largest non-poisonous snakes of the United States. They are generally docile and feed well in captivity, and hence are a favorite with "snake charmers." The common form often has an iridescent bluish appearance, which has earned for it the name "indigo snake." They are also known as gopher snakes.

In spite of their large size and fairly wide distribution, little is known of the habits and behavior of these snakes. In Florida *couperi* is said to inhabit high pine areas in the north and central parts of the state, and dry glades, tropical hammock, and muckland fields in the south. They often inhabit the burrows of the "gopher" tortoise.

Size.—Adults average about 5 feet. The longest recorded specimen measured 7 feet 9 inches (Ditmars).

Food.—Captive specimens are indiscriminate feeders. Records of food taken in nature are singularly rare; a Florida specimen disgorged a large eastern coachwhip snake. Prey is not constricted.

Breeding Habits.—Egg-laying; breeding habits otherwise unknown.

THE PATCH-NOSED SNAKES
(Salvadora)
Plate 15

The patch-nosed snakes, so-called because of the peculiar form of the rostral shield, are most closely related to the racers of the genus *Coluber*. The rostral is enlarged, flattened, curved back over the top of the snout, and free at the edges; it appears to have been stuck carelessly on the tip of the nose as an afterthought. There is a less specialized species in Central America in which the rostral is quite normal.

Scales smooth. Anal plate divided.

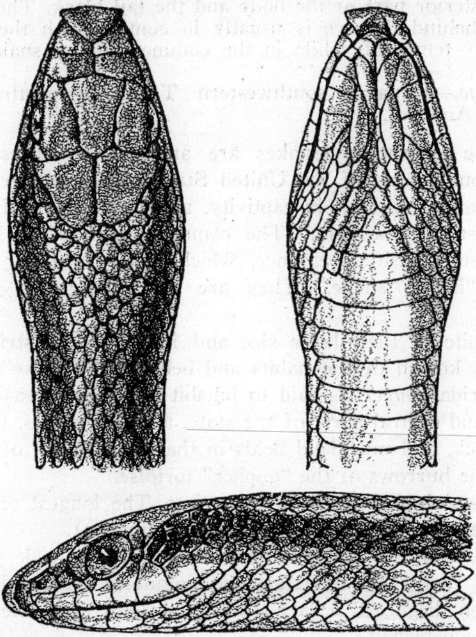

Fig. 34. Big Bend patch-nosed snake (*Salvadora hexalepis deserticola*). Note great development of rostral shield.

Mountain Patch-nosed Snake.—*Salvadora grahamiae* Baird and Girard. The second pair of chin shields in contact or nearly so, upper labials usually 8, loreal usually single, no narrow dark line on the third or fourth scale row. (Fig. 35). The rostral shield is not very greatly enlarged.

Range.—Forested mountain areas of western Texas and southeastern Arizona.

Rio Grande Patch-nosed Snake.—*Salvadora lineata* Schmidt. Agreeing with the mountain patch-nosed snake in scale characters, but with a well-defined narrow black line on the third scale row, and larger in size. (Fig. 35).

Range.—Central and southern Texas.

Desert Patch-nosed Snake.—*Salvadora hexalepis hexalepis* Cope. Second pair of chin shields separated by two

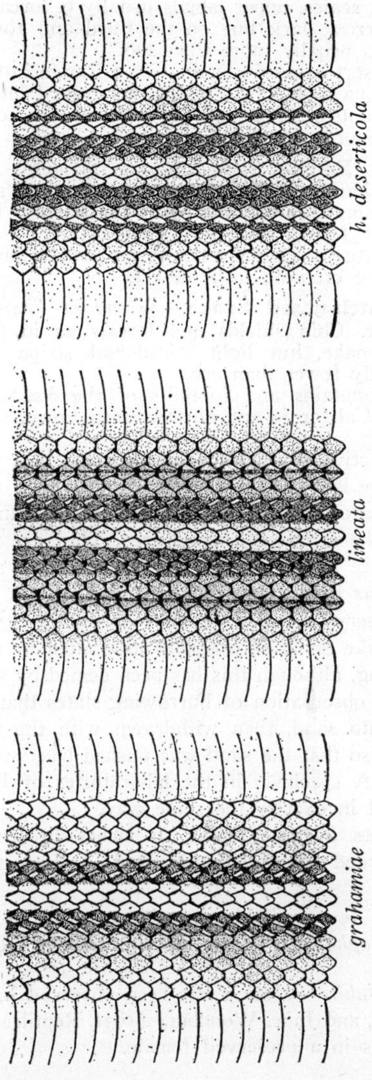

Fig. 35. Patterns of patch-nosed snakes.

or three small scales, upper labials usually 9, loreals usually 2 or 3; a narrow dark line on the third and fourth scale rows; ventrals usually more than 200.

Range.—Desert areas from the Coast Range in California through Arizona and New Mexico, northward into Nevada and extreme southwestern Utah; southward into Lower California and Sonora.

Big Bend Patch-nosed Snake.—*Salvadora hexalepis deserticola* Schmidt. Like the desert patch-nosed snake, but with only a single loreal and with the narrow black line confined to the fourth scale row. (Fig. 35).

Range.—Plateaus of western Texas and adjacent New Mexico, in the creosote bush desert.

Pacific Patch-nosed Snake.—*Salvadora hexalepis virgultea* Bogert. Chin shields and loreals as in the desert patch-nosed snake, but light mid-dorsal stripe narrower; ventrals usually fewer than 200.

Range.—Mountains and foothills of the coastal area of southwestern California and northwestern Lower California.

These are active, diurnal snakes occurring in a variety of habitats. There is a definite tendency for each of the forms to occupy a particular habitat, and thus more than one may be found in the same geographic area. They are terrestrial snakes, and are able to crawl with considerable swiftness; their speed has been compared with that of the racers by competent observers.

The augurlike snout is probably associated in some way with burrowing, although this has been denied by some. The only recorded observation of burrowing states that the head was thrust into sand, then withdrawn with the neck bent into S-shape, so that the sand was pushed back with a loop of the neck. A specimen in the laboratories of Field Museum behaved in exactly the same way.

Size.—Adults average about 30 inches in length. The longest recorded specimen measured 4 feet 10 inches (Bogert).

Food.—The few available records are of whip-tailed lizards (*Cnemidophorus*). Captive specimens have fed on other lizards.

Breeding Habits.—Mating has been observed in captivity in April, May, and June. Woodbury (1931, Reptiles of Utah) found 10 eggs in a preserved female.

Bogert, C. M., 1939, A Study of the Genus *Salvadora*, the Patch-nosed Snakes. *Publ. Univ. Calif. at Los Angeles, Biol.*, vol. 1, pp. 177-236, il.

THE LEAF-NOSED SNAKES
(*Phyllorhynchus*)
Plate 15

The leaf-nosed snakes are small heavy-bodied snakes apparently most closely related to the patch-nosed snakes, which they resemble in having the rostral shield enlarged and modified into an augurlike structure. There are two species, *browni* with fewer than 17 dorsal blotches on the

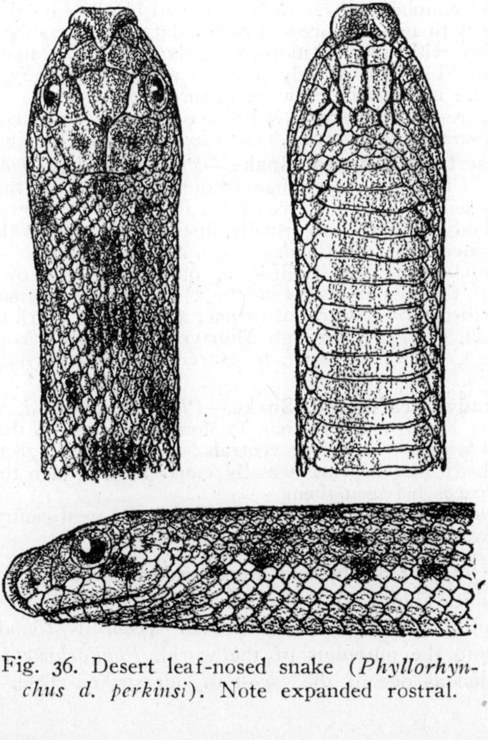

Fig. 36. Desert leaf-nosed snake (*Phyllorhynchus d. perkinsi*). Note expanded rostral.

body (not including tail) and *decurtatus* with more than 17. These have recently been divided by Klauber (1940) into five subspecies, one of which does not reach the United States.

Scales keeled (sometimes very faintly). Anal plate single.

Pima Leaf-nosed Snake.—*Phyllorhynchus browni browni* Stejneger. Fewer than 17 dorsal blotches on the body. Males with 166 or fewer ventrals and 36 or fewer subcaudals; females with 179 or fewer ventrals and 26 or fewer subcaudals. The dorsal body blotches are considerably longer than the interspaces between them.

Range.—Southeastern Pinal County and eastern Pima County, west to Organ Pipe Cactus National Monument, Pima County, Arizona.

Maricopa Leaf-nosed Snake.—*Phyllorhynchus browni lucidus* Klauber. Fewer than 17 dorsal blotches on the body. Males with 167 or more ventrals and 37 or more subcaudals; females with 180 or more ventrals and 27 or more subcaudals. The dorsal body blotches are little, if any, longer than the interspaces between them.

Range.—Northeastern Maricopa County, Arizona, along the mountain bases, from near Cave Creek to Indian Wells.

Desert Leaf-nosed Snake.—*Phyllorhynchus decurtatus perkinsi* Klauber. More than 17 dorsal blotches on the body. Males with 168 or more ventrals; females with 179 or more. The body blotches are usually distinctly narrower than the interspaces between them.

Range.—Southern California, on the eastern or desert side of the mountains, from the Death Valley region south to northeastern Lower California; also central Clark County, Nevada, southeast through Mohave, western Maricopa, and Yuma Counties, Arizona, to extreme northwestern Sonora, Mexico.

Cloudy Leaf-nosed Snake.—*Phyllorhynchus decurtatus nubilus* Klauber. More than 17 dorsal blotches on the body. Males with 167 or fewer ventrals; females with 178 or less. The body blotches are usually equal to or wider than the interspaces between them.

Range.—Vicinity of Tucson, Arizona; west-central and northwestern Sonora, Mexico.

The history of the leaf-nosed snakes has been most remarkable. They were first discovered in 1868, and from that date until 1922 only ten additional specimens found their way into the museums of the world. *Phyllorhynchus* was regarded as one of the rarest of our snakes. Then L. M.

Klauber, of San Diego, discovered that they could be collected in great numbers by driving an auto at night along highways in regions inhabited by these snakes, and picking up individuals that appeared in the headlight beam. Hundreds were collected in this way, often more in a single night than in all the preceding 65 years. It was found that *Phyllorhynchus* was actually one of the most abundant snakes of the region.

The leaf-nosed snakes are desert inhabitants, and like other desert animals they are nocturnal, spending the day underground. The pupil of the eye is vertical, as in many other nocturnal animals. The peculiar rostral shield is used in burrowing in sand, although *Phyllorhynchus* is much less efficient in this activity than some other sand-burrowing snakes. Some other factor, still unknown, may have been partly responsible for the development of the rostral.

These snakes defend themselves by assuming a striking coil, ridiculously similar to that of a cornered rattlesnake, from which they lunge forward in an exaggerated and usually poorly aimed strike. The lunge is accompanied by a slight hiss, and may be made with the mouth open.

Size.—The average length of adults is about 15 inches. The longest on record was a male *perkinsi* that measured 495 mm. (19½ in.).

Food.—According to Klauber these snakes seem to feed largely on lizard eggs, particularly of the gecko *Coleonyx*, in the spring. At other times they presumably eat insects and lizards, and have been observed to eat geckos in captivity.

Breeding Habits.—From 2 to 4 (usually 4) eggs are laid. These measure about ⅜ x 1⅜ inches (10 x 35 mm.), which as Klauber pointed out "seems very large proportionate to the size of the snake."

Klauber, L. M., 1935, *Phyllorhynchus,* the Leaf-Nosed Snake. *Bull. Zool. Soc. San Diego,* vol. 12, pp. 1-31, il.—1940, Two New Subspecies of *Phyllorhynchus,* the Leaf-Nosed Snake, with Notes on the Genus. *Trans. San Diego Soc. Nat. Hist.,* vol. 9, pp. 195-214, il.

THE RAT SNAKES AND THEIR RELATIVES
(*Elaphe*)

The rat snakes, or chicken snakes, are among the largest and most richly colored snakes in the United States. The genus is more characteristic of the eastern part of the country than of the west, although several forms are found west of the Mississippi River. The color pattern is usually quite distinctive, and is usually characteristic in each species.

The rat snakes, along with the water snakes and garter snakes, are noted for the readiness with which they dis-

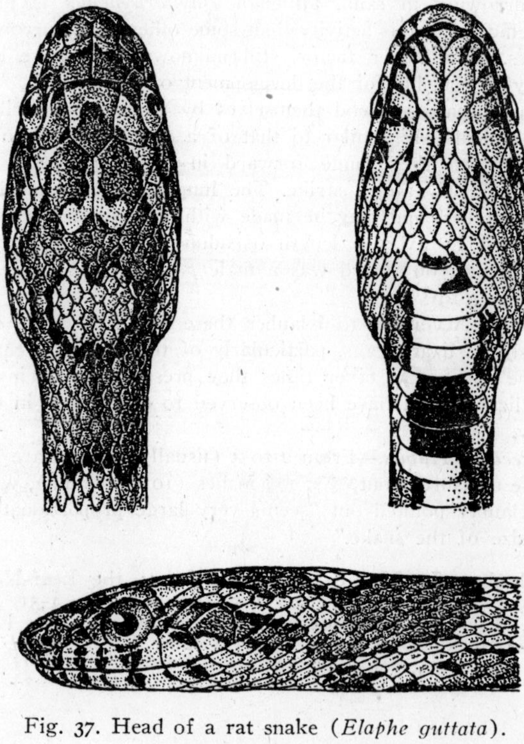

Fig. 37. Head of a rat snake (*Elaphe guttata*).

charge the offensive contents of their anal scent glands when they are annoyed.

Scales feebly keeled at the middle of the back, smooth on the sides of the body. Anal plate divided.

KEY TO SPECIES OF *ELAPHE**

1 a. Suboculars present
...Davis Mountain rat snake (*E. subocularis*) p. 153

1 b. No suboculars (upper labials in contact with eye) 2

2 a. Upper surface uniform grayish or greenish; uniform whitish below
......Green rat snake (*E. chlorosoma*) p. 144

2 b. Upper surface dark brown or black, or with blotches or stripes 3

3 a. Dorsal pattern consisting of 50 or more (usually more) narrow dark cross-bands
......Juvenile Baird's rat snake (*E. bairdi*) p. 144

3 b. Dorsal pattern not of 50 or more narrow dark cross-bands 4

4 a. Neck bands traversing parietals and uniting on frontal 5

4 b. No neck bands traversing parietals and uniting on frontal 7

5 a. More than 222 ventrals 6

5 b. Fewer than 222 ventrals; dorsal color gray and brown
......Emory's rat snake (*E. laeta*) p. 146

6 a. A great deal of black on the yellowish belly
......Corn snake (*E. guttata*) p. 146

6 b. No black (or very little) on pinkish belly
......Pink rat snake (*E. rosacea*) p. 152

7 a. More than 220 ventrals 9

7 b. Fewer than 220 ventrals 8

8 a. About 34 (28 to 39) dorsal blotches on the body, not including tail
......Eastern fox snake (*E. vulpina gloydi*) p. 153

---

* Adapted from Perkins, C. B., "A Key to the Snakes of the United States." *Bull. Zool. Soc. San Diego*, No. 16, 1940.

8 b. About 41 (33 to 51) dorsal blotches on the body, not including tail
.....Western fox snake (*E. vulpina vulpina*) p. 153

9 a. Dorsal pattern without well-defined blotches or longitudinal lines 10

9 b. Dorsal pattern with bold blotches, sharply defined lines, or a combination of lines and blotches 11

10 a. General dorsal color brown, with obscure broad lighter bands along the body
......Baird's rat snake (*E. bairdi*) p. 144

10 b. General dorsal color black, with obscure white cross-bands or lines, the white mostly between the scales
......Pilot black snake (*E. obsoleta obsoleta*) p. 148

11 a. Dorsal pattern of blotches, without sharply defined longitudinal lines
......Gray rat snake (*E. obsoleta confinis*) p. 150

11 b. Dorsal pattern with two pairs of longitudinal dark lines, blotches present or absent 12

12 a. Ground color light gray, uppermost pair of lines connected by blotches
...West Florida chicken snake (*E. williamsi*) p. 151

12 b. Ground color yellow, tan or orange, with dark longitudinal stripes 13

13 a. Ground color orange, belly with bright orange spots, dorsal stripes sometimes diffuse, sometimes with juvenile blotches persistent
......Deckert's chicken snake
(*E. quadrivittata deckerti*) p. 151

13 b. Ground color yellow or tan, no orange blotches, on belly, dorsal stripes sharply defined, juvenile blotches not persistent in adults
......Four-lined chicken snake (*E. quadrivittata quadrivittata*) p. 151

Baird's Rat Snake.—*Elaphe bairdi* Yarrow. Differs from other rat snakes in having nine upper labials, and in the larger number (about 80) of narrow brown crossbands on the body in juvenile specimens, with a corresponding series of faint blotches on the side of the body. Belly yellow, marked with small black blotches. Adults lose the spotted pattern, and are dark brown above with obscure lighter longitudinal bands. (Fig. 38).

Range.—Davis and Chisos Mountains in Jeff Davis and Brewster Counties, Texas; also Coahuila, Mexico.

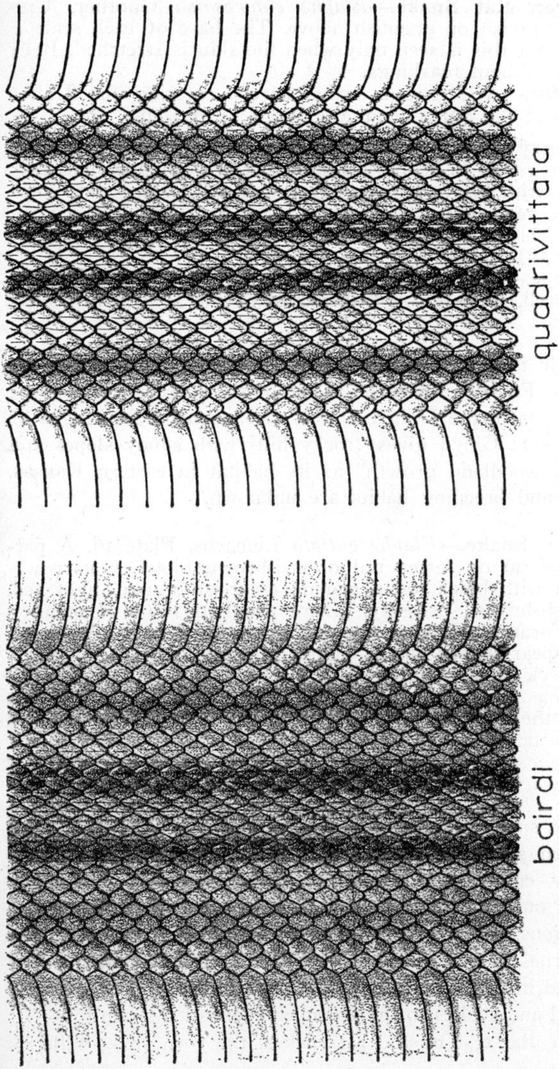

Fig. 38. Patterns of adult Baird's rat snake (*Elaphe bairdi*), and four-lined chicken snake (*Elaphe q. quadrivittata*).

Green Rat Snake.—*Elaphe chlorosoma* Günther. Uniform grayish or greenish above. The base of each scale is black, but this is seen only when the skin is stretched. Belly white, without markings.

Range.—A Mexican snake, barely entering the United States in the Santa Rita Mountains of Arizona.

Emory's Rat Snake.—*Elaphe laeta* Baird and Girard. A pattern of 39 to 48 dark gray or brown blotches, narrowly edged with black, on a gray ground color. The first blotch on the neck extends forward in spear shape between the eyes. Belly yellowish-white with gray or black blotches. (Fig. 39).

Range.—Missouri and southeastern Nebraska west to eastern Utah, south through Texas and New Mexico to central Mexico.

Little is known of the habits of these three western rat snakes. Emory's rat snake is one of the smaller members of the genus in the United States, rarely reaching a length of four feet; Gloyd gives "rocky hills with sunny slopes and sparse woodland growth" as its habitat in eastern Kansas. Food and breeding habits are unknown.

Corn Snake.—*Elaphe guttata* Linnaeus. Plate 16. A pattern of 40 or fewer red or red-brown blotches, narrowly edged with black, on a ground color of orange, light red, reddish-brown, or gray. There are two rows of smaller, more orange, blotches on each side of the body. A prominent spear-shaped blotch, lighter in the center, extends from the neck forward between the eyes. Belly yellowish-white, prominently checkered with large black squares. Large adults have the blotched pattern somewhat less sharply defined than young and half-grown specimens. (Figs. 37, 39).

Range.—New Jersey to Florida, west to Louisiana and northward in the Mississippi valley to Missouri.

This snake, which is also known as the red rat snake, red chicken snake, or house snake, is one of the most beautifully colored of North American snakes. It is usually found on the ground in fields and thickets in relatively dry situations, but is able to climb with fair agility. It is chiefly nocturnal. Often when cornered the corn snake will hold its ground instead of trying to escape. At such times it vibrates its tail and strikes to the accompaniment of a sharp hiss.

Like the rest of the rat snakes, the corn snake kills its

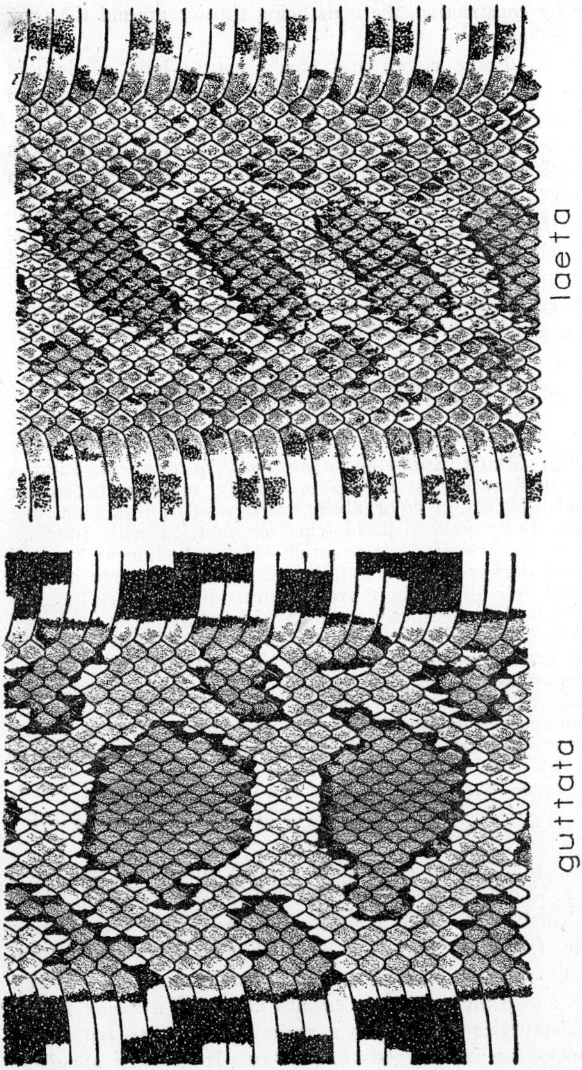

Fig. 39. Corn snake (*Elaphe guttata*) and Emory's rat snake (*E. laeta*).

prey by constriction, the coils being thrown around the prey like a flash.

Its handsome colors and hardy nature have made this species a favorite pet. It usually feeds readily on mice in captivity.

Size.—Adults average about 3 feet in length. Ditmars records a specimen "a fraction of an inch over six feet in length."

Food.—Rice rats (*Oryzomys*) have been found in the stomachs of captured individuals, and a specimen captured by Ditmars disgorged a quail.

Breeding Habits.—From "one to two dozen yellowish-white eggs" are laid (Ditmars).

PILOT BLACK SNAKES

Plate 16

Pilot Black Snake.—*Elaphe obsoleta obsoleta* Say. A large and rather stout snake, usually uniform brown or blackish-brown in color above, with whitish lips, chin, and throat. Belly yellowish, blotched or mottled with four alternating rows of dark squarish spots which near the tail become darker and run together. Often, particularly in light colored individuals, there are obscure, squarish dark blotches on the back, indistinctly outlined with white. (Fig. 40).

Juveniles have a vivid pattern of about 35 brown blotches on a gray ground color. Alternating with these there is a series of smaller brown blotches on the sides. These may closely resemble young fox snakes and Emory's rat snake, but may be distinguished from the former by the higher number of ventral plates (more than 220) and by the fewer dark blotches from the latter.

Range.—Massachusetts, southern Ontario, southern Michigan and central Illinois, southward to northern Georgia, and westward to eastern Kansas.

The pilot black snake, also called the mountain black snake, is one of the largest and best-known snakes in eastern North America. It is often confused with the true black snake (p. 125), but may be distinguished by its faintly keeled scales and highly polished appearance; in the true black snake the scales are smooth and have a satiny luster.

This species is found in a variety of habitats, but rarely wanders far from woods or thickets. It is often abundant

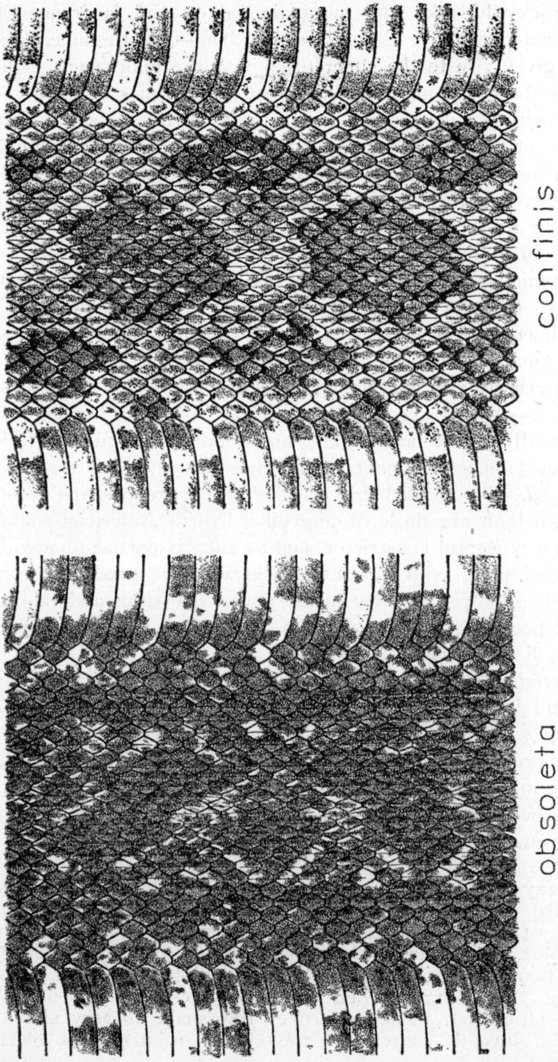

Fig. 40. Pilot black snake (*Elaphe o. obsoleta*), and gray rat snake (*E. o. confinis*).

on rocky hillsides and mountain ledges, and is frequently associated with the copperhead and banded rattlesnake. This has given rise to the superstition that the pilot black snake leads these venomous snakes to safety in times of danger—hence its popular name. It apparently is less arboreal than some of the other rat snakes, although it is able to climb with ease and is occasionally found in trees at a considerable distance from the ground. Gloyd states that they were "seen among the branches of trees at heights from ten to thirty feet" in eastern Kansas.

Opinions differ as to the behavior of this snake in captivity. Ditmars says that "the majority of the author's specimens cannot be trusted," while Conant and Bridges aver that "many specimens become very tame in captivity, taking food readily and making good pets."

Size.—Adults average about 4 feet in length, but are occasionally much larger. The maximum recorded length is 8 feet 5 inches (Conant and Bridges).

Food.—The food habits of this snake are perhaps better known than are those of any other North American snake. It is a powerful constrictor, and as such is partial to warm-blooded prey, with various species of mice predominating, closely followed by song birds. Young opossums and rabbits have been found in its stomach. Its diet also includes birds' eggs, lizards, snakes, and frogs.

Breeding Habits.—Matings have been reported for May 25 and June 19 and eggs are laid during July, in loose earth, damp sawdust, or manure piles. Seven recorded clutches numbered from 10 to 22 eggs each, with an average of 14. They measure about 1¾ x ⅞ inches (45 x 21.5 mm.). Eggs have been recorded as hatching on Aug. 22 and on Oct. 9, the young snakes measuring 14 inches (360 mm.).

Gray Rat Snake.—*Elaphe obsoleta confinis* Baird and Girard. Differs from the pilot black snake in having a pattern of large blotches, black, dark gray, or dark brown in color, on a ground color of gray, orange, or yellow. There are two rows of smaller alternating blotches on the sides. Belly yellowish, blotched with gray, especially near the tail. (Fig. 40). (The pattern of this snake is very similar to the juvenile pattern of the closely related pilot black snake.)

Range.—North Carolina, through the Gulf states.

No careful study has been made of the habits and behavior of this snake. They are probably similar to those of its northern relative, the pilot black snake. The gray rat snake, often referred to as the spotted chicken snake, is famous throughout the South for its depredations on chicken houses, which it visits in search of eggs. The relations of this subspecies with the pilot black snake and with the following form are by no means well understood.

CHICKEN SNAKES

Plate 16

West Florida Chicken Snake.—*Elaphe williamsi* Barbour and Carr. A blotched pattern in the adult, with the blotches connected by longitudinal dark stripes; a second pair of dark stripes on the sides. Ground color white or gray instead of yellow as in the four-lined chicken snake.
Range.—Known only from Levy County, western Florida.

Four-lined Chicken Snake.—*Elaphe quadrivittata quadrivittata* Holbrook. A large and moderately stout snake, yellow to olive in color with four prominent black or dark brown stripes running the entire length of body and tail. Belly yellow. (Fig. 38).

Juveniles have a spotted pattern quite different from adults, and are like the young of the pilot black snake and gray rat snake. According to Conant and Bridges the dark line running backward from the eye is narrow and broken in young chicken snakes, while in the others it is broad and continuous. The stripes of the adult pattern begin to appear when the snakes are about a year old.
Range.—Eastern North Carolina south throughout Florida and west to the Mississippi River.

Deckert's Chicken Snake.—*Elaphe quadrivittata deckerti* Brady. Differs from the four-lined chicken snake in having the dark dorsal lines less sharply defined, gray blotches sometimes persistent. Belly yellow to bright orange.
Range.—Restricted to southern Florida.

Nothing is known of the habits of Deckert's chicken snake. The four-lined chicken snake, sometimes called the common chicken snake or yellow rat snake, is more arboreal than the other rat snakes. It is often found about barns and poultry houses, which it frequents in search of rats and mice.

These snakes are usually described as bold and fearless compared with most snakes. When cornered they will usually coil with head and neck raised, vibrate the tail rapidly, and strike repeatedly. In captivity they usually become fairly tame.

Size.—Adults average about 4 feet in length. The maximum length is about 7 feet (Ditmars).

Food.—Little has been recorded regarding the specific food habits of these snakes. Their food is probably similar to that of the pilot black snake.

Breeding Habits.—Eggs number up to 24, and are laid during June or July; they measure 1¼ x ⅞ inches (Ditmars). The young measure about 12 inches at hatching.

Pink Rat Snake.—*Elaphe rosacea* Cope. The markings of this rare and little-known snake are very similar to those of the corn snake, except that they are less intense. It looks much like a pale-colored example of that species. The ground color is light pinkish- or grayish-tan, with a series

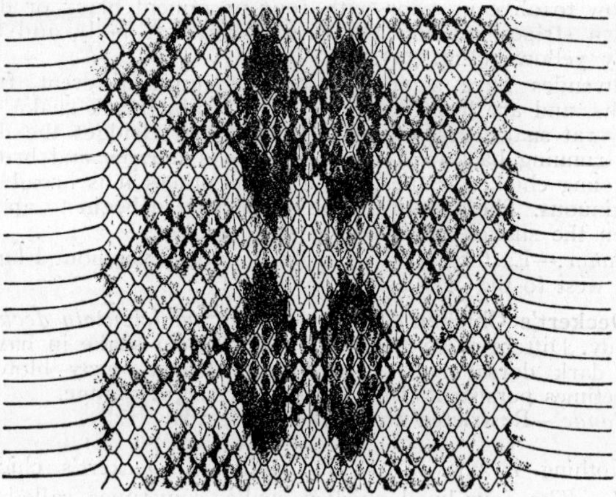

Fig. 41. Davis Mountain rat snake (*Elaphe subocularis*).

of reddish-brown blotches, narrowly edged with black, down the back. There is a row of smaller and less well-defined blotches on each side. The spear-shaped blotch on the head, which is found in many rat snakes, is present. Belly orange-yellow, with squarish blotches on the forward part and rather faint streaks of gray toward the tail. Average length about four feet.

Range.—Restricted to the lower Florida Keys.

Davis Mountain Rat Snake.—*Elaphe subocularis* Brown. Differs from all other rat snakes in having a row of small scales (suboculars) between the lower border of the eye and the upper labials. The ground color is orange-yellow to gray, with a series of dark blotches down the back, the corners of which tend to form a pair of bold black lines. There is a row of smaller and more obscure blotches on each side. Belly yellowish-white. Average length more than three feet. (Fig. 41).

Range.—Extreme southwestern Texas southward to near Saltillo, Mexico.

FOX SNAKES

(Elaphe vulpina)

Plates 5, 17

Western Fox Snake.—*Elaphe vulpina vulpina* Baird and Girard. A large heavy snake with a series of 33 to 51 (av. 41) chocolate to black blotches on a ground color ranging from yellowish to light brown. There is a series of smaller and somewhat less distinct blotches on each side. The head is coppery-brown. Belly yellow, prominently checked with black. (Fig. 42).

Range.—Northwestern Indiana and the northern peninsula of Michigan southwestward to eastern Missouri, eastern Nebraska, and southeastern South Dakota.

Eastern Fox Snake.—*Elaphe vulpina gloydi* Conant. Differs from the western fox snake in the smaller number and larger size of the dorsal blotches. These range from 28 to 39 (av. 34) in number, and are 4, 5, or 6 scales in length while in the western fox snake they are 3 or 4 (rarely 5). Specimens are best identified on the basis of range, as the characters used in separating the two forms are averages based on large collections and many individual exceptions will be found.

Range.—Along and near the shores of Lakes Huron and Erie, from Georgian and Saginaw Bays southward to north central Ohio, and eastward along the northern shore of Lake Erie to Long Point and perhaps Buffalo.

Fig. 42. Fox snake (*Elaphe vulpina vulpina*).

The fox snakes are usually called "pine snakes" or "spotted adders." The book name, "fox snake," is a translation of the Latin name *vulpina*. Because the spotted pattern is vaguely similar to the bold pattern of the timber rattlesnake they are often confused with that venomous species. The fact that the tail is vibrated when they are cornered, which in dry leaves produces a sound similar to that of a rattler, contributes to this mistaken identity. The coppery color of the head leads many people to mistake them for copperheads.

The western fox snake occurs in a variety of habitats—cultivated fields, prairie, woods, and stream valleys. The eastern form, on the contrary, is restricted to marsh lands and their immediate environs. These snakes are much more terrestrial than other rat snakes are, and are rarely found in trees or bushes. They are much less agile climbers, perhaps because of their stouter bodies.

Fox snakes make hardy captives and usually feed readily on mice and sparrows.

Size.—Adults average about 3½ feet in length. The subspecies *gloydi* averages slightly larger than *vulpina;* the maximum known length of the former is 5 feet 5 inches, of the latter 5 feet (Conant).

Food.—Prey is killed by constriction. Conant states that "freshly caught individuals disgorged mice (*Microtus* and *Peromyscus*), fledgling birds (probably red-winged blackbirds) and quail eggs." Hay found a half-grown rabbit in a stomach.

Breeding Habits.—Eggs are laid in July, usually during the last half. Seven clutches from Ohio numbered from 11 to 21, with an average of 15. A female from Illinois laid 8 eggs during the first week of July, in the laboratories of Field Museum. The eggs measure about 1¾ x 1 inches (45 x 24 mm.) and are adherent to one another. Hatching takes place in September and October, the young measuring about 10½ inches.

THE FADED SNAKES
(Arizona)
Plate 17

These snakes apparently are most closely related to the bull snakes (*Pituophis*), which they resemble in general appearance and color pattern. They differ from the bull snakes in lacking any keels on the scales. The anal plate is not divided.

Faded Snake.—*Arizona elegans elegans* Kennicott. A pale-colored, spotted snake with a small, flat-topped head not sharply distinct from the neck. A series of about 55 dark-edged brown or gray blotches down the back, on a ground color of cream, pale brown, or yellowish-gray, lighter near the middle of the back. The sides are marbled with two alternating rows of similar but smaller blotches. Belly yellowish-white, without markings. (Fig. 44).

Range.—Central Kansas, western Oklahoma, and the west-

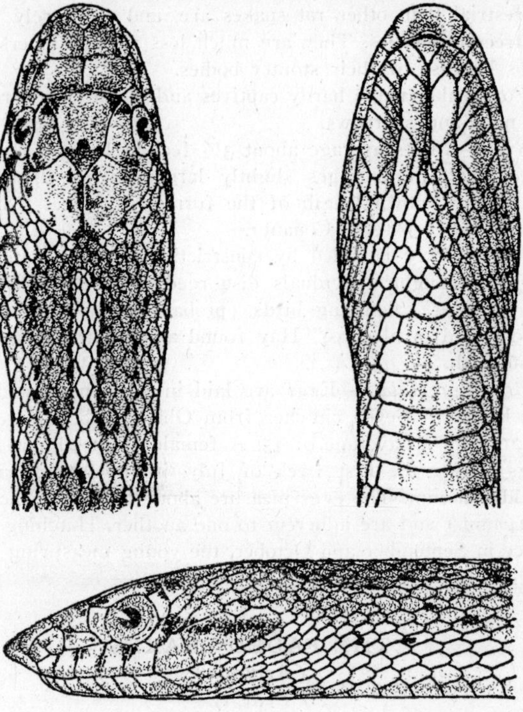

Fig. 43. Western faded snake (*Arizona elegans occidentalis*).

ern two-thirds of Texas, westward to southern New Mexico and adjacent Mexico.

Western Faded Snake.—*Arizona elegans occidentalis* Blanchard. Differs from the common faded snake in having a higher average number of dorsal blotches (60), a shorter tail (10 to 14 per cent, as compared with 13 to 15 per cent in *Arizona e. elegans*), and fewer scale rows (27, as compared with 29 or 31 in *Arizona e. elegans*). The dorsal blotches are narrow, covering 1½ to 2 longitudinal rows of scales; in *A. e. elegans* they cover 2 to 3 rows. (Fig. 44).

Range.—Southeastern Arizona, extreme southwestern Utah, southern California and Lower California.

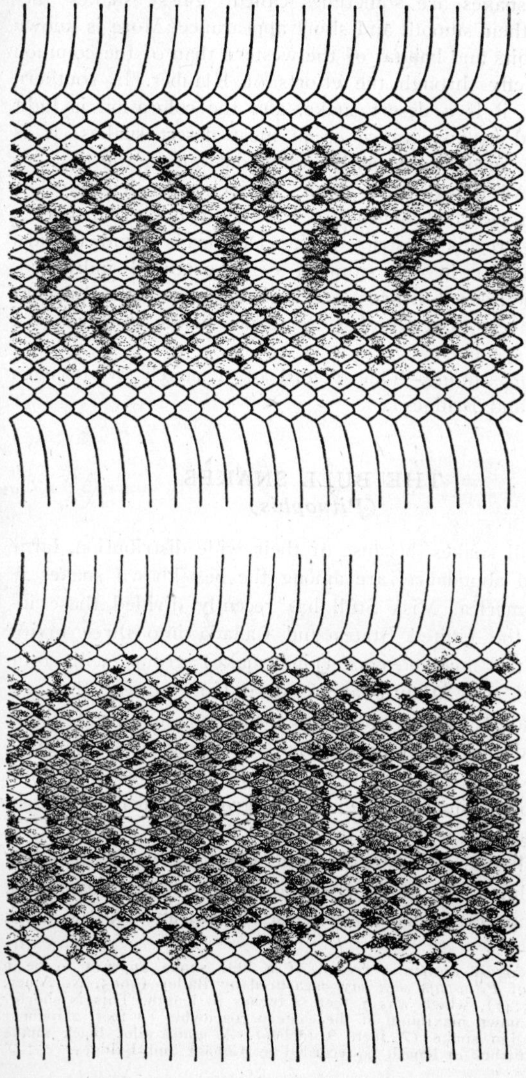

Fig. 44. Patterns of eastern and western faded snakes (*Arizona e. elegans* and *A. e. occidentalis*).

These snakes are sometimes called "glossy snakes" because of their smooth and shiny appearance. More is known of the habits and habitat of the western than of the common form, chiefly through the efforts of Klauber. In southern California it is a desert snake, and the coloration is light and faded in appearance as in most desert snakes. It is strictly nocturnal, apparently hiding out during the day.

Size.—Adults average about 30 inches in length. The maximum recorded length is 3 feet 8½ inches (Blanchard).

Food.—Prey is constricted. Van Denburgh found a lizard (*Dipsosaurus*) in the stomach of a captured individual. Brown-shouldered lizards (*Uta*) have been eaten by captive specimens, and Klauber found one in the stomach of a captured specimen.

Breeding Habits.—One record of a clutch of 10 eggs (Conant and Bridges).

THE BULL SNAKES
(Pituophis)

The bull snakes, because of their wide distribution, large size,* and abundance, are among the best-known snakes in North America. Miss Stull has recently divided those inhabiting the United States and Canada into three major groups: the *melanoleucus* (pine snake) group, with four forms, of the Atlantic and eastern Gulf states; the *sayi* (bull snake) group with two forms, of the great plains area; and the *catenifer* (gopher snake) group, with three forms, of the Pacific region. There are three additional forms, belonging to the *deppei* group, which occur in Mexico and do not enter the United States.

All bull snakes have the rostral plate enlarged, elongated, and modified for burrowing. (Fig. 45). This adaptation, which imparts a very characteristic appearance to the head,

* The longest authentic record of a bull snake appears to be a specimen of *Pituophis sayi sayi* measured by Bailey (1905, N. Amer. Fauna, 25:47), which was 7 feet, 8 inches in length. This is shorter than the known maximum of the eastern coachwhip (8 feet, 2 inches) or the indigo snake (7 feet, 9 inches). A giant pilot black snake 8 feet, 5 inches in length is recorded by Conant and Bridges.

varies considerably in the three groups; it is most extreme in *melanoleucus,* moderate in *sayi,* and least in *catenifer.*

These snakes have long been noted for the peculiar modification of the epiglottis, which is thin, erect, and flexible, and which apparently vibrates in a stream of air forced out of the wind pipe to produce the peculiarly loud and hoarse hissing for which bull snakes are famous.

Scales keeled. Anal plate entire.

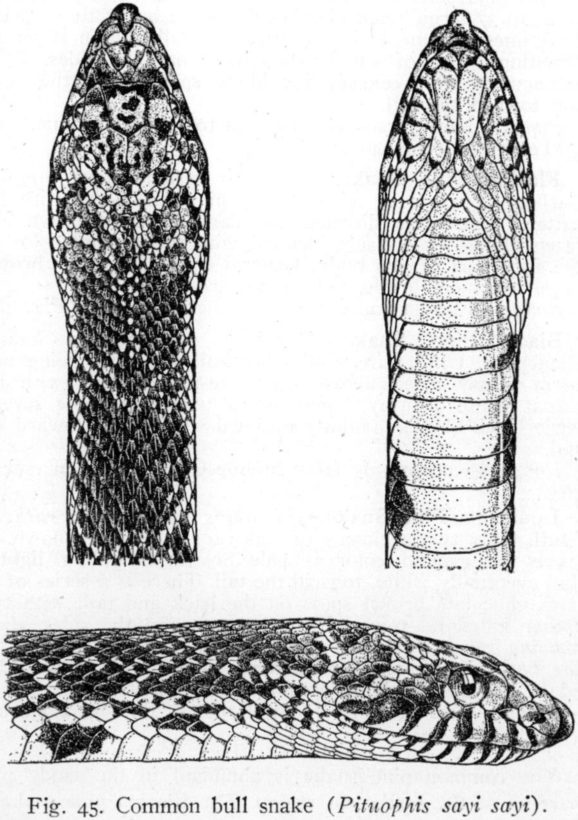

Fig. 45. Common bull snake (*Pituophis sayi sayi*).

Stull, O. G., 1940, Variations and Relationships in the Snakes of the Genus *Pituophis. Bull. U. S. Nat. Mus.*, No. 175; **Klauber, L. M.** *Copeia*, 1941, pp. 57-60 (critique of Miss Stull's monograph); **White, C. A.**, 1884, *Amer. Nat.*, vol. 18:19-21, 2 figs. (structure and function of epiglottis).

PINE SNAKES

Common Pine Snake.—*Pituophis melanoleucus melanoleucus* Daudin. This is a distinctly black and white snake. The ground color is dull white or light gray, with a series of 25 to 37 large black blotches down the back; the blotches sometimes become brown toward the tail. There is an alternating series of smaller blotches along the sides. Belly immaculate white except for black spots along the sides and toward the tail.

Range.—New Jersey pine barrens to South Carolina, west to Tennessee (Fig. 46).

Florida Pine Snake.—*Pituophis melanoleucus mugitus* Barbour. Similar to the common pine snake but with the pattern much less distinct, the dark blotches brown and often almost or entirely blended with the ground color on the fore part of the body. General coloration rusty brown, often becoming bright reddish toward the tail.

Range.—Florida and extreme southern Georgia (Fig. 46).

Black Pine Snake.—*Pituophis melanoleucus lodingi* Blanchard. Differs from all other bull snakes in being uniform glossy black above and slate-gray below, with the throat white or gray. Small individuals may show several large black blotches, faintly outlined with white, toward the tail.

Range.—Known only from Mobile County, Alabama (Fig. 46).

Louisiana Pine Snake.—*Pituophis melanoleucus ruthveni* Stull. Only two speimens of this rare snake are known. In these the ground color is pale brown, becoming lighter, and eventually white, toward the tail. There is a series of 50 dark chocolate brown spots on the back and tail, with two rather indefinite rows of smaller spots on the sides, these running together toward the tail and fusing with those of the back. Belly white, with dark brown spots toward the edges and marked with irregular brown spots.

Range.—Known only from Rapides Parish, Louisiana (Fig. 46).

The common pine snake is abundant in the sandy pine barrens of the east coast region. The Florida pine snake is

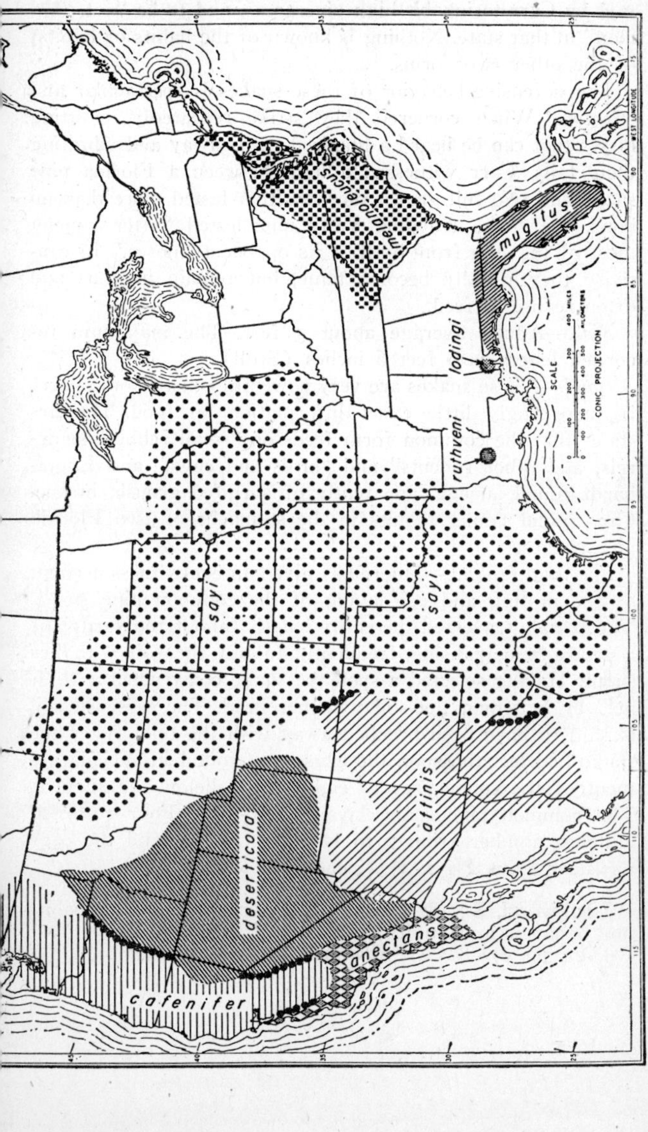

Fig. 46. Distribution of various forms of *Pituophis*. Black circles indicate points of intergradation.

said by Carr to inhabit high pine areas, and to be "not common" in that state. Nothing is known of the habits or habitat of the other two forms.

The defensive behavior of these snakes is spectacular and effective. When cornered they strike repeatedly, emitting hisses that can be heard a hundred yards away and vibrating their tails. Carr witnessed a fight between a Florida pine snake and two full grown raccoons that lasted more than an hour, the snake crawling away unmolested "after ripping most of the skin from both of its opponents' noses." In captivity they usually become tame, but remain nervous and often refuse to feed.

Size.—Adults average about 5 feet. The maximum recorded length is 6 feet 6 inches (Stull).

Food.—These snakes are very powerful constrictors. There is surprisingly little exact information on food. Ditmars states that the common form feeds on "small rabbits, squirrels, and other rodents" and "birds and eggs," and Engelhardt found an egg, apparently of a ruffed grouse, in one. Carr found young rabbits in the stomachs of two Florida pine snakes.

Breeding Habits.—Moore has given an eye-witness account of the nesting and egg-laying of the common pine snake. The female traversed the entire length (about 100 yards) of a sandy field, pausing frequently to test the soil with her snout. Having selected a spot, the snake constructed a "tunnel" by loosening the soil with her head. The loosened soil is said to have been brushed away with the tail! After the snake had left the spot, the eggs were found in an enlargement of the tunnel, six to eight inches below the surface. The common pine snake lays in mid-July. Four recorded clutches number from 7 to 12 eggs (av. 9), and the eggs measure about 2¼ x 1¼ inches (56 x 31.3 mm.).

Lockwood, S., 1875, *Amer. Nat.*, vol. 9, pp. 1-14 (habits and behavior in captivity).—**Moore, J. P.**, 1893, *Amer. Nat.*, vol. 27, pp. 878-885 (egg-laying).

BULL SNAKES
Plate 18

Common Bull Snake.—*Pituophis sayi sayi* Schlegel. A large and rather stout blotched snake, with more than 40 (av. 64) large squarish blotches, black, brown, or reddish-brown in color, on the body and tail. Ground color yellowish. Belly yellow, conspicuously spotted with large dark blotches, chiefly along the sides. The rostral plate is nearly twice as high as it is broad.

Range.—Throughout the Great Plains region, from northern Mexico and Texas north to Indiana, Wisconsin, and Alberta (Fig. 46).

Arizona Bull Snake.—*Pituophis sayi affinis* Hallowell. Differs from the common bull snake in that the rostral plate is only slightly higher than broad and the dorsal blotches are saddle-shaped and reddish brown to reddish in color.

Range.—Southern Colorado south through New Mexico into Chihuahua, Mexico; west through Arizona to southern California (Fig. 46).

The common bull snake is one of the best known of North American snakes, perhaps because of its size and very wide distribution. It is a typical prairie inhabitant. At the eastern edge of its range it is restricted to sandy situations but farther west it occurs in a wider variety of habitats. The Arizona bull snake is most abundant in the mesquite association of the plains area, but also occurs in the true desert areas and occasionally at high elevations in the coniferous forest. The bull snake is the snake oftenest killed by autos in most parts of the Great Plains region; trunk highways are sometimes littered with the mashed bodies of this large snake.

These snakes are apparently more docile than pine snakes are, although when cornered in the field their actions are similar and equally threatening. They are usually tame and hardy in captivity. Their spectacular size and striking colors have made them favorites among showmen.

The bull snakes, more than any other North American snakes, have achieved a reputation for being useful to agriculture. Their food habits qualify them as an important natural check on the numerous small rodents regarded as agricultural pests. There are instances of farmers having bought bull snakes and releasing them on their land. Hisaw and Gloyd have attempted to compute the cash value of an individual bull snake by determining the number of pocket gophers it would destroy in a season, the economic loss per pocket gopher being known through Biological Survey studies. They computed that the annual value to agriculture of a single snake is about $3.75.

Size.—Adults average about 5 feet in length. The maximum recorded length for the common bull snake is 7 feet 8 inches (Bailey).

Food.—Larger prey is killed by constriction, while smaller and weaker animals are simply swallowed alive. Hisaw and Gloyd found that these snakes are able to kill rats in narrow tunnels by compressing them against one of the walls with a loop of the body. They surmised that pocket gophers are killed in their burrows in this way. There are authentic records of bull snakes feeding on pocket gophers, ground squirrels, rabbits, wood rats, and birds' eggs. Undoubtedly they also eat other rodents and occasional birds.

Breeding Habits.—A clutch of eggs was found "partially embedded in soft earth under a stone" (Gloyd). Eggs are laid early in July. Four recorded clutches numbered from 10 to 18 (av. 14). They are adherent to one another, and measure about 2 by 1½ inches (52 x 38 mm.). Hatching takes place in September, the young measuring about 15½ inches.

Hisaw and Gloyd, 1926, *Jour. Mammalogy,* vol. 7:200-205, 3 fig. (feeding habits and economic importance).

GOPHER SNAKES

Plate 18

Pacific Gopher Snake.—*Pituophis catenifer catenifer* Blainville. A large and rather slender blotched snake, with more than 60 (av. 87) squarish blotches, black, brown, or grayish brown in color, on the body and tail. The blotches are much wider than the lighter interspaces. Ground color yellowish-white or pale brown. Belly whitish, with a row of small dark spots along each edge. The rostral plate is wider than it is high.

Range.—Los Angeles County, California north through

western Oregon and Washington into British Columbia (Fig. 46).

Great Basin Gopher Snake.—*Pituophis catenifer deserticola* Stejneger. Differs from the Pacific gopher snake in having more than 228 (av. 236) ventral plates; in the Pacific gopher snake these usually number less than 228 (av. 220). Each of the light-colored scales on the sides and interspaces between the blotches often has a small black central spot.

Range.—The Great Basin area of southeastern California, Nevada, Utah, western Colorado, Idaho, and eastern parts of Oregon and Washington (Fig. 46).

San Diegan Gopher Snake.—*Pituophis catenifer annectans* Baird and Girard. Dorsal blotches more than 90 (av. 100) on body and tail. The blotches are little, if any, wider than the light interspaces, and are often fused with the lateral spots to give a checkerboard or banded appearance.

Range.—Coast region of southern California and northern Lower California (Fig. 46).

The gopher snakes are found in a wide variety of habitats, specimens having been taken at altitudes above 6,000 feet. The Great Basin gopher snake is typically a desert snake, and although by no means limited to that environment it is much more restricted in its habitat preferences than are the other two forms. Like other desert snakes it is crepuscular or nocturnal, while the other two gopher snakes are diurnal. Klauber found that the San Diegan gopher snake was the commonest snake of the San Diego region, with more than 2,500 individuals recorded in a 16-year census.

Many writers have emphasized the economic importance of the gopher snakes. Like the bull snakes of the Great Plains region, they are important natural enemies of mice, pocket gophers, and other rodents. Pack recorded an instance of 35 small mice being found in a 5-foot gopher snake killed in an alfalfa field at haying time.

Captives generally become quite tame, taking either living or freshly killed food readily.

Size.—Adults average about 4½ feet in length. The longest authentic record is a 5 foot 9 inch specimen of the Great Basin form.

Food.—The food and feeding habits of these snakes resemble those of the bull snakes. There are authentic records of pocket gophers, ground squirrels, rabbits, mice, and small birds. Several writers have emphasized the enormous numbers of mice often found in the stomachs of these snakes.

Breeding Habits.—Mating has been observed in late April, and egg-laying takes place in the last half of July and August. Two recorded clutches numbered 10 and 19 eggs, respectively.

THE KING SNAKES

(Lampropeltis)

The king snakes and milk snakes are widely distributed, being found from southeastern Canada to southern Ecuador in South America. They display an enormous range of colors and patterns, but Blanchard showed that those found

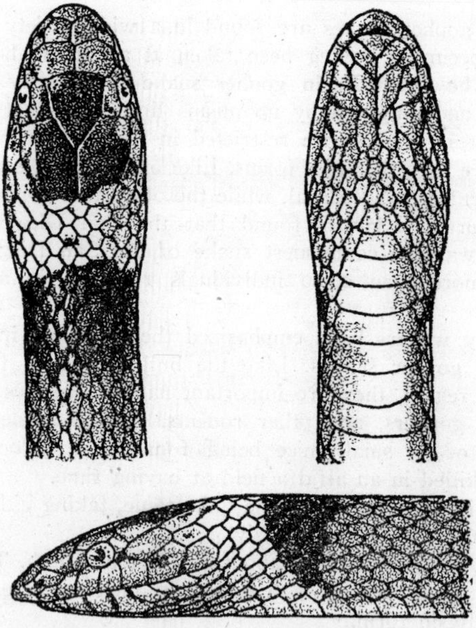

Fig. 47. Head of a king snake (*Lampropeltis e. elapsoides*).

in the United States fall into three main groups. These are: the *getulus* group, in which the pattern is fundamentally an oval white center in a black scale; the *calligaster* group, with a pattern of numerous black-edged brown blotches set on a ground color of lighter brown; and the *triangulum* group, with a basic pattern of encircling rings of white or yellow, bordered with black, and separated by red. One form, *alterna*, has a peculiar pattern that does not fit into any of these groups.

All king snakes are moderate-sized terrestrial snakes, with rather small heads, slight neck constriction, and short tails.

Scales not keeled. Anal plate not divided.

Blanchard, F. N., 1921, A Revision of the King Snakes: Genus *Lampropeltis*. *Bull. U. S. Nat. Mus.*, No. 114.

KEY TO SPECIES OF *LAMPROPELTIS* *

1 a. Pattern of narrow cross-bands of black, the alternate bands mixed or split with red; ground color above slate gray
.....Davis Mountain king snake (*L. alterna*) p. 170

1 b. Pattern not as described above 2

2 a. Pattern with red, or with dorsal blotches of brown, gray, or red, with black borders 11

2 b. Pattern without red; no black-bordered dorsal blotches 3

3 a. Pattern of rings, cross-bands, or stripes; or chiefly of scales white at base shading gradually into a black edge, but not chiefly of sharply defined white or yellow spots on black scales 6

3 b. Scales chiefly black with sharply defined white or yellow spots often so grouped as to form 50 or more narrow cross-bands on body and tail 4

4 a. Usually 21 scale rows at the middle of the body.. 5

4 b. Mid-body scale rows 23 or 25; no light centers dorsally on the scales between the cross-bands; head mostly black
...Sonoran king snake (*L. getulus splendida*) p. 178

5 a. A yellow spot on practically every dorsal scale
...Speckled king snake (*L. getulus holbrooki*) p. 176

* Adapted from Perkins, C. B., "A Key to the Snakes of the United States." *Bull. Zool. Soc. San Diego*, No. 16, 1940.

5 b. Scales between the cross-bands without light centers or with only a very few small ones
......Black king snake (*L. getulus nigra*) p. 178

6 a. Pattern consisting of rings, or of longitudinal stripes of white or yellowish; posterior chin shields generally much shorter and narrower than anterior and separated by 1 or 2 small scales.... 9
6 b. No rings or stripes; posterior chin shields nearly as long and nearly as wide as anterior ones, and in contact or separated by not more than 1 small scale 7

7 a. Many dorsal cross-bands of white or yellow 8
7 b. No dorsal cross-bands distinguishable; dorsal scales light at base, shading gradually into a dark edge
......Brook's king snake (*L. getulus brooksi*) p. 174

8 a. Fewer than 50 cross-bands
....Common king snake (*L. getulus getulus*) p. 174
8 b. More than 50 cross-bands, or cross-bands nearly indistinguishable
.....Florida king snake (*L. getulus floridana*) p. 174

9 a. Pattern of rings 10
9 b. A dorsal longitudinal stripe
..California king snake (*L. getulus californiae*) p. 180

10 a. White scales white to their bases; white bars on prefrontals broad
California king snake (*L. getulus californiae*) p. 180
10 b. White scales mostly brown at their bases; white bars on prefrontals narrow
....Arizona king snake (*L. getulus yumensis*) p. 180

11 a. Pattern of black-edged dorsal blotches of brownish or dark red, only narrowly in contact with fifth row of scales, or extending no lower than the sixth or seventh rows 12
11 b. Pattern of rings or cross-bands; or if of blotches or saddles of brown, gray, or red, these are broadly in contact with the fifth or a lower row of scales 13

12 a. Scale rows 25 or 27; dorsal blotches with concave anterior and posterior margins; lower labials 9 or 10, rarely 8
....Yellow-bellied king snake (*L. calligaster*) p. 170

12 b. Scale rows 23 or 21; dorsal blotches with straight or convex anterior and posterior margins; blotches often indistinct; lower labials 8, less often 9
......Mole snake (*L. rhombomaculata*) p. 172

13 a. Whitish cross-bands on body and tail fewer than 40; or if more than 40, snout not uniformly whitish 14

13 b. Whitish cross-bands more than 40; top of head black, snout uniformly white
......Banded king snake (*L. pyromelana*) p. 183

14 a. Whitish cross-bands usually distinctly widened on first row of scales, or scale rows anteriorly not more than 17 18

14 b. Whitish cross-bands little, if any, widened on the lower rows of scales, and scale rows more than 17 on anterior end of body 15

15 a. Whitish rings usually more than 30; snout black
......Coral king snake (*L. multicincta*) p. 182

15 b. Whitish rings fewer than 30 16

16 a. Dorsal red areas usually continuous across the belly; snout reddish speckled with black
...Cope's milk snake (*L. triangulum amaura*) p. 188

16 b. Spaces on the belly between the yellow rings filled with black; snout totally black or only very slightly lightened on top or sides 17

17 a. Yellowish rings 19 to 25; black spaces on the belly usually longer than the intervening yellow ones
.Mexican milk snake (*L. triangulum annulata*) p. 191

17 b. Yellowish rings usually 25 to 30; black spaces on belly usually shorter than the intervening yellow ones
..Western milk snake (*L. triangulum gentilis*) p. 188

18 a. Black on the head practically restricted to the posterior part, or to various black-edged light markings 20

18 b. Black practically uniform over head except for snout region, which is more or less lightened, at least on the sides 19

19 a. Whitish rings or cross-bands usually 25 to 30
..Western milk snake (*L. triangulum gentilis*) p. 188

19 b. Whitish rings or cross-bands 18 to 25
...Cope's milk snake (*L. triangulum amaura*) p. 188

20 a. Usually two anterior temporals; scale formula very rarely lower than 19-21-19-17 22

20 b. Usually one anterior temporal; scale formula generally 17-19-17, rarely higher than 19-17 21

21 a. Red areas continuous across the belly
..Scarlet king snake (*L. elapsoides elapsoides*) p. 173

21 b. Red not continuous across the belly but restricted to black-bordered dorsal saddles that extend upon the ventrals
......Northern scarlet king snake
(*L. elapsoides virginiana*) p. 173

22 a. Dorsal pattern of saddles, or of blotches of red or brown; whitish cross-bands 23 to 60 23

22 b. Dorsal pattern practically of rings; whitish cross-bands 18 to 30
...Cope's milk snake (*L. triangulum amaura*) p. 188

23 a. Dorsal saddles usually more than 25, reaching down to the fifth or third row of scales above the ventrals; often two rows of lateral alternating blotches; a dark band on the posterior part of prefrontals; a black-bordered light band from the eye to the angle of the mouth; usually a Y-shaped light spot on the back of the head
......Milk snake (*L. triangulum triangulum*) p. 186

23 b. Dorsal saddles usually fewer than 35, extending down to the third row of scales or lower; only one series of alternating spots; head markings only partially or not at all developed
......Red milk snake (*L. triangulum syspila*) p. 188

Davis Mountain King Snake.—*Lampropeltis alterna* Brown. A moderate-sized long-tailed snake differing from all other king snakes in its pattern. The ground color is slate gray, with a pattern of very narrow black cross-bands alternating at intervals of 3 to 5 scales with wider black cross-bands split transversely with scarlet. There are 19 red and black bands on the body, and an equal number of the narrower black ones. Belly grayish white, heavily blotched with black.

Range.—Known only from the Davis and Chisos Mountains in Texas and adjacent Mexico.

Only five specimens of this rare snake are known. The original specimen measures 28 inches in total length.

Yellow-bellied King Snake.—*Lampropeltis calligaster* Harlan. (Plate 19). A pattern of 46 to 78 (av. 60) squarish

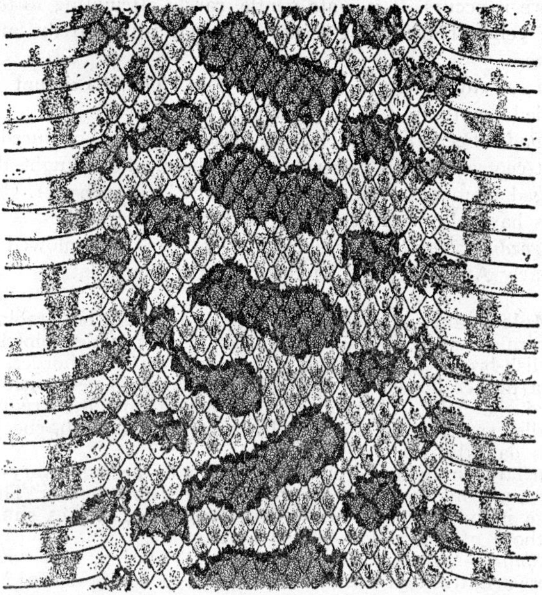

Fig. 48. Yellow-bellied king snake (*Lampropeltis calligaster*).

blotches, brownish, reddish, or greenish in color and with a narrow black edge, set on a ground color of lighter brown. These blotches are concave before and behind, and are sometimes split at the midline. There are two alternating rows of smaller, rounded blotches on the sides. In many adults the pattern becomes very obscure due to darkening of the ground color, and these individuals may appear striped, with four poorly defined dark stripes running the length of the body. Belly marked with square yellow or brown blotches, which are sometimes restricted to the sides of the plates. (Fig. 48).

Range.—Indiana west to western Kansas, and south to Mississippi, through Louisiana, to western Texas.

This is a prairie snake usually found in pastures or open woods, often under rocks or other cover. It is chiefly diurnal, although occasionally individuals are found prowling at night. This species is often quite abundant in regions where it occurs. It is quite gentle, rarely attempting to bite. The yellow-bellied king snake is closely allied to the mole snake.

Size.—Adults average about 3 feet. The maximum recorded length is 4 feet, 5 inches (Blanchard).

Food.—Feeds largely on mice in nature; of 38 captured in west-central Illinois "every one of them when caught disgorged from 1 to 8 mice, mostly young" (Blanchard). Captives have also eaten small birds, lizards, and snakes.

Breeding Habits.—One clutch of 11 eggs was plowed up in early August. These hatched about a month later.

Mole Snake.—*Lampropeltis rhombomaculata* Holbrook. A pattern of 48 to 68 (av. 55) rather small rounded blotches, reddish-brown in color and with a narrow black border, set on a lighter brown ground color changing to yellowish toward the belly. There is an alternating row of irregular smaller spots on the sides. Belly white or yellowish, checked with dark brown.

In large individuals this pattern usually becomes very obscure, and many specimens are nearly uniform brown. These large individuals may show dark lengthwise stripes similar to those of the yellow-bellied king snake.

Range.—Maryland south to central Florida, and southwestward through eastern Tennessee to southeastern Mississippi.

The mole snake, sometimes called the brown king snake, is a burrowing and more or less subterranean form as its name implies. Specimens are usually found by being turned out by the plow or during excavating operations, although they are occasionally found in the open.

The habits of this interesting snake are little known, because of its secretive nature. Blanchard wrote in 1921 that "accurate observations on the natural history of this form are very much to be desired," but little seems to have been learned since that time.

Size.—Adults average about 3 feet in length. The longest recorded individual measured 3 feet 9 inches (Hay).

Food.—A captured specimen disgorged a mouse. Otherwise unknown.

Breeding Habits.—Unknown. Presumably oviparous like other king snakes.

Scarlet King Snake.—*Lampropeltis elapsoides elapsoides* Holbrook (Plate 6). A small snake with a brilliant pattern of red, yellow, and black rings. The rings, except for occasional black rings, are continued across the belly and are arranged in the following order: red, black, yellow, black, red, black, yellow, black, etc. In other words, each yellow ring is enclosed by a pair of black ones. The red rings are much the widest, the black ones the narrowest. The head, which is small and pointed, is red to behind the eyes; the back of the head is black.

In occasional specimens the rings fail to cross the belly. Such specimens can be distinguished from the scarlet snake (*Cemophora*) by the absence of the loreal shield in the scarlet king snake.

Range.—Kentucky, Tennessee, and North Carolina southward throughout the southeastern coastal plain.

Northern Scarlet King Snake.—*Lampropeltis elapsoides virginiana* Blanchard. Differs from the preceding form in that the red rings fail to cross the belly, so that they form black-bordered dorsal saddles that extend onto the ends of the ventral plates.

Range.—Northern North Carolina to Delaware, east of the Allegheny Mountains. Specimens from the vicinity of Raleigh, North Carolina, are intermediate between this form and the common scarlet king snake.

The scarlet king snakes are famous for their close resemblance to the deadly coral snake (p. 274), and because of this similarity are often called "false coral snakes." In the true coral snake *the red and yellow rings are in contact,* which is not the case in any of the harmless snakes that resemble it, and the snout is black in the coral snake, while in the scarlet king snakes it is red.

These are the smallest of the king snakes, rarely exceeding 18 inches in length. They are very secretive burrowing forms, usually found in rotting logs or under the loose bark of logs and stumps, especially of pine. Captives are gentle, rarely attempting to bite.

Size.—Adults average about 15 inches in length. The maximum known length is 23½ inches (Blanchard).

Food.—Skinks and other lizards, snakes, small fish, and insects have been found in stomach contents. Captives also eat young mice.

Breeding Habits.—Oviparous; otherwise unknown.

EASTERN KING SNAKES

Common King Snake.—*Lampropeltis getulus getulus* Linnaeus. (Plate 19). A moderate-sized shiny black snake with 23 to 52 (av. 35) narrow white or yellow cross-bands that fork on the sides and connect with adjacent bands to form a chainlike pattern, whence another common name, "chain snake." Belly black with many white or yellow markings. In specimens from the southern part of the range the ground color tends to be brownish and the markings more yellowish. (Fig. 49).

Range.—Southern New Jersey to northern Florida and southeastern Alabama. (Fig. 52).

Florida King Snake.—*Lampropeltis getulus floridana* Blanchard. Differs from the preceding form in having more than 50 (46 to 85, av. 66) yellowish cross-bands. The forking of the cross-bands on the sides has usually disappeared, and is replaced by a series of light vertical spots that alternate with the cross-bands. Ground color brown to dull black, but each scale with some white or yellowish, often so much as to obscure the cross-bands. Belly black or brown, checked with white or yellow. (Fig. 49).

Range.—Central and southern Florida. Intergrades with the chain snake in north-central Florida. (Fig. 52).

Brooks' King Snake.—*Lampropeltis getulus brooksi* Barbour. Similar to the Florida king snake, but without a pattern. General coloration dull yellow, with a dark brown area on the tip of each scale. (Fig. 49).

Range.—Limited to the tropical southern tip of Florida (Collier, Dade, and Monroe Counties). Intergrades with the Florida king snake to the north. (Fig. 52).

The king snakes are among the best-known snakes in eastern United States. They are characteristic of the pine belt of that region, and are usually found in dry patches of timber, although by no means confined to that situation. Several writers have emphasized their fondness for the vicinity of streams and ponds, and Carr says that in Florida they "have definite aquatic tendencies." He has seen individuals swimming voluntarily.

These snakes are inclined to be secretive and apparently are more or less nocturnal. Although occasionally found basking in the sun, they are usually discovered under logs or other debris. When first captured a specimen may show its resentment by biting and chewing its captor, but this be-

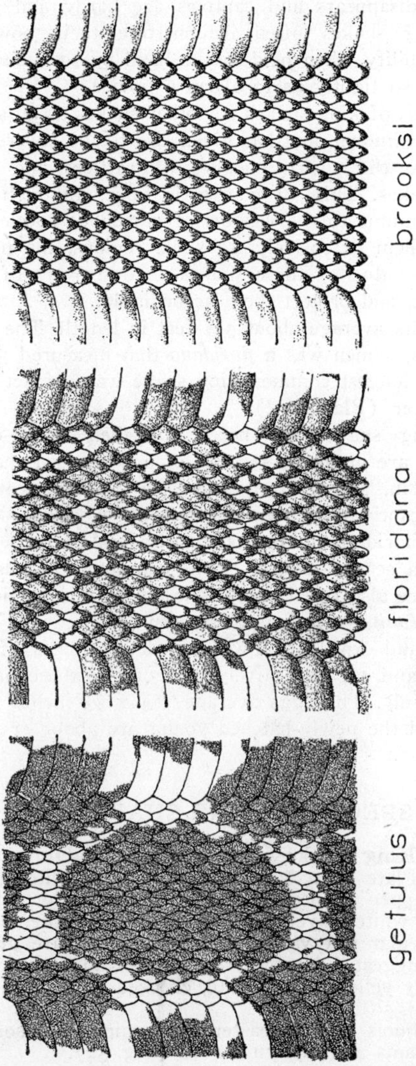

Fig. 49. Patterns of common king snake (*Left*) Florida king snake (*Middle*) and Brook's king snake (*Right*). These form a color pattern gradient from north to south. (After Blanchard).

havior soon disappears and captives are hardy and good-natured. King snakes often demonstrate their powerful constricting ability when held in the hand by squeezing the hand or arm so tightly as to alarm a novice.

The fondness of king snakes for other snakes as an article of diet is well known, and has given rise to the superstition that they are the sworn enemies of rattlers and other venomous snakes. This, of course, is false, although king snakes are immune to the venoms of poisonous species and do feed on them extensively. In some regions, the natives recognize the value of these snakes as destroyers of dangerous snakes, and protect them accordingly.

Size.—Adults average about 3½ feet in length. The longest recorded specimen was a *floridana* that measured 5 feet, 9 inches; the longest common king snake was a fraction of an inch shorter (Blanchard).

Food.—King snakes are noted for their snake-eating habits. There are authentic records of a hog-nosed snake, a water moccasin, and a coral snake having been eaten in nature, and captives have eaten many other kinds. Wright says that in Florida they are particularly fond of turtle eggs, with snakes a second choice. Small mammals, lizards, and amphibians are also eaten. Prey is killed by constriction.

Breeding Habits.—Matings have been observed in Florida on May 19 and April 19. Two recorded clutches of eggs numbered 7 and 11, respectively, and one of these hatched during late July. The eggs average 1⅝ x ⅞ inches (41 x 23 mm.), and the newly-hatched young are about 11 inches long.

SPECKLED KING SNAKES

Speckled King Snake.—*Lampropeltis getulus holbrooki* Stejneger. (Plate 19). A large, shiny snake with general "salt and pepper" appearance. The ground color is blue-black, with a white or yellowish spot near the center of each scale. At regular intervals some of the spots are grouped together to suggest distinct narrow cross-bands, 50 to 100 in number. Belly yellowish or white, checked with large black blotches. (Fig. 50).

Range.—Illinois to southeastern Wyoming, and south to western Alabama and eastern Texas. (Fig. 52).

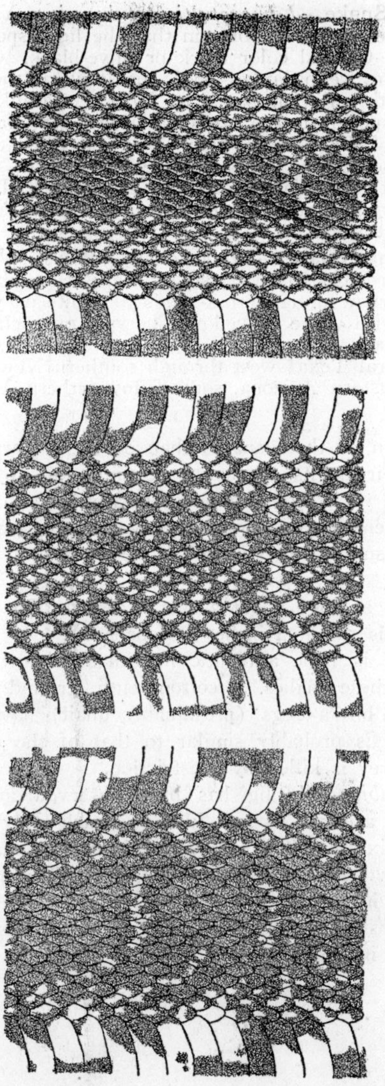

Fig. 50. Patterns of black king snake, speckled king snake, and Sonoran king snake. (After Blanchard).

Black King Snake.—*Lampropeltis getulus nigra* Yarrow. Differs from the preceding form in that the light spots are usually lacking. Ground color black or olive-black, with 50 to 90 very narrow yellow cross-bands that fork on the sides and connect with adjacent bands to form a chainlike pattern. In some specimens the cross-bands are very faint or entirely absent. Belly checked with black and white or yellow, the black sometimes predominating. (Fig. 50).

Range.—West Virginia to extreme east-central Illinois, and south through Kentucky and Tennessee to central Alabama. (Fig. 52).

Sonoran King Snake.—*Lampropeltis getulus splendida* Baird and Girard. Center of back black, crossed with 40 to 85 (av. 70) narrow dotted cross-bands of white or yellow. Sides spotted with white or yellow, one spot on each scale. Belly mostly black. (Fig. 50).

Range.—Central Texas west through southern New Mexico into southeastern Arizona, south into northern Mexico. (Fig. 52).

Less is known of these snakes than of the eastern king snakes, but their habits appear to be similar. They have been found in a variety of situations, usually beneath stones or logs. Specimens are occasionally plowed or dug out. The speckled king snake is often called the "salt and pepper snake."

Size.—Adults average about 3 feet in length. The maximum recorded is 5 feet 4 inches (Blanchard).

Food.—There is little authentic information on the natural food of these snakes. A cottonmouth, ground snakes (*Haldea*), and bird's eggs (presumably quail) have been recorded. Food is probably similar to that of the eastern king snakes. Prey is killed by constriction.

Breeding Habits.—Mating has been observed in early May, and eggs are laid in late June and early July (June 22-July 17). Six recorded clutches of *holbrooki* numbered from 6 to 10 eggs each, with an average of 9. They measure about 1⅜ x ¾ inches (35 x 18 mm.). Hatching takes place from late August to early October, the young snakes measuring about 10 inches at hatching.

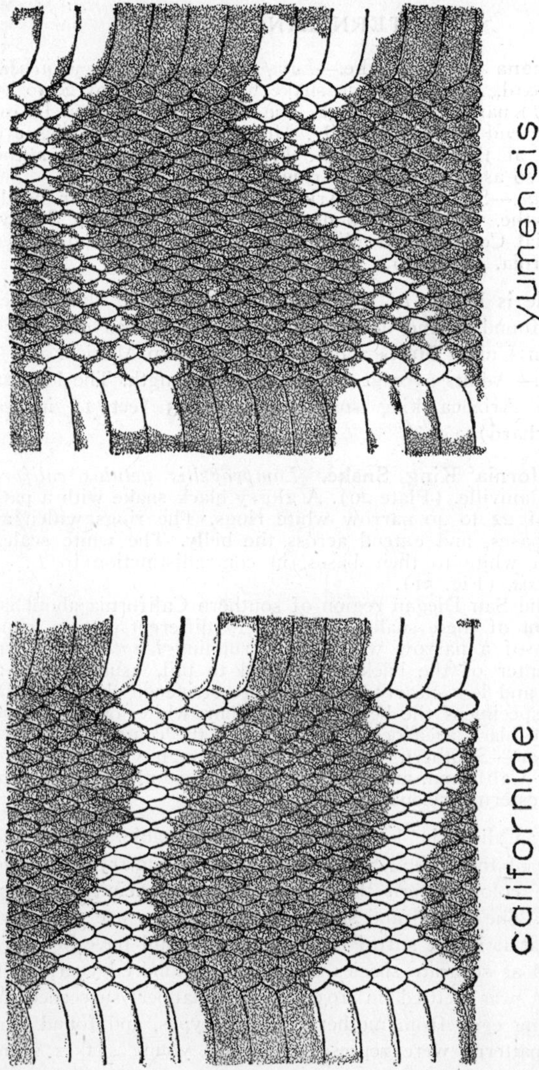

Fig. 51. Distinction between California king snake (with cross-bands) and Arizona king snake.

WESTERN KING SNAKES

Arizona King Snake.—*Lampropeltis getulus yumensis* Blanchard. A glossy black snake with a pattern of 29 to 45 (av. 37) narrow white rings. The rings widen at their bases, and extend across the belly. Most of the white scales are brown at the base, and the brown may extend over the scales so as to obscure the rings. (Fig. 51).

Range.—Southwestern Arizona; California, as far north as Blythe, Riverside County, and as far west as Seeley, Imperial County; and adjacent areas of Sonora and Lower California. (Fig. 52).

Little is known of the habits or behavior of this snake. It is found in the desert and semidesert areas of southwestern United States and adjacent northern Mexico.

Size.—Adults average about 3 feet in length. The longest known Arizona king snake measured 3 feet 11 inches (Blanchard).

California King Snake.—*Lampropeltis getulus californiae* Blainville. (Plate 20). A glossy black snake with a pattern of 22 to 49 narrow white rings. The rings widen at their bases, and extend across the belly. The white scales remain white to their bases, in contradistinction to *L. g. yumensis.* (Fig. 51).

In the San Diegan region of southern California about 40 per cent of these snakes have a very different pattern, consisting of a narrow white stripe running *lengthwise* down the center of the back from head to tail, usually with a wider and less clearly defined white stripe on the sides. In these specimens the belly may be plain white, or may have a large black area occupying most of the center.

Range.—Southern Oregon south through California into Lower California, and east into Nevada, southwestern Utah, and western Arizona. (Fig. 52).

The California king snake is remarkable among the snakes of the United States for the extraordinary difference in the color pattern that appears in the vicinity of San Diego. The ringed and striped pattern phases are so different that it is not surprising that they should have been regarded as separate species for nearly a hundred years. The matter was settled in 1936, when Klauber succeeded in hatching eggs from mothers of both types, and found that both patterns were represented in the young snakes from

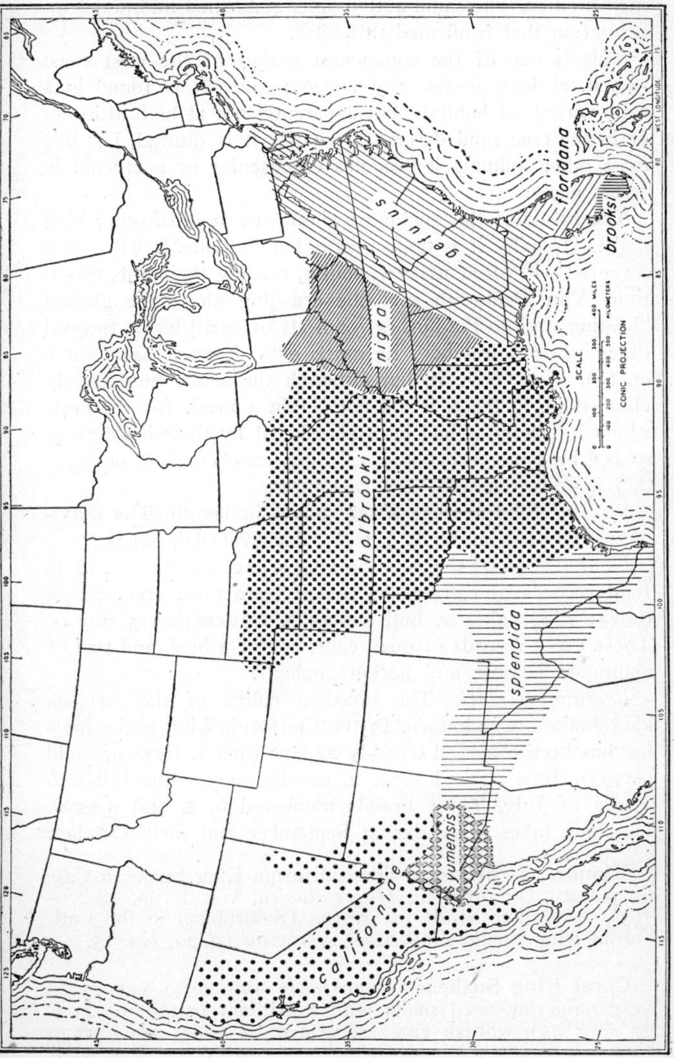

Fig. 52. Distribution map of the *getulus* group of king snakes. (After Blanchard).

each mother. The same author later published additional information that confirmed this view.

This is one of the commonest snakes of the west coast region, at least in the San Diego region. It is found in a wide variety of habitats, but apparently not at high altitudes or in the true sand desert. Ordinarily it is diurnal, but like most other animals it becomes crepuscular or nocturnal in desert areas.

The habits of this snake are similar to those of other king snakes. Usually it is quite gentle, but individuals when first cornered will often strike viciously, rattling their tails meantime. Van Denburgh saw one crawling along the ground "looking up into the bushes for nests of small birds. Several times while I watched, its quick eyes detected nests three or four feet above it, but although the snake immediately climbed up to these, it did not obtain a meal, for the nests which it examined had been abandoned by their builders or robbed by some earlier comer." Such excellent field observation is unfortunately very rare.

Size.—Adults average about 3 feet in length. The maximum recorded length is 4 feet 2 inches (Blanchard).

Food.—Food of the Arizona king snake is unknown. In 13 food records of *californiae,* snakes were most frequent (8 times: whipsnakes 2, bull snakes 3, rattlesnakes 3 times). There are 3 records of quail eggs, one of a bird, and two of mammals (mouse and pocket gopher).

Breeding Habits.—The breeding habits of the Arizona king snake are unknown. In the California king snake mating has been observed on May 22 and June 1. Eggs are laid between June 23 and Aug. 2, usually during the last two weeks of July. Three broods numbered 6, 7, and 9 eggs. Hatching takes place during September and early October.

Klauber, L. M., 1936. The California King Snake, a Case of pattern Dimorphism. *Herpetologica,* vol. 1, pp. 18-27—1939. A further Study of pattern Dimorphism in the California King Snake. *Bull. Zool. Soc. San Diego,* No. 15.

Coral King Snake.—*Lampropeltis multicincta* Yarrow. A very moderate-sized snake with a brilliant pattern of 23 to 57 (av. 45) whitish rings separated by wider black rings that are more or less completely split with red. The white

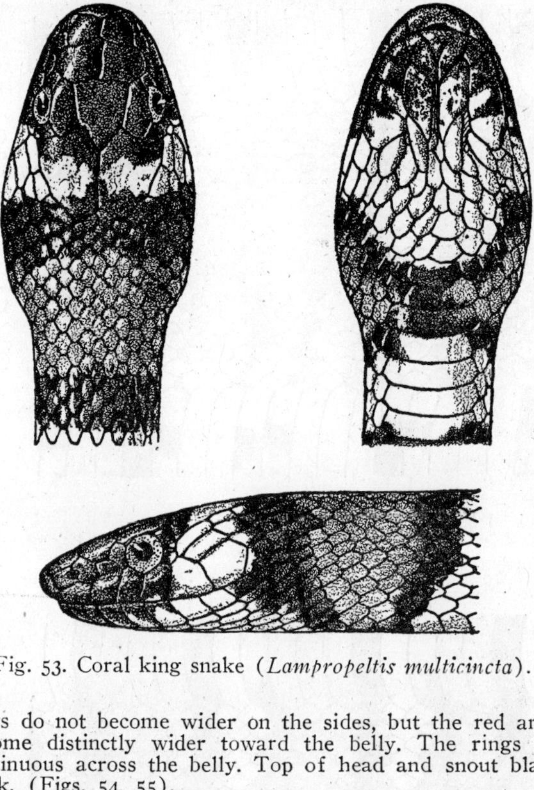

Fig. 53. Coral king snake (*Lampropeltis multicincta*).

rings do not become wider on the sides, but the red areas become distinctly wider toward the belly. The rings are continuous across the belly. Top of head and snout black: black. (Figs. 54, 55).

Range.—California and Lower California (Fig. 58).

Banded King Snake.—*Lampropeltis pyromelana* Cope. (Plate 20). A pattern of 35 to 61 (av. 50) whitish rings on body and tail, separated by black which is more or less completely split with red. The black becomes much narrower or sometimes disappears completely on the sides. The rings are continuous across the belly, although the white may be obstructed with black at the midline. Differs from the coral king snake in that the whole snout is whitish, instead of black. (Figs. 54, 55).

Range.—From northern Mexico through southwestern New Mexico and Arizona into Utah (Fig. 58).

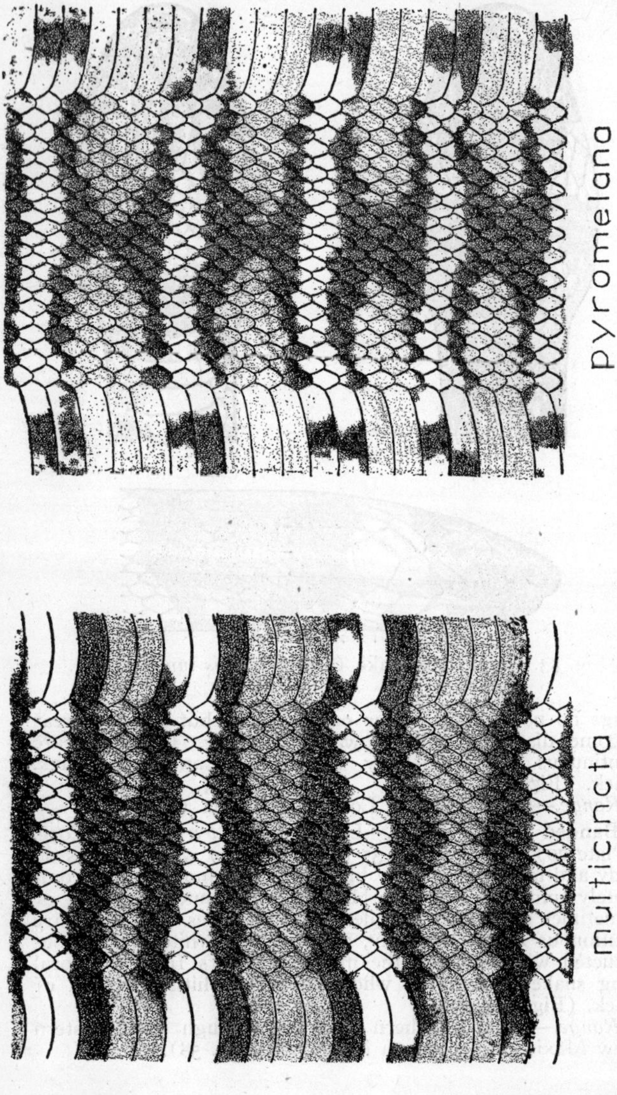

Fig. 54. Patterns of coral king snake and banded king snake.

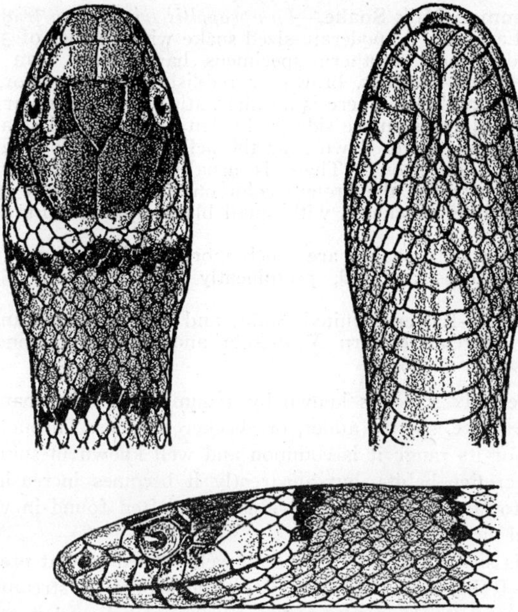

Fig. 55. Banded king snake (*Lampropeltis pyromelana*).

Little is known of the habits of these two snakes. Both are mountain forms not found on desert or plains, and apparently they are partial to the pine forest zones.

Size.—The coral king snake averages about two feet in length, with a maximum of 41 inches (Blanchard).

MILK SNAKES

Plate 20

The common name of this group of snakes refers to one of the most persistent and widespread of all snake myths—that they suck cows in the pasture. This snake story was discussed on p. 7.

Common Milk Snake.—*Lampropeltis triangulum triangulum* Lacépède. A moderate-sized snake with a series of 35 to 62 (occasional southern specimens have fewer than 30) black-edged blotches, brown or reddish-brown in color, on the body and tail. There is an alternating row of similar but smaller blotches on the side, and often a row of still smaller, darker spots lower down near the belly. Ground color gray, tan, or light brown. There is usually a Y-shaped or V-shaped patch of the ground color on the back of the head. Belly white, checkered with small black squares. (Figs. 56, 57).

Young milk snakes are much more brilliant than adults. The blotches are red, prominently bordered with black. (Plate 5).

Range.—Eastern United States and southeastern Canada, from extreme eastern Minnesota and southern Maine to Florida (Fig. 58).

The milk snake is known by a number of other names: house snake, spotted adder, or checkered adder. Throughout most of its range it is common and well known in spite of its secretive habits, but apparently it becomes increasingly rare toward the south. Individuals are often found in well-settled urban areas.

This snake appears to have no well-defined habitat preference. It has even been found on the shores of streams in Illinois, the only situation that Blanchard believed it might avoid. The milk snake is seldom seen abroad during daylight, individuals almost invariably being found under flat stones, the bark of rotting logs or stumps, boards, pieces of discarded sheet-iron, or other cover. It probably does its prowling at night.

Like other king snakes, the milk snake is usually quite fearless when first encountered. When molested it is likely to assume a defensive pose, vibrate its tail, and strike rather viciously. In common with other king snakes, it chews instead of merely biting if it succeeds in grasping a finger. Individuals usually become tame soon after capture, but often refuse to feed and do not flourish in captivity.

Size.—Adults average about 30 inches in length. The longest authentic record is 3 feet 6½ inches (Blanchard).

Food.—Milk snakes are less addicted to snake-eating than are other king snakes. Surface analyzed the stomach contents of 42 milk snakes from Pennsylvania and found that snakes made up only 6 per cent of the diet. Mice, chiefly field mice (*Microtus*), were by far the commonest food, accounting for about 72 per cent of the food. Other small

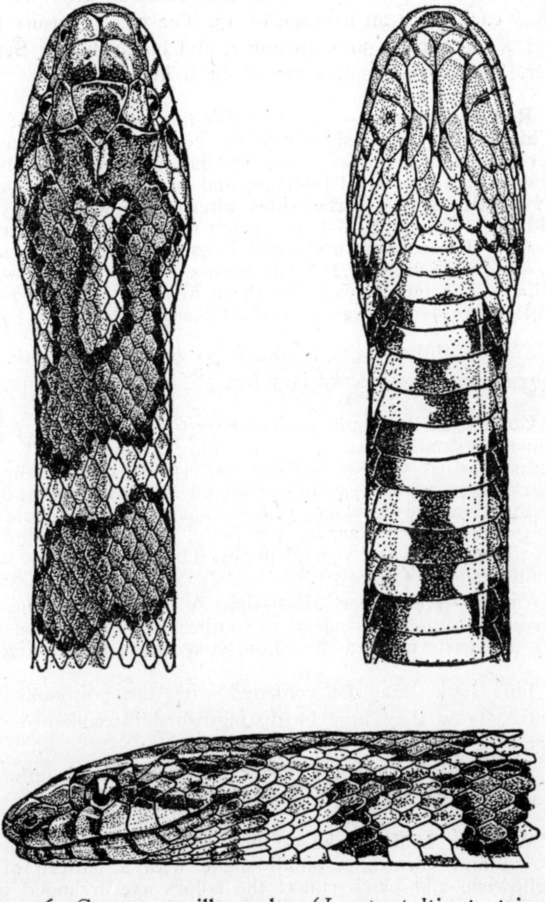

Fig. 56. Common milk snake (*Lampropeltis t. triangulum*).

mammals made up 11 per cent, birds 5.5 per cent, and slugs 3 per cent.

Breeding Habits.—Eggs are laid during late June and early July in manure piles, decaying sawdust piles, or similar situations. Four recorded clutches numbered from 11 to 16 eggs each, with an average of 13. The eggs measure about 1¼ x ⅝ inches (30 x 16 mm.), and hatch during September. The young snakes are about 9 inches long.

Red Milk Snake.—*Lampropeltis triangulum syspila* Cope. This snake is very similar to the common milk snake, differing from it in its more reddish coloration, in having fewer than 35 dorsal blotches, and in having only one row of small spots on the sides alternating with the dorsal blotches. The light V-shaped patch found on the back of the head in the common milk snake is usually lacking. (Fig. 57).

Range.—Southern Indiana across southern and western Illinois, through Iowa to southern Minnesota; south to central Arkansas and west to central Kansas (Fig. 58).

Size.—Adults average about 30 inches in length. The longest authentic record is 3 feet 5½ inches (Blanchard).

Cope's Milk Snake.—*Lampropeltis triangulum amaura* Cope. A small snake, rarely reaching a length of two feet. It is marked with a brilliant pattern of red, yellow, and black rings, with the colors arranged in the following order: yellow, black, red, black, yellow, black, red, black, etc. The rings may extend across the belly, but usually they end on the edges of the ventral plates. The head is black with a reddish snout. (Fig. 57).

Range.—The lower Mississippi Valley. Mississippi west through southern Arkansas to southeastern Oklahoma, south through eastern Texas and Louisiana to the Gulf (Fig. 58).

This snake may be confused with the poisonous coral snake. How they may be distinguished is explained on p. 173.

Size.—Adults average about 18 inches in length. The maximum known length is 25 inches (Blanchard).

Western Milk Snake.—*Lampropeltis triangulum gentilis* Baird and Girard. A small snake with a pattern of red, yellowish, and black rings; the colors are arranged in the same order as in Cope's milk snake. The red rings are narrow and are often broken up with black along the middle of

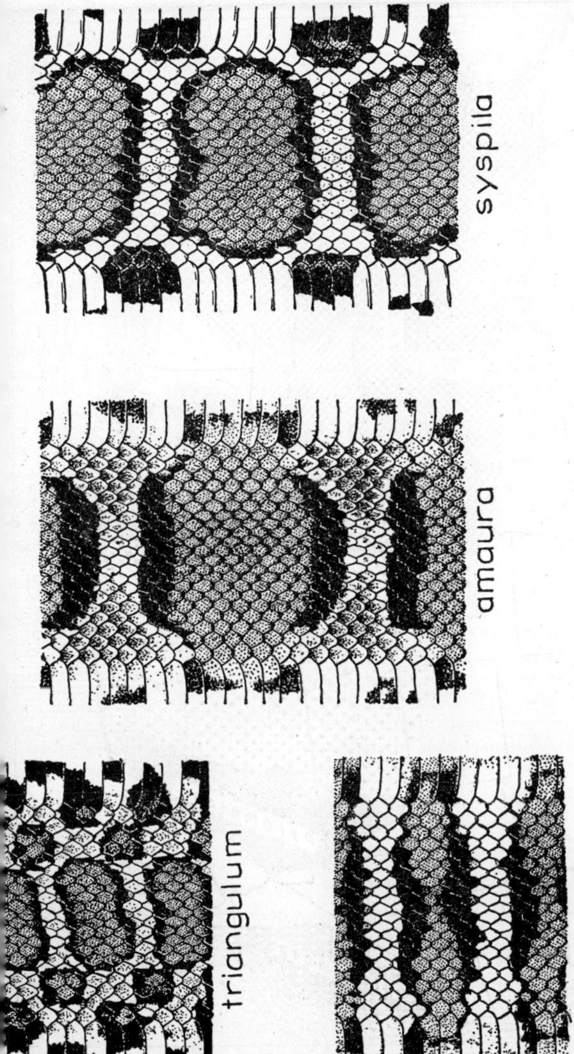

Fig. 57. Patterns of common milk snake (*Lampropeltis t. triangulum*), western milk snake (*L. t. gentilis*), Cope's milk snake (*L. t. amaura*), and red milk snake (*L. t. syspila*).

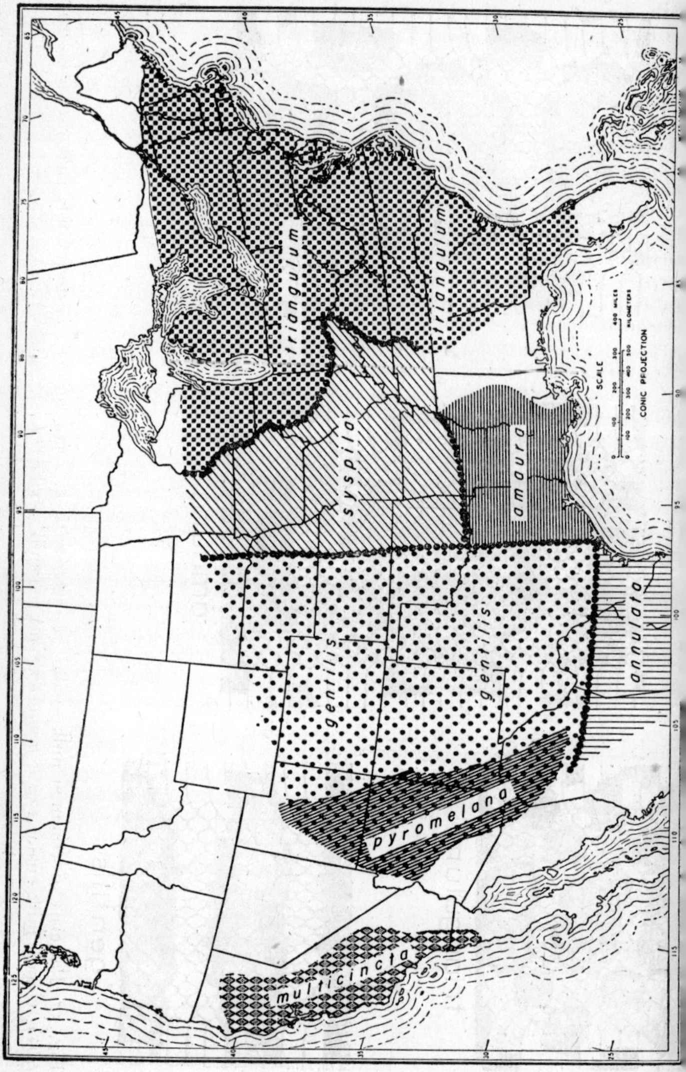
triangulum
triangulum
syspila
amaura
gentilis
gentilis
annulata
pyromelana
multicincta
SCALE
CONIC PROJECTION

the back. The yellowish rings number from 25 to 40. Back of the head black, snout mottled with red and black. (Fig. 57).

Range.—South Dakota to Utah, south to south central Texas and west to Arizona (Fig. 58).

Size.—Adults average about 20 inches in length. The maximum known length is 28 inches (Blanchard).

Mexican Milk Snake.—*Lampropeltis triangulum annulata* Kennicott. A pattern of 19 to 26 narrow white or yellow rings bordered by black and separated by broader areas of red. The black areas become wider toward the middle of the back, and may completely crowd out the red there. The head is usually entirely black above. Belly with large squarish black areas separated by much narrower bands of white or yellow.

Range.—Eastern Mexico, reaching the United States only at the extreme southern tip of Texas (Fig. 58).

Size.—Adults average about 28 inches. The longest authentic record is 33 inches (Blanchard).

Very little is known of the habits or behavior of these snakes. Probably they do not differ greatly from those of the common milk snake.

SHORT-TAILED SNAKE
(*Stilosoma extenuatum* Brown)
Plate 21

A small slender snake with a very short tail. Silvery gray above with 60 to 70 irregular dark brown spots with black borders on the body and about 12 similar spots on the tail. The spaces between the spots may be reddish or yellowish. Belly blotched with black or brown, the blotches usually extending up onto the sides.

Scales smooth. Anal plate single.

Range.—The central part of peninsular Florida.

This is a rare burrowing snake, occasionally seen foraging above ground, inhabiting high pine, upland hammock, and rosemary scrub in a restricted area in Florida. Carr states that "when handled although alert, it seems quite unafraid, and if treated roughly it becomes enraged, coiling, vibrating its meager tail and striking like an irate blacksnake." Carr's observations are supported by the behavior of living specimens in the laboratories of Field Museum. The posture in these specimens was peculiarly stiff and springy.

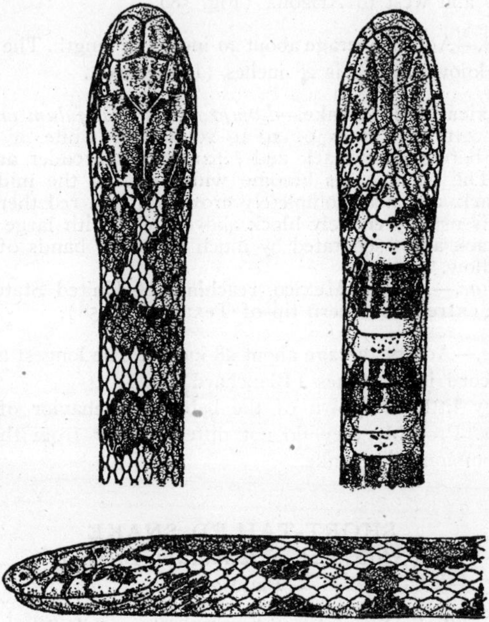

Fig. 59. Short-tailed snake (*Stilosoma extenuatum*).

Size.—Adults average about 18 inches in length.

Food.—Prey is killed by constriction. Carr's captive specimen ate a black-headed snake (*Tantilla*) that was two-thirds as long as itself. The process took two hours and fifteen minutes.

Breeding Habits.—Unknown.

Carr, A. F. Jr., 1934, Notes on the Habits of the Short-tailed Snake, *Stilosoma extenuatum* Brown. *Copeia,* 1934, pp. 138-139.

SCARLET SNAKE
(*Cemophora coccinea* Blumenbach)

A small, rather slender snake that appears to be ringed with red, black, and yellow when viewed from above. It is important to note, however, that *none of the rings extends onto the belly.* The pattern consists of wide red blotches separated by pairs of narrow black bands, each pair of black bands enclosing a band of yellow. Belly immaculate white or yellow. The top of the head is red, with a black band just behind the eyes, followed by a yellow ring. The snout is pointed, and projects beyond the lower jaw.

Scales smooth. Anal plate single.

Range.—Southern New Jersey south through Florida, west through Tennessee and Louisiana to eastern Oklahoma.

This snake bears a certain resemblance to the poisonous coral snake, and hence is sometimes called the "false coral

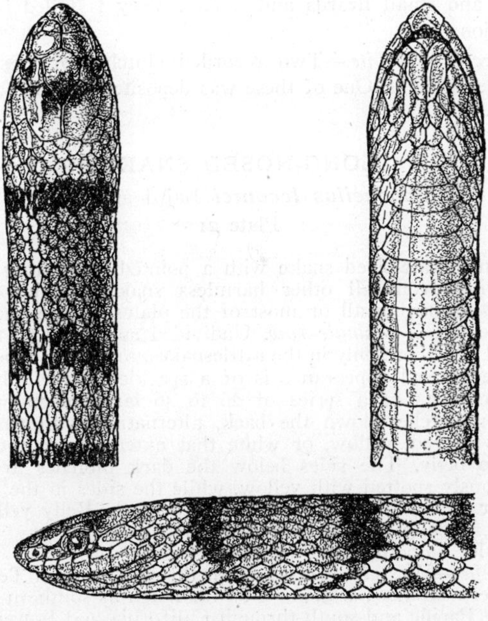

Fig. 60. Scarlet snake (*Cemophora coccinea*).

snake." It is readily distinguished by the different arrangement of colors (see p. 274). It is also similar to the scarlet king snake (p. 173) but may easily be distinguished by the fact that the bright colors do not extend onto the belly.

The scarlet snake is a rather uncommon burrowing snake, occasionally found wandering above ground at night but usually found under the bark of rotting logs or beneath the surface in fairly moist soil. It is sometimes turned up by the plow or in excavating operations. The head is obviously modified for burrowing, but there are no observations on precisely how it is employed. Captives rarely attempt to bite when handled.

Size.—Adults are about 16 inches long. Ditmars records a specimen that measured 25 inches.

Food.—Natural food unknown. Captives have eaten young mice and small lizards and snakes. Prey is killed by constriction.

Breeding Habits.—Two recorded clutches of eggs each numbered eight. One of these was deposited on June 23.

LONG-NOSED SNAKE

(*Rhinocheilus lecontei* Baird and Girard)

Plate 21

A moderate-sized snake with a pointed, projecting snout, differing from all other harmless snakes in the United States in having all or most of the plates on the underside of the tail *in a single row.* Undivided subcaudal plates are found elsewhere only in the rattlesnakes, moccasins, and boas.

The general appearance is of a speckled snake. The pattern consists of a series of 26 to 46 large black or dark brown blotches down the back, alternating with narrower bands of red, yellow, or white that extend down the sides to the belly. The sides below the dark blotches are conspicuously spotted with yellow, while the sides in the lighter red or yellow areas are spotted with black. Belly yellow or white, usually with a few black spots.

Scales smooth. Anal plate single.

Range.—Western Kansas south through western Texas to northern Mexico; westward, as far north as southern Idaho, to the Pacific and south through California and Lower California.

The long-nosed snake is found in a wide variety of habitats from pond and river banks to barren and sandy desert. It does not inhabit forest areas, and is almost or quite absent in mountains above the foothills. The red of

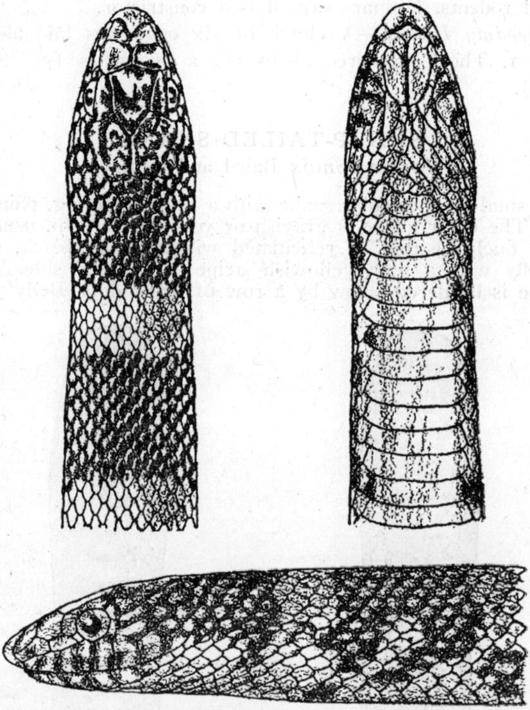

Fig. 61. Long-nosed snake (*Rhinocheilus lecontei*).

the color pattern is reduced in specimens from desert areas, and in extreme cases may be entirely replaced by yellow or white.

Little is known of the habits of this interesting snake. It is almost exclusively nocturnal. The form of the snout indicates that it is a burrower, but there are no observations to substantiate this.

Size.—Adults average about two feet in length. Van Denburgh recorded a specimen that measured 3 feet one inch.

Food.—Unknown, but presumably lizards, snakes, and small rodents. Ditmars says it is a constrictor.

Breeding Habits.—A clutch of six eggs was laid about July 1. These measured about 1⅜ x ⅝ inches (36 x 16 mm.).

SHARP-TAILED SNAKE

(*Contia tenuis* Baird and Girard)

A small, rather stout snake with a short, tapering, pointed tail. The color above is grayish or yellowish brown, usually very finely spotted or reticulated with slate or black, and usually with a light yellowish stripe along each side. The stripe is bordered below by a row of black dots. Belly yel-

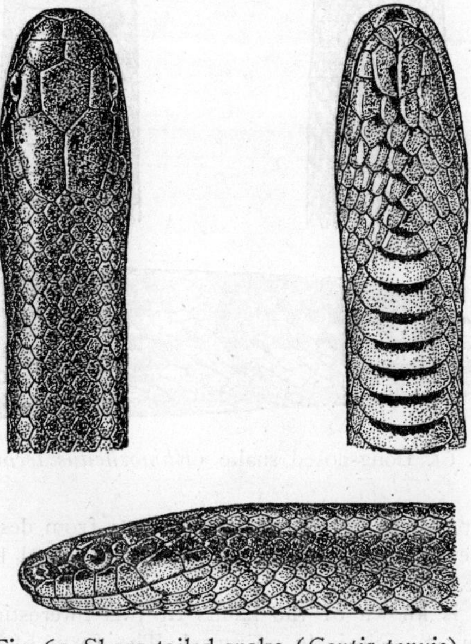

Fig. 62. Sharp-tailed snake (*Contia tenuis*).

lowish, with a transverse black band on each plate. Chin and throat spotted with black.

Scales smooth. Anal plate divided.

Range.—The Pacific Coast region, from Puget Sound to south central California.

The habits of this harmless little snake are virtually unknown. Fitch (1936, Amer. Midland Nat., 17:647) states that one was found under a board near a creek, and that another kept in captivity "was secretive and seldom showed itself during the daytime, but it became active and crawled about the cage after dark."

Size.—Adults measure about 11 inches in length. Van Denburgh recorded a specimen that measured 16¼ inches.

Food.—Unknown.

Breeding Habits.—Unknown.

WESTERN GROUND SNAKES
(Sonora)
Plate 21

The western ground snakes are small snakes, with small heads and slight neck constriction. Many have a banded color pattern. They are closely allied to *Contia,* from which they differ in having a kind of false groove on the posterior tooth, by an undivided nasal, and in having the dorsal scale reduction (when there is one) proceeding by loss of the median scale row. The scale formula of a *Sonora* may accordingly alternate from odd to even and from even to odd (15-14 in *semiannulata,* 15-14-13 in the Lower Californian *mosaueri,* 14-13-14 in *taylori*).

Scales smooth. Anal plate divided.

These snakes have only recently been revised and the Key below is that of William Stickel.

KEY TO THE WESTERN GROUND SNAKES OF THE UNITED STATES

1 a. Snout normal; abdomen rounded or but slightly angulate; scale rows various.................... 2

1 b. Snout distinctly flattened and extending beyond lower jaw; abdomen strongly angulate; scale rows 15-15 ......Mohave ground snake (*S. occipitalis*)

2a. Anterior scale rows 15, rarely 14 or 16........... 3

2b. Anterior scale rows 13, rarely 14; ventrals in males 126-139, in females 136-148
......South Texas ground snake (*S. taylori*)

3a. Scale rows near anus 15 in 90 per cent of specimens, but 14 in 10 per cent; ventrals in males 134-155 (av. 147), in females 140-162 (av. 153); caudals in males 39-52 (av. 43.5), in females 31-44 (av. 37); unicolor, bicolor, streaked, or with 1-25 dark cross-bands on body exclusive of tail
......Great Plains ground snake, (*S. episcopa*)

3b. Scale rows near anus 14, very rarely 15 or 13; ventrals or caudals running distinctly higher........ 4

4a. Ventrals in males 153-168 (av. 161), in females 162-183 (av. 172); caudals in males 41-57 (av. 53), in females 37-54 (av. 47)..................... 5

4b. Ventrals in males 147-155 (av. 151), in females 157-166 (av. 160); caudals in males 53-59 (av. 56), in females 46-51 (av. 48.5); color varying from unicolor to a regular series of 28-42 dark cross-bands on body
......Blanchard's western ground snake
(*S. semiannulata blanchardi*)

5a. A regular series of dark cross-bands present....... 6

5b. No series of bands present........................ 7

6a. Most of the body bands meeting across the abdomen; lateral scales heavily shaded with gray
......Gloyd's western ground snake
(*S. semiannulata gloydi*)

6b. Bands not meeting across abdomen, or only a few so meeting; lateral scales lightly shaded with gray, or not shaded
......Arizona ground snake (*S. s. semiannulata*)

7a. A sharp-edged dorsal pink stripe present; stripe contrasting with the bluish-gray to brownish-gray lateral scales
Vermilion-lined ground snake (*S. miniata linearis*)

7b. Dorsal pink stripe absent or blending gradually with the grayish to reddish color of the sides
......Vermilion ground snake (*S. m. miniata*)

Mohave Ground Snake.—*Sonora occipitalis* Hallowell. Snout projecting and spadelike, abdomen angulate. The ground color is yellowish, with a pattern of sharply defined black rings on the body and tail, usually encircling the body but sometimes not continued across the belly. Between each pair of black rings there is a bright orange half ring. (Fig. 63).

Range.—Desert areas of southern California, southern Nevada, and western Arizona.

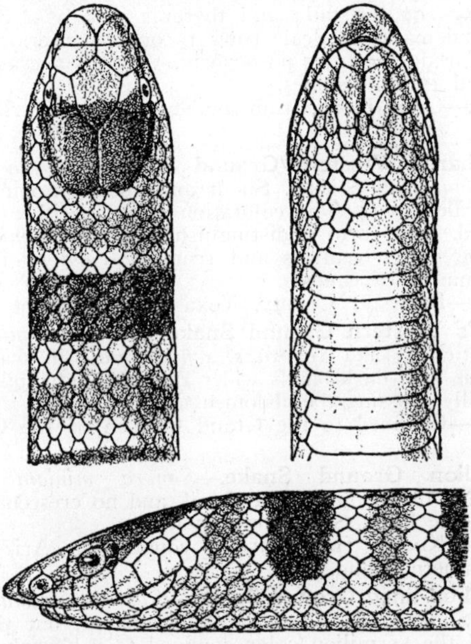

Fig. 63. Mohave ground snake (*Sonora occipitalis*).

South Texas Ground Snake.—*Sonora taylori* Boulenger. Snout little projecting, and ventral plates not angulate. Color brown above, the center of each scale darker than the outer edges. Belly, throat, and lips white. Dorsal scale rows 13-13; ventrals fewest in the genus (126-148).

Range.—Southern Texas and adjacent Mexico.

Great Plains Ground Snake.—*Sonora episcopa* Kennicott. Snout rounded, and ventrals not angulate. Scales in 15 rows. The coloration is extremely variable, ranging through gray to red and dark brown, and may be uniform or with a varying number of dark cross-bands on the back. (Fig. 64; Plate 21).

Range.—Kansas and Colorado south through Texas and New Mexico.

Arizona Ground Snake.—*Sonora semiannulata semiannulata* Baird and Girard. Snout rounded, ventrals not angulate. The body and tail are marked with black bands, which form rings on the tail; and there is usually a crescentic black head marking. Scale rows 15 on the anterior half of the body, reducing to 14 posteriorly. Ventrals average 160 in males and 171 in females.

Range.—Great Basin, from southern Idaho to Arizona and Utah.

Blanchard's Western Ground Snake.—*Sonora semiannulata blanchardi* Stickel. Snout and abdomen unmodified; dorsal scales 15-14. The coloration may be either uniform or banded. This form is distinguished from *s. semiannulata* by having fewer ventrals and from *episcopa* by having a higher number of caudals.

Range.—Brewster County, Texas, and adjacent Mexico.

Gloyd's Western Ground Snake.—*Sonora semiannulata gloydi* Stickel. Like *Sonora s. semiannulata* in scale characters, but with dark bands wider than the light interspaces, and usually crossing the abdomen.

Range.—Confined to the Grand Canyon of the Colorado River.

Vermilion Ground Snake.—*Sonora miniata miniata* Stickel. No bands on body and tail, and no crescentic black mark on the head. Scale rows 15-14.

Range.—Known from various counties in Arizona and from southern Idaho.

Vermilion-lined Ground Snake.—*Sonora miniata linearis* Stickel. Similar to *Sonora miniata miniata,* but the sides gray and the vermilion color confined to a sharply defined dorsal stripe.

Range.—Southern California and adjacent Nevada, southward into Lower California.

The habits of the western ground snakes are little known, and some of the species and subspecies are still quite inadequately represented in museum collections. It would be especially interesting to obtain broods of young of the variable *episcopa* and *semiannulata blanchardi.* These snakes are doubtless all secretive forms, to be found under rocks or hummocks formed by vegetation, like those of the sotol in western Texas. Specimens of the Mohave form (*occipitalis*) have been dug out from one or two feet below the surface of desert sand dunes.

Size.—The Mohave ground snake (*occipitalis*) seems to be the largest species, averaging about a foot long. The abundant Great Plains ground snake (*episcopa*) averages about 10 inches in length, with a maximum of about 14 inches. The South Texas ground snake averages a foot in length, maximum about 15 inches.

Food.—Unknown, but presumably insects and small invertebrates.

Breeding Habits.—Egg laying; *Sonora taylori* is reported to produce about 6 eggs, four-fifths of an inch long and a little more than a fifth of an inch in diameter.

Mulaik, S. and D., Variation in *Sonora taylori*. *Copeia,* 1941.

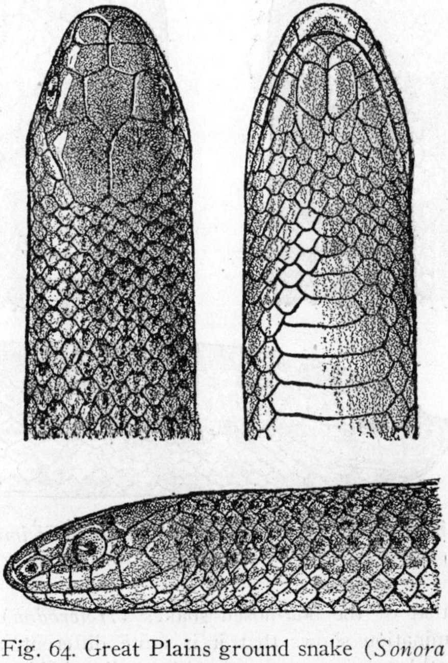

Fig. 64. Great Plains ground snake (*Sonora episcopa*).

HOOK-NOSED SNAKES
(*Ficimia*)

The hook-nosed snakes have the rostral much enlarged with a flattened upper surface and turned up in front into a hooklike point. The species within the borders of the United States are small, but a related species in Yucatan is a good-sized snake. The shovellike rostral scale is reminis-

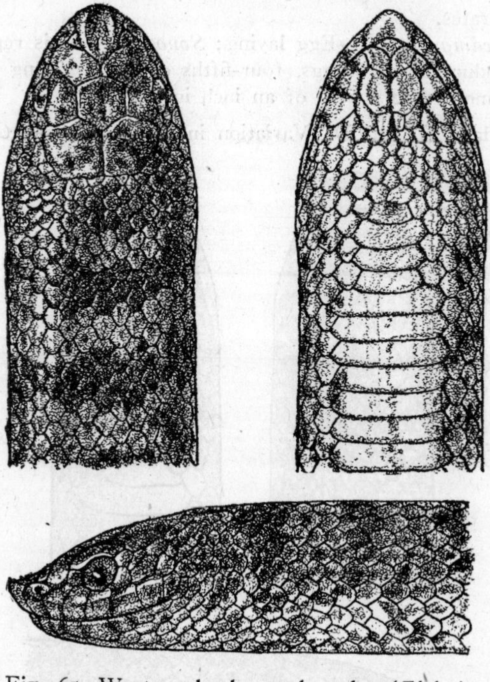

Fig. 65. Western hook-nosed snake (*Ficimia cana*).

cent of that of the hog-nosed snakes (*Heterodon*). Attentive examination shows that it is quite different, and that this resemblance is associated with similar habits and not with relationship. *Heterodon* is further distinguished by having keeled scales.

Scales smooth. Anal plate divided.

KEY TO THE SPECIES OF *FICIMIA* IN THE UNITED STATES

Rostral separating the very small internasals and in contact with prefrontals
......Western hook-nosed snake (*Ficimia cana*)

Rostral separating the prefrontals and in contact with the frontal; no internasals
......South Texas hook-nosed snake (*Ficimia streckeri*)

Western Hook-nosed Snake.—*Ficimia cana* Cope. General coloration grayish brown, with 30 or more dark-edged dorsal cross-bands on the body and 8 to 12 on the tail; a brown band across the eyes and down to the labials and another across the parietals. Dorsal scales 19-17-17; ventrals 134-143, caudals 29-35.

Range.—Trans-Pecos Texas to southern Arizona and presumably in adjacent Mexico.

South Texas Hook-nosed Snake.—*Ficimia streckeri* Taylor. General coloration gray with darker narrow cross-bands, 46 on the body and 11 on the tail; head without cross-bands. Dorsal scales 17, ventrals 144, caudals 30.

Range.—Southern Texas.

The hook-nosed snakes appear to be burrowers, as may be inferred from their rarity in collections and from their shovellike snout. Taylor reports a remarkable defensive behavior in specimens collected at night in New Mexico, consisting of continued spasmodic writhing after being touched and eversion and retraction of the cloaca with a popping sound.

Size.—The species of *Ficimia* seem to be genuinely small snakes. Most specimens are about 8 inches long, with a maximum known of about 12 inches.

Food.—Unknown.

Breeding Habits.—Unknown.

Taylor, E. H., 1931, Notes on two Specimens of the rare Snake *Ficimia cana* and the Description of a new Species of *Ficimia* from Texas. *Copeia,* 1931, pp. 4-7.

BANDED SAND SNAKE
(*Chilomeniscus cinctus* Cope)
Plate 22

The banded sand snake represents an extreme of adaptation to sand burrowing, with a shovel-shaped snout and countersunk lower jaw, cylindrical body, and consolidated head shields. Other species of *Chilomeniscus* are found in Lower California.

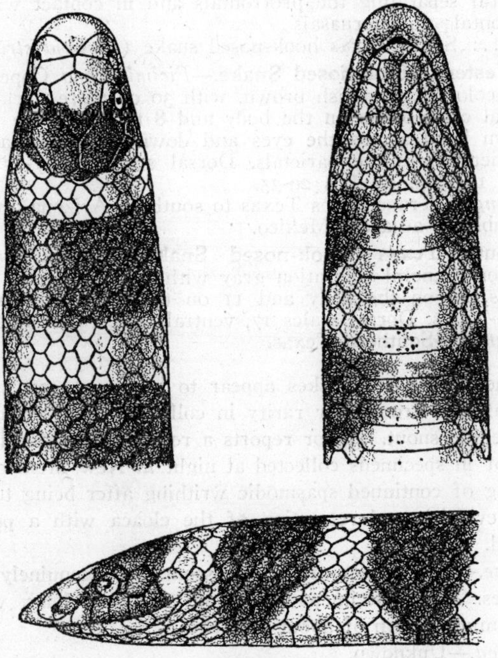

Fig. 66. Banded sand snake (*Chilomeniscus cinctus*).

A small, rather heavy bodied, banded snake with a shovel-shaped snout and highly polished scales. The ground color is yellow or red, with 18 to 28 dark brown or black bands on the body and from three to five on the tail. The bands may extend across the belly, and usually form complete rings on the tail. Belly whitish.

Scales smooth and in 13 rows; ventrals 109-125; caudals 22-28; rostral much enlarged; anal plate divided.

Range.—Southeastern California and southwestern Arizona, southward into Lower California and Sonora.

The banded sand snake is a desert inhabitant, remarkably adapted to burrowing in the loose sand of true sand deserts. It is nocturnal, like most desert animals. The habits of this snake were studied by Dr. Walter Mosauer, who found that individuals crawl about freely just beneath the surface of the sand. The sand caves in behind the moving snake, so that it leaves a very characteristic groovelike track. In some places bewildering mazes of these tracks may be found. These snakes often emerge at night, and are then found moving about on the surface.

Size.—Adults are 9 or 10 inches long.

Food.—Said to live on ant larvae.

Breeding Habits.—Unknown.

Mosauer, Walter, 1936, *Occ. Papers Mus. Zool. Univ. Mich.*, No. 329, pp. 12-14, pl. 2 (sand adaptations and locomotion; photo of sand track).

THE WATER SNAKES
(Natrix)

The water snake group is extremely well represented in eastern North America, with a great variety of species, only two of which are found in tropical Mexico. They are completely absent in western North America. A somewhat similar series of species is found in eastern Asia. There the geographic parallel ends, as *Natrix* has a great number of species in the Oriental tropics. Europe has only two species, and western North America none. Such peculiarities of distribution in the world as a whole form a part of the subject matter of the broad field of Animal Geography. The relations of the animal life of eastern North America with that of eastern Asia are further illustrated among our familiar snakes by *Elaphe, Opheodrys,* and *Agkistrodon.*

The North American water snakes exhibit a slight tendency to upward displacement of the nostrils, as is shown also by narrowing of the internasals, which reaches an extreme in other more completely aquatic snakes. Only one of our species exhibits even a beginning of compression of the tail to form an oarlike scull. It is evident that our water snakes are adapted to life in the water primarily by adjustments of behavior and physiology. Most obvious of these adjustments are the taking of refuge in the water when alarmed, with voluntary submergence, the accompanying association with permanent bodies of water, and the development of corresponding food habits.

The arrangement of the species of *Natrix* which follows is that of William M. Clay, and the Key is adapted directly from his (*Copeia*, 1938, pp. 174-175).

KEY TO THE WATER SNAKES OF THE UNITED STATES AND CANADA

1 a. Scale rows 19, at mid-body 2
1 b. Scale rows more than 19.......................... 5

2 a. Lower labials 7, a single preocular
......Kirtland's water snake (*N. kirtlandii*) p. 209
2 b. Lower labials 9-11, usually 2 preoculars.......... 3

3 a. One long dark median stripe on the belly, or no markings on belly except those on the ends of the ventrals
......Graham's water snake (*N. grahami*) p. 210
3 b. Two long dark stripes near middle of belly, at least anteriorly 4

4 a. Light stripes present at the sides of the belly
......Queen snake (*N. septemvittata*) p. 211
4 b. No light lateral stripes at the sides of the belly
......Striped water snake (*N. rigida*) p. 213

5 a. Scale rows 27-33 (sometimes 25 in *rhombifera*, in which the pattern of alternating dorsal and lateral spots with oblique connecting bars is distinctive); lower labials usually 11-13 6
5 b. Scale rows 21-25 (rarely 27, in *transversa*); lower labials usually 10 8

6 a. Two anterior temporals; a mid-dorsal row of 21-25 isolated quadrate spots on the body (without tail)
......Brown water snake (*N. taxispilota*) p. 213

6 b. A single anterior temporal 7

7 a. Eye in contact with upper labials
Diamond-backed water snake (*N. rhombifera*) p. 217

7 b. Eye separated from labials by suboculars
......Green water snake (*N. cyclopion*) p. 215

8 a. A median row of light spots on belly (sometimes irregular) 9

8 b. No median row of light spots on belly 10

9 a. Back spotted or unicolor, the spots occasionally forming longitudinal lines, especially anteriorly
......Flat-tailed water snake
(*N. sipedon compressicauda*) p. 222

9 b. Back with four well-marked dark stripes
.....Clark's water snake (*N. sipedon clarkii*) p. 223

10 a. Body unspotted above 11

10 b. Back with cross-bands or spots.................. 12

11 a. Back gray, belly yellow to cream dusky posteriorly, especially the tail
Lake Erie water snake (*N. sipedon insularum*) p. 220

11 b. Back uniform dark brown, reddish, or black (or spots faintly visible), belly yellow or red, and underside of tail without markings at tip
......Red-bellied water snake (*N. erythrogaster erythrogaster*) p. 224

12 a. Belly immaculate or with dark antero-lateral margins of ventrals, tip of tail immaculate beneath. 13

12 b. Lower surface with well-defined markings, tip of tail never immaculate beneath................... 15

13 a. Paired dark dorsal spots, two scales long, alternating with similar lateral spots, spots on body more than 58
......Harter's water snake (*N. harteri*) p. 225

13 b. Dorsal spots on body less numerous (less than 45), not paired on middle of back 14

14 a. Neck region with 1-7 cross-bands, followed posteriorly by a median series of spots in alternation with a lateral series; this pattern becomes

obsolete and uniformly dark with maturity
......Immature red-bellied water snake
(*N. e. erythrogaster*) p. 224

14 b. Pattern similar but with 0-2 anterior transverse bands and not becoming obsolete
Yellow-bellied water snake (*N. e. transversa*) p. 224

15 a. A dorsal pattern of 3-15 anterior transverse bands, posterior to which a series of median dorsal blotches alternates with a series of lateral spots (rarely a complete series of transverse bands, but then belly has half-moon-shaped spots); ventrals 128-155 16

15 b. Dorsal pattern wholly of transverse bands or rarely with a few alternating spots; ventrals 121-143 17

16 a. Usually 3-10 (rarely more) anterior transverse bands and a total of more than 30 bands and dorsal spots on body; ventrals 135-155, many with 2 dark or red half-moon-shaped marks with flecking and mottling; dorsal spots and bands generally darker, less distinct from the ground color, and separated by interspaces narrower than those of *pleuralis* (lateral interspaces narrower than lateral bars)
Common northern water snake (*N. s. sipedon*) p. 219

16 b. Usually 5-15 anterior transverse bands and a total of fewer than 30 bands and dorsal spots; ventrals 128-146, many with 2 reddish-brown, crescent-shaped marks which are somewhat more restricted than those of *sipedon* and tend more to form 2 longitudinal rows; dorsal spots generally lighter, more distinct from pale ground color, and separated by interspaces wider than those of *sipedon* (lateral interspaces wider than lateral bars
......Midwest water snake (*N. s. pleuralis*) p. 220

17 a. Dorsal bands about 10-18; ventrals 129-138; belly with squarish markings
Mississippi River water snake (*N. s. confluens*) p. 222

17 b. Dorsal bands more than 18; ventrals 120-137; belly with squarish markings or not 18

18 a. Dorsal bands about 24 (19-33); ventrals 126-137; belly with quadrate dark or red spots; sometimes small lateral spots alternate with the transverse bands
Southern banded water snake (*N. s. fasciata*) p. 222

18 b. Dorsal saddles about 29 (24-35); ventrals 120-129; belly with reddish or dark anterior borders to ventrals, these often narrowed in center leaving a light area suggestive of the spots of *compressicauda*
......Florida water snake (*N. s. pictiventris*) p. *222*

Kirtland's Water Snake.—*Natrix kirtlandii* Kennicott (Plate 22). The smallest of the water snakes, rarely exceeding 18 inches in length. A checkered snake, with a pattern of four rows of about 50 round black blotches on a ground color of light brown to gray. The blotches are arranged in two alternating rows on either side of the midline. Occasionally there is a series of small spots low down on the side, alternating with the blotches of the outer row. Belly bright red or brick red, with a row of conspicuous black spots, one pair of spots to each plate, down each side. Small specimens are dark, usually with the dorsal pattern very obscure.

Range.—Wisconsin and southern Michigan south through northern and central Illinois and Indiana to Louisville, Kentucky, and east throughout Ohio to Pennsylvania and western New Jersey.

Kirtland's water snake is quite spotty in its distribution, occurring in local "islands" over its range and entirely absent in wide areas. It is much less aquatic than other water snakes, and is seldom found along streams or about ponds or swamps. It prefers damp situations, however, and is most often seen in marshy meadows or near small woodland pools. As with many small snakes, individuals are most often located under boards or flat stones.

When alarmed, this snake defends itself by flattening its body until it appears almost ribbonlike. This flattening, which involves the whole body and not just the head and neck as in the hog-nosed snakes, is often accompanied by a rigid immobility, followed by ineffectual strikes. In spite of this extraordinary behavior it is not known to bite when handled. A similar flattening of the body is frequent in water snakes and in some related forms.

Size.—Adults average about 15 inches in length. The longest authentic record is 21 inches (Conant).

Food.—Specimens captured by Conant "disgorged slugs and earthworms."

Breeding Habits.—Hay found 6 young in one female and

8 in another, while six broods recorded by Conant numbered from 5 to 11 (av. 8). The young are born during August and early September, and measure from 5 to 6⅝ inches in length.

Conant, R., 1938, The Reptiles of Ohio. *Amer. Midland Nat.* vol. 20, pp. 74-77 (habits and behavior).

Graham's Water Snake.—*Natrix grahamii* Baird and Girard. A rather slender striped snake. The ground color of the back is dark brown, with a broad yellow band on the first three rows of scales bordered below by a narrow black stripe, often irregular or zig-zag, along the edges of the belly plates. There is often an indistinct pale stripe, narrowly bordered with black, down the center of the back, particularly in small specimens. Belly yellowish, usually with a median row of small dark spots posteriorly and under the tail. (Fig. 67).

This snake is often mistaken for a garter snake, but is easily distinguished by its divided anal plate and by the fact that all the garter snakes in its area have a prominent yellow stripe down the center of the back.

Range.—Illinois to southern Nebraska, south to Louisiana and eastern Texas.

The habits of Graham's water snake are similar to those of the typical water snakes. It frequents the borders of streams and ponds, where it is either seen in trees and bushes overhanging the water or is found under flat rocks, logs, or brush piles along the water's edge. Strecker found them abundant in crayfish chimneys in Texas. It is a rather timid snake, promptly taking refuge in the water when alarmed.

Size.—Adults average about two feet in length. The longest authentic record was a Texas specimen that measured 29½ inches (Strecker).

Food.—Little is known of the natural food of this snake. According to Strecker it feeds on crustaceans, small fish, frogs and salamanders, "largely on crayfish and a small species of fresh-water prawn."

Breeding Habits.—From 10 to 15 young are born (Strecker). They measure about 8 inches at birth.

Strecker, J. K., 1926, On the Habits of some southern Snakes. *Contrib. Baylor Univ. Mus.*, No. 4.

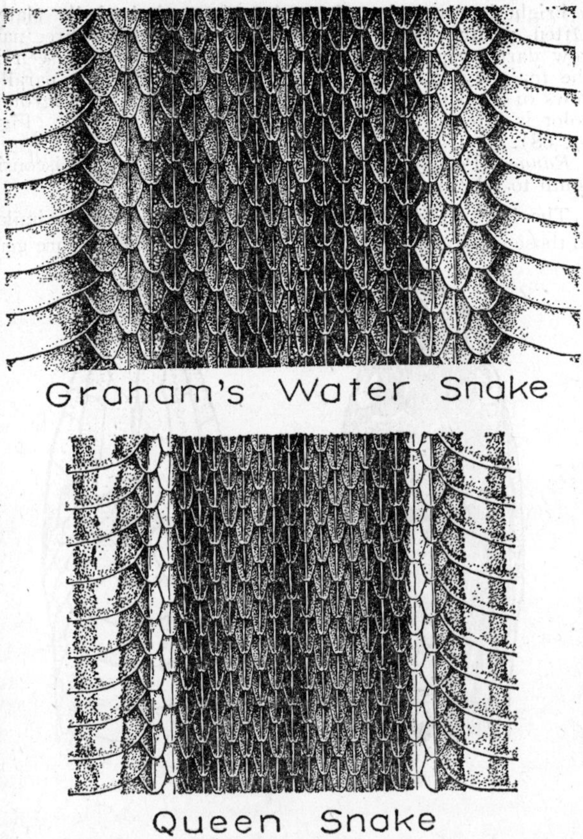

Fig. 67. Patterns of Queen snake and of Graham's water snake (*Natrix grahamii*).

Queen Snake.—*Natrix septemvittata* Say (Plate 22). A slender striped snake, similar to the preceding form but differing in having two dark stripes down the middle of the belly. The ground color of the back is chocolate brown to chestnut, with a narrow yellow stripe occupying the second and upper half of the first row of scales bordered below by a bright brown stripe along the edges of the belly plates. Often, particularly in small specimens, there are three narrow dark stripes down the back; these cannot be seen in the majority of adults. Belly yellowish, with two parallel rows of brown or gray spots down the midline. The ground color is often greenish between these rows of spots. (Figs. 67, 68).

Range.—Pennsylvania, Ohio, Michigan, and Wisconsin south to Alabama and Georgia.

The habits and behavior of this snake are very similar to those of Graham's water snake. It is a timid creature gen-

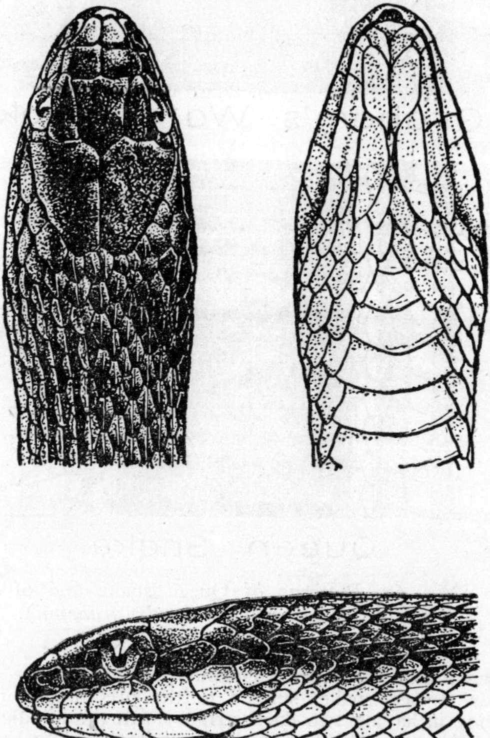

Fig. 68. Queen snake (*Natrix septemvittata*).

erally found along streams or the borders of ponds, in the bottom of which it promptly takes refuge when alarmed. In northern Illinois, at least, it is very spotty in its distribution, being extremely abundant in some localities and entirely absent in others.

Size.—Adults average about 20 inches in length. Conant recorded an Ohio specimen that measured 33 inches.

Food.—The queen snake is noted for its selective food habits, its diet consisting almost wholly of crayfish. Of six stomachs that contained food, five contained only crayfish while the sixth snake had eaten a toad. Conant says that Ohio specimens disgorged crayfish and small fish, chiefly crayfish, when captured.

Breeding Habits.—Young are born in late August. Four recorded broods numbered from 8 to 11 (av. 10). The young measure about 8 inches at birth.

Striped Water Snake.—*Natrix rigida* Say. A small heavy-bodied snake with a striped pattern. The ground color is brown to olive-brown, with two parallel dark brown stripes down the back. The sides are paler than the back. Belly yellow, with two parallel rows of black or brown spots down the midline. The underside of the tail is unspotted or marked with an irregular median stripe. (Fig. 69).

Differs from the two preceding species in lacking the yellow stripe on the side.

Range.—South Carolina along the coastal plain to western Louisiana, south into northern Florida.

The striped water snake, like the two preceding forms, is a timid snake. It apparently differs from them in its habits, however, since it seems to be a mud-burrower rarely seen in the open.

Size.—Adults average about 16 inches in length. The largest specimen in the collection of Field Museum measures 29 inches.

Food.—Strecker states that "it feeds to a large extent on small sirens and fish."

Breeding Habits.—Unknown.

Brown Water Snake.—*Natrix taxispilota* Holbrook. (Plate 23). A large, very heavy-bodied snake, with the neck distinctly narrower than the head. The ground color is brown or rusty brown. There is a row of about 25 large squarish

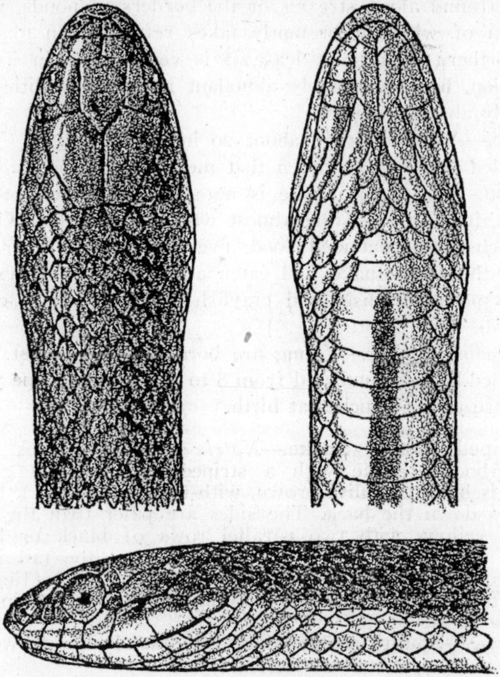

Fig. 69. Striped water snake (*Natrix rigida*).

blotches, black or dark brown in color, down the back; a row of similar but smaller blotches alternates with these on the sides. All the blotches are well separated from each other, those on the back being almost as far apart as the width of the blotches. Belly usually yellow heavily blotched with black or dark brown; in occasional specimens the belly is almost entirely black.

This species has a larger number of scale rows (27 to 33) than any other North American water snake.

Range.—Coastal region from North Carolina to central Florida, westward through the Gulf states to Louisiana.

This snake, which is sometimes called the "water rattle" or "water pilot," exceeds all other North American water snakes in size. In the Gulf states it is one of the commonest water snakes in rivers, creeks, and lakes. The brown water snake is one of the most arboreal of the large southern water snakes. It loves to climb upon the dead branches and live shrubs that line the water courses, individuals occasionally being found in trees twenty-five feet above the water. From these they drop into the water with a great crashing of branches and resounding splash at the approach of danger, for like all water snakes they are very shy unless cornered. In the water they are swift and active swimmers.

A cornered or captured individual is a vicious and powerful adversary, and if large is capable of inflicting considerable damage with its teeth. In addition, captured specimens almost invariably throw out the vile-smelling contents of their anal scent glands. Because of their behavior and venomous appearance these creatures are considered as poisonous as rattlesnakes or true moccasins by most residents of the south.

Size.—Adults average about 3½ feet in length. The maximum recorded length is 4½ feet, although it is reputed to reach a length of 6 feet.

Food.—Carr states that these snakes "feed on fish more regularly than any other Florida snake; where fish are concentrated in holes, during times of low water, the brown water snakes stuff themselves until they can scarcely move." Wright and Bishop found two frogs in one specimen, and fish remains in two others.

Breeding Habits.—Mating has been observed on March 20. Three females dissected by Wright and Bishop contained 14, 40, and 58 embryos respectively. The young measure about 12 inches at birth.

Green Water Snake.—*Natrix cyclopion cyclopion* Duméril and Bibron. (Plate 23). A large, very heavy-bodied snake. Dark green, greenish-brown or brown above, with a poorly-defined pattern of about 50 narrow blackish cross-bars. The cross-bars are often lacking in large individuals, which are then uniform dull olive or brown. The belly is yellowish on the anterior third; the posterior two-thirds is dark brown marked with numerous semi-circles of white or yellow.

This, and the following form, differ from all other North American water snakes in having one or more small scales under the eye, so that the eye appears to be surrounded by a ring of small plates (Fig. 70).

Range.—Lowlands of the Mississippi Valley from southern Illinois south to Louisiana, east along the Gulf coast to Alabama and possibly west into Texas.

Florida Green Water Snake.—*Natrix cyclopion floridana* Goff. Very similar to the preceding form, but differing in that the belly is uniformly whitish except for small dark spots along the edges, especially toward the tail. The underside of the tail is gray, but each scale is marked with a white spot.

Range.—Coastal region of South Carolina, southern Georgia, and throughout Florida.

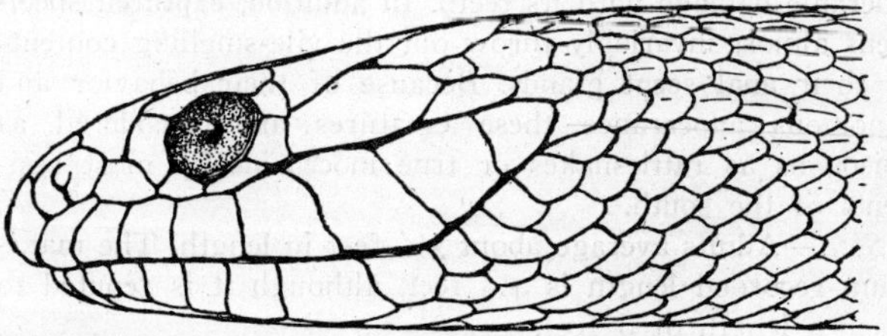

Fig. 70. Green water snake (*Natrix c. cyclopion*), showing the ring of scales around the eye.

The green water snakes are more restricted in habitat than most other water snakes are, although their habits and behavior are otherwise quite similar to those of the other larger water snakes. They are quite partial to the quiet waters of sluggish streams, lakes, or ponds. Brackish coastal marshes, open rice fields, and the bayous of rivers are favorite habitats.

Size.—Adults average about three feet in length. The maximum length (*floridana*) is five feet (Conant and Bridges).

Food.—Van Hyning examined 75 stomachs, only 13 of which contained food. Frogs were present in 10, fish in 4, and a salamander in one.

Breeding Habits.—Young are born in late July and August. Two broods born in captivity (*floridana*) numbered 10 and 14. The young snakes measure about 10 inches at birth.

Diamond-backed Water Snake.—*Natrix rhombifera rhombifera* Hallowell.* (Plate 23). A large, very heavy-

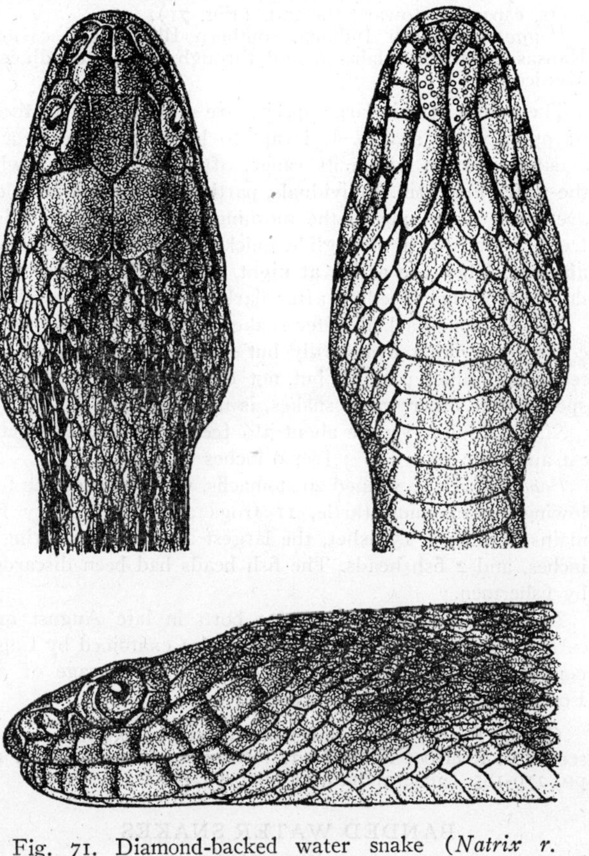

Fig. 71. Diamond-backed water snake (*Natrix r. rhombifera*). Note the chin tubercles characteristic of males in this species.

* There is a related subspecies in southern Mexico.

bodied snake, brown or olive in color with a chain of diamond-shaped markings along the back. Each diamond is composed of a narrow black or dark brown border enclosing a central area of the ground color, and a dark band extends downward from the bottom of the diamond to the edges of the belly plates. Belly yellow, marked with semilunar brown spots, especially toward the tail. (Fig. 71).

Range.—Southern Indiana, southern Illinois and eastern Kansas, south to Alabama and through Texas to adjacent Mexico.

The habits of this large species are quite similar to those of other water snakes. It is apt to be encountered in any aquatic situation within its range, often in association with the water moccasin. Individuals, particularly gravid females, are fond of basking in the morning sun on logs or fallen trees, from which they glide quickly into the water when alarmed. They are active at night, and Cagle believes they do most of their feeding after dark.

The diamond-backed water snake is a vicious fighter when cornered, striking awkwardly but rapidly. Its sharp, strong teeth can inflict painful, but not dangerous, wounds. This species, like other water snakes, is nonpoisonous.

Size.—Adults average about 3½ feet in length. The longest authentic record is 4 feet 9 inches (Cagle).

Food.—Cagle examined 20 stomachs, which yielded the following: 1 snapping turtle, 11 frogs and fragmentary remains of others, 15 fishes, the largest a catfish measuring 9 inches, and 2 fish heads. The fish heads had been discarded by fishermen.

Breeding Habits.—Young are born in late August and early September. Twelve gravid females examined by Cagle contained 18 to 42 embryos each with an average of 30. Force recorded a captive brood of 43.

Cagle, F. R., 1937, Notes on *Natrix rhombifera* as observed at Reelfoot Lake. *Jour. Tennessee Acad. Sci.*, vol. 12, pp. 179-185 (general natural history).

BANDED WATER SNAKES

Plate 24

These snakes, which are the most abundant water snakes in eastern North America, form a chain of intergrading subspecies. These geographic races are by no means easy to identify, and it will be well for the beginning student to supplement the key by consideration of the geographic probabilities. (See map, Fig. 72).

Common Water Snake.—*Natrix sipedon sipedon* Linnaeus. (Plate 24). A heavy-bodied blotched snake always found in the vicinity of water. On the anterior third of the body the pattern consists of a series of wide cross-bands, brown, reddish-brown, or dark gray in color; farther back the cross-bands are replaced by squarish blotches on the back, which alternate with smaller blotches on the sides. Ground color light gray or tan to dark gray or brown. Belly yellowish or gray, usually brilliantly marked with many half-moons of gray, brown, or red. The pattern often becomes obliterated in large individuals, which are then uniformly dark above.

Very young snakes are brilliantly marked. They are pale gray, with markings similar to adults but with the pattern on both the back and the belly jet black in color.

Range.—Southern parts of Maine, Quebec, and Ontario west to Wisconsin and eastern Colorado; south to northern South Carolina, Tennessee, and eastern Oklahoma. (Fig. 72).

This snake, sometimes called the northern banded water snake, is one of the most abundant reptiles in the eastern and central states. It is never found far from water, but because it is to be seen around nearly every river, brook, or pond it is probably as well known as any snake in the United States. Like other water snakes, it is very timid, plunging precipitately into the water when alarmed.

Because of its heavy body, alarmingly pugnacious behavior when cornered, and constant association with water this snake is almost invariably supposed by the layman to be the venomous water moccasin, particularly in the north where the true water moccasin does not occur. In southern Illinois the junior author found that the water snake is called "water moccasin," while the true moccasin is carefully distinguished as the "cottonmouth"; both are firmly believed to be poisonous. Actually there is no easy way of distinguishing these snakes at a distance, and in country where moccasins are known to occur it is an excellent idea to treat *all* water snakes with respect. A dead specimen may be distinguished as follows:

WATER SNAKE	WATER MOCCASIN
Plates under tail in a double row throughout.	Plates under tail in a single row except near tip.
No pit between eye and nostril.	A prominent pit between eye and nostril (Fig. 94).
Pupil of eye round.	Pupil of eye elliptical.
Upper teeth small and uniform.	A pair of large folding fangs in front part of upper jaw.

Size.—Adults average about 30 inches in length. The maximum known length is 4 feet 3 inches (Conant and Bridges).

Food.—This snake feeds almost exclusively on cold-blooded vertebrates. A recent analysis of the contents of 30 stomachs (Uhler, Cottam and Clarke, 1941) gave the following percentages by bulk: fishes (mostly non-game), 61 per cent; frogs and toads, 22 per cent; salamanders, 13 per cent; insects, 2.5 per cent. Conant also found crayfish, and Surface recorded mice and shrews as occasional food.

Breeding Habits.—Mating takes place in April, and young are born between August and early October. Eight recorded broods numbered 16 to 40 with an average of 31. Fowler (1915, *Copeia,* No. 19) reported finding 76 embryos in a very large female "little short of five feet" in length. The young measure about 9 inches at birth.

Lake Erie Water Snake.—*Natrix sipedon insularum* Conant and Clay. Differs from the common water snake in the almost complete absence of a color pattern. Usually uniform gray, greenish-gray, or brownish-gray above and uniform white or yellowish-white on the belly. Small individuals may have faint indications of dark blotches on the back and lower sides.

Range.—Restricted to Pelee and other islands in the western part of Lake Erie. (Fig. 72).

Midwest Water Snake.—*Natrix sipedon pleuralis* Cope. Differs from the common water snake in being lighter in color, in the larger size of the areas of ground color, and in having the belly spots arranged *chiefly in two rows.* Ground color above grayish-buff, the markings brown or reddish; the areas of ground color are usually as large as the mark-

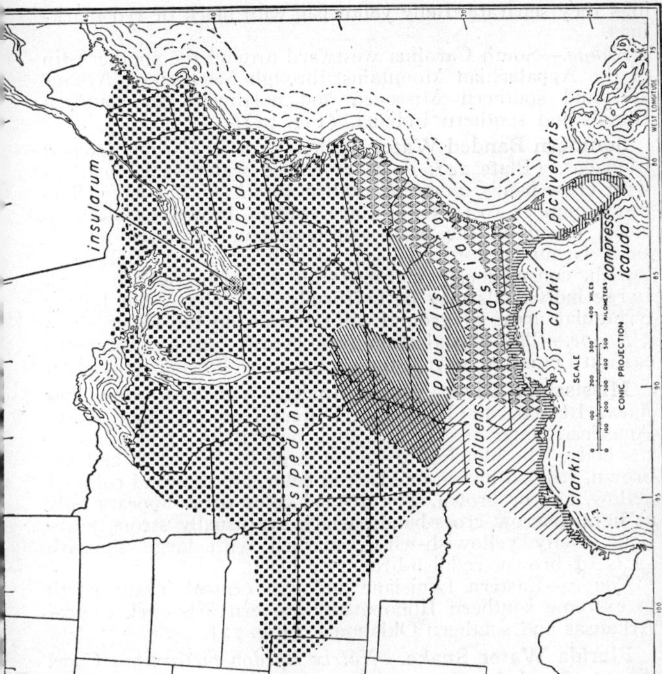

Fig. 72. Distribution of the subspecies of the common water snake (*Natrix sipedon*). Note that the ranges of *pleuralis* and *confluens* overlap.

ings they separate. Belly yellowish, with black or red markings.

Range.—South Carolina westward around the southern tip of the Appalachian Mountains, through Mississippi, Arkansas, and southern Missouri, and northward to southern Illinois and southern Indiana. (Fig. 72).

Southern Banded Water Snake.—*Natrix sipedon fasciata* Linnaeus. (Plate 24). A heavy-bodied water snake marked with cross-bands *along the entire length of the body*. The bands number 19 to 30, and are reddish, brown, or black in color, broad on the back and becoming narrower on the sides. Ground color yellowish, reddish, or brown. Belly yellowish, conspicuously marked with squarish, reddish spots. Large individuals may be uniformly dark above, but lighter triangular areas of ground color remain on the lower sides.

Range.—The coastal plain from North Carolina to southeastern Louisiana, except the peninsula of Florida. (Fig. 72).

Mississippi River Water Snake.—*Natrix sipedon confluens* Blanchard. (Plate 24). Differs from all other North American water snakes in having only 10 to 17 blotches on the body. The blotches are quite large on the back, and are brown, reddish-brown or black in color, on a ground color of yellow, tan, or brown. The ground color often appears only as light, narrow cross-bands, which are usually strongly oblique. Belly yellowish-white, marked with large squarish spots of brown, reddish-brown or black.

Range.—Eastern Louisiana and east central Texas north to extreme southern Illinois, southeastern Missouri, central Arkansas and southern Oklahoma. (Fig. 72).

Florida Water Snake.—*Natrix sipedon pictiventris* Cope. A cross-banded water snake very similar to the southern banded water snake, from which it differs chiefly in the shape of the markings on the belly. These markings consist of blotches extending transversely across the belly plates in *pictiventris,* many of them enclosing an oval light spot, while in *fasciata* they are solid squarish spots.

The ground color above is light brown or yellowish, and the bands, which number from 26 to 35, are reddish-brown to black. The belly is yellow or white, with reddish-brown or black markings. In large adult individuals the bands of the ground color on the lower sides sometimes become darker than the parts of the cross-bands extending onto the lower sides, thus producing an appearance of alternating blotches on the back and sides.

Range.—Nearly all of the peninsula of Florida. (Fig. 72).

Flat-tailed Water Snake.—*Natrix sipedon compressicauda* Kennicott. Differs from all other North American water snakes except Clark's water snake in having the first third of the tail vertically compressed, instead of round. The most constant color character is a row of light spots, one to each plate, down the middle of the belly.

The pattern on the back is extremely variable. There is usually a series of about 30 dark, poorly defined cross-bands on a dark green or brown ground color, each of which is so expanded and constricted at intervals as to tend to produce longitudinal stripes. The presence of two or four longitudinal stripes is not unusual, especially in the neck region. Belly dark, with a row of light spots down the center. Some specimens are almost entirely black, while others are reddish or straw-colored above and entirely without markings.

Range.—Coast of the southern half of peninsular Florida and adjacent coast of Cuba, mainly in brackish water. (Fig. 72).

Clark's Water Snake.—*Natrix sipedon clarkii* Baird and Girard. A striped water snake, with the base of the tail flattened as in the preceding species. The pattern consists of four blackish-brown or olive-brown longitudinal stripes on a ground color varying from brown to grayish-yellow. The stripes are more or less irregular, the lowermost ones sometimes broken by patches of the ground color. Belly blackish-brown to brick-red, with a yellowish stripe running down the center.

This snake may be distinguished from the other striped water snakes (the queen snake, Graham's water snake, and the striped water snake) by the larger number of scale rows around the body. It has 21 or 23 rows, while the others have only 19.

Range.—Brackish waters of the Gulf coastal region, from northwestern Florida to about Corpus Christi, Texas.

All the water snakes of the "sipedon" group are closely related to the northern banded water snake, and most of them are quite similar to it in habits and behavior. The flat-tailed water snake and Clark's water snake have forsaken fresh water for the brackish waters, chiefly of the mangrove swamps and coastal island beaches of the coastal areas.

The flat-tailed and Clark's water snakes are the smallest forms in this group, averaging about two feet in length; the southern banded water snake is the largest, averaging about three feet; while the others agree closely with the northern banded water snake.

Food also is similar to that of the common northern water snake, except that the two brackish water forms seem to feed largely on fish. Breeding habits are also similar, all bearing their young alive.

Red-bellied Water Snake.—*Natrix erythrogaster erythrogaster* Forster. A large, heavy-bodied snake, uniform black to reddish-brown above and solid reddish beneath. Small (young) individuals are differently marked, as described below. The back may exhibit faint cross-lines, and each belly plate has a dark area at each end, the dark area largely confined to the front part of each plate. Individuals from the lower Mississippi Valley and farther west usually have yellow bellies, while those to the east and north are bright red beneath.

Young individuals have a conspicuous pattern of dark blotches on a reddish or brownish ground color, with a row of smaller alternating blotches on the side. They may be distinguished by the belly, however, which is marked as in the adult.

Range.—Extreme southeastern Pennsylvania, Virginia, and the Carolinas to eastern Oklahoma and eastern Texas; northward in the central states to central Missouri and southern Michigan.

Yellow-bellied Water Snake.—*Natrix erythrogaster transversa* Hallowell. A large, heavy-bodied snake, blotched above and with a plain yellowish belly. There is a series of large, squarish, dark blotches down the back, separated by narrow light lines; an alternating row of similar but smaller blotches on the side extends onto the edges of the belly plates. Ground color gray, olive, or brown, darkest in old specimens. The belly is yellowish (whitish in young individuals) and almost without definite markings.

Range.—Western Missouri and eastern Kansas through western Oklahoma to southeastern New Mexico, east to Fort Worth and Houston, Texas, and south into Mexico.

These snakes are found in much the same situations as are the other water snakes, although the red-bellied water snake seems to be less partial to a thoroughly aquatic environment and is often found about small ponds that dry up during the summer. Their habits are those of the other water snakes. The eastern form, which is sometimes called the "copper-belly," is active and aggressive, striking and biting viciously when cornered or captured.

Size.—Adults average three feet in length. The longest authentic record for the red-belly is 4 feet 7½ inches (Conant).

Food.—Appears to be similar to that of the banded water snakes. Stomach contents of three individuals included 11 suckers, 3 sunfish, one crayfish, one leopard frog, 7 frog tadpoles, and one salamander larva.

Breeding Habits.—Mating has been observed in April and May, and young are born in late September and early October. The number of young is smaller than in the banded water snakes. Three recorded broods of the red-belly numbered from 8 to 27, with an average of 18, and a brood of the yellow-belly numbered 21.

Harter's Water Snake.—*Natrix harteri* Trapido.* Dark dorsal spots in two rows, more or less distinctly paired, and alternating with lateral spots below them. The spots are about two scales long, and number 58 to 65 on the body, thus much more numerous than in any other water snake. Belly pink, nearly immaculate. Scales in 23 rows.

Range.—Known only from Palo Pinto County, Texas, along the upper Brazos River.

This newly described water snake appears to be restricted to a river bank habitat, where it is found under rocks or logs.

Size.—The longest specimen recorded measured 35½ inches.

Food.—Unknown.

Breeding Habits.—Young are born alive as in other water snakes. Otherwise unknown.

BLACK SWAMP SNAKE
(*Seminatrix pygaea* Cope)
Plate 25

A small, shiny, rather stout-bodied snake. The color above is uniform black or bluish-black, except that each of the scales may have a pale line down its center, most strongly marked on the sides of the body. The belly is red, with a conspicuous narrow black bar extending in from either end of each belly plate. These bars usually end abruptly before reaching the middle of the belly, producing a curious effect suggesting the widely spaced teeth of a comb.

---

* Trapido, Harold, 1941. A new species of *Natrix* from Texas. *Amer. Midl. Nat.*, Vol. 25, pp. 673-680, 5 figs.

Scales smooth, except for a few on the tail that are keeled. Anal plate divided.

Range.—North Carolina, south through Florida.

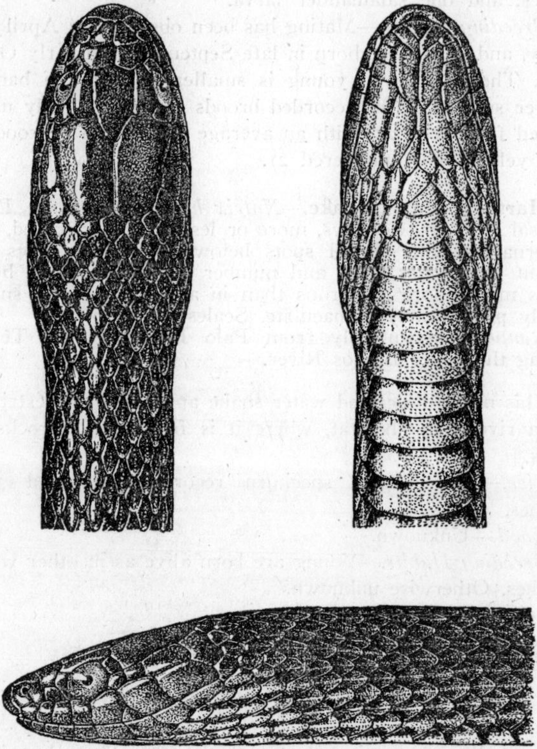

Fig. 73. Black swamp snake (*Seminatrix pygaea*).

This snake, sometimes called the red-bellied mud snake, appears to have been derived from the true water snakes (*Natrix*). It is quite abundant locally, but little is known of its habits. As its name implies, it is seldom found far from water. Carr regards it as partly fossorial, and states that it may sometimes be collected in numbers by rolling up masses of water hyacinths growing in shallow water.

Size.—Adults average about a foot in length. The longest recorded individual measured 16¾ inches (Ditmars).

Food.—Unknown. Presumably fishes and other small aquatic animals.

Breeding Habits.—Young are born alive, apparently in late August. There is one record of a brood of 11 and another of 13.

BROWN SNAKES
(Storeria)
Plate 25

The brown snakes are dwarfed relatives of the water snakes. Our species are distinguished primarily by the absence of the loreal plate. This is associated with a shortened snout, which gives them a peculiar physiognomy. A species of the Mexican plateau has the loreal shield present, so that a formal definition distinguishing *Storeria* from *Natrix* is by no means simple. The head is shortened in the brown snakes. This condition seems to be associated with slug-eating habits, since some tropical slug-eating snakes (*Dipsas,* for example) have the head extremely shortened.

Scales keeled. Anal plate divided.

KEY TO THE SPECIES OF *STORERIA*

1 a. Scales in 17 rows .... *S. dekayi*
1 b. Scales in 15 rows 2
2 a. Belly red, dark color of sides of body extending onto it .... *S. occipitomaculata*
2 b. Belly pale, with a row of dark spots on each side ...... *S. victa*

De Kay's Snake.—*Storeria dekayi* Holbrook. (Plate 25). General color above brown or gray, with a clay-colored stripe about 4 scales wide down the middle of the back, bordered more or less by small black spots. The coloration is often nearly uniform. Belly brown or pink with small black dots at the sides on the ends of the ventrals. Ventrals 120-140, caudals, 40-63; preocular single; upper labials 7, lower labials 7.

At birth a conspicuous yellow band, 2 or 2½ scales wide, crosses the neck. This band soon darkens to the same shade as the surrounding area, however.

Range.—Southern Maine to Minnesota and Kansas, southward to the Gulf of Mexico except for peninsular Florida.

De Kay's snake, or the brown snake, is one of the most persistent snakes in urban regions, where it may be found in vacant lots under trash of all kinds, and especially under pieces of old linoleum or roofing. It is evident that under natural conditions it was equally secretive, living under logs and bark. It is an extremely inoffensive creature, flattening of the body and the secretion of the anal glands being its only means of defense. In spite of its abundance this species is not well known to the layman, its small size, drab color, and secretive habits combining to make it extremely inconspicuous.

These snakes are sometimes found in immense numbers in small areas. More than 350 individuals were collected recently in two areas, each approximately 30 feet square, near Flushing, N. Y. They also congregate in considerable numbers to hibernate, and such hibernating colonies have been found in ant hills and abandoned rat burrows.

Size.—Adults average about 10 inches in length. The longest authentic record is 16½ inches (Conant).

Food.—The food of this snake in Pennsylvania was studied by Surface in 1906. He reported its diet to be: slugs and snails, 67 per cent; insect larvae, 16 per cent; and earthworms, 17 per cent. Conant found that Ohio specimens had eaten slugs and earthworms.

Breeding Habits.—Studied in detail by Clausen. Mating takes place in late March and early April, and the young are born in the last half of July and early August. Fourteen broods numbered 9 to 20, with an average of 14; Conant, however, found only 3 young in one female from Ohio and 24 in another. The young measure 3½ to 4½, av. 3⅝ inches (88-105 mm., av. 93) at birth.

Clausen, H. J., 1936. Observations on the Brown Snake *Storeria dekayi* (Holbrook), with especial Reference to the Habits and Birth of Young. *Copeia,* 1936, pp. 98-102.

Red-bellied Snake.—*Storeria occipitomaculata* Storer. A small snake characterized by its dark dorsal color with three well-defined yellowish spots behind the head. Belly red, the dark gray color of the sides extending onto the ends of the ventral plates. Ventrals 116-133, caudals 43-54; 2 preoculars; 5 or 6 upper labials, lower labials 7, rarely 8.

Range.—Southern Canada and the northern states of the United States west to Minnesota; more irregularly distributed farther south, extending to Florida and Louisiana.

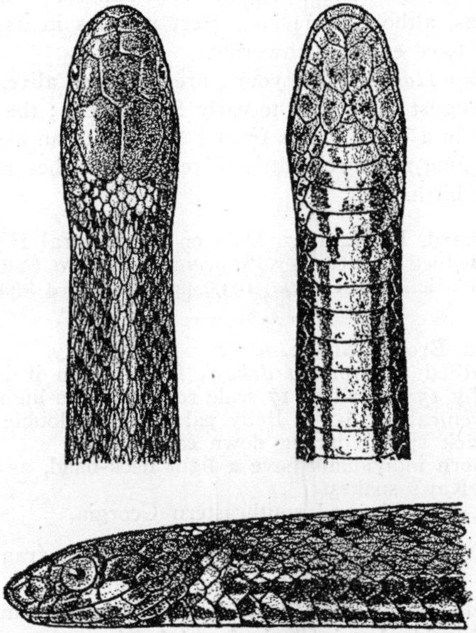

Fig. 74. Red-bellied snake (*Storeria occipitomaculata*).

The contrast between the abundance of this snake at the north and its erratic distribution to the south is unexplained. In northern Wisconsin, for example, it occurs widespread as the only *Storeria,* while in the Chicago Region it is found only in a limited area (Schmidt and Necker, 1935, Bull.

Chicago Acad. Sci., 5:71). It is especially a woodland species, found beneath logs and bark. It seems to demand a more moist environment than the closely related De Kay's snake does, and like De Kay's snake it is a completely inoffensive creature.

Size.—Average adult length about 10 inches; maximum recorded length 14 inches (Surface).

Food.—Apparently these little snakes subsist almost exclusively on slugs. The stomachs of seven individuals contained only slugs, although one had insect remains in its rectum. Captives have eaten earthworms.

Breeding Habits.—The young are produced alive, usually in mid-August (late July to early September); the number of young in a brood varies from 1 to 14, with an average of 7. The young measure a little more than 3 inches (67 to 98 mm.) at birth.

Blanchard, F. N., 1937. Data on the Natural History of the Red-bellied Snake, *Storeria occipitomaculata* (Storer), in Northern Michigan. *Copeia,* 1937, pp. 151-162, 4 figs.

Florida Brown Snake.—*Storeria victa* Hay. Apparently closely allied to *Storeria dekayi,* from which it is distinguished by 15 instead of 17 scale rows and the higher number of ventrals, 138-150. Belly pale, with a double row of small black spots running down each side.

New-born individuals have a light neck-band, as in newborn De Kay's snakes.

Range.—Florida and southeastern Georgia.

This form was described on the basis of a fragmentary specimen from the stomach of a coral snake, and is still far from well known. Carr states that it is fairly common locally in Florida, but is rarely found far from water. It usually occurs among water-hyacinth roots, or under logs along canals in the everglades.

Size.—Twelve to fourteen inches long.

Food.—Unknown.

Breeding Habits.—A captive female produced 11 young on June 6. They measured about 4¼ inches (107-109 mm.) at birth.

GROUND SNAKES
(Haldea)
Plate 25

The two species *Haldea valeriae* and *Haldea striatula* have only recently been referred to the same genus, the scales being apparently smooth in the former and sharply keeled in the latter. These forms acordingly appear even in relatively recent literature as *Virginia valeriae* and *Potamophis striatulus.* The discovery that the scales on the posterior part of the body of *valeriae* may be weakly keeled, as is more evident in its western subspecies, together with the fact that the normally single internasal of *striatula* may be divided, erases the sharp distinction between these species and justifies their reference to the same genus. It should be noted that the names of the species have been more stable than the generic arrangement.

Anal plate divided.

Southern Ground Snake.—*Haldea striatula* Linnaeus. A small snake, uniform reddish or grayish brown above, yellowish or pink beneath; occasionally there is an obscure light band across the back of the head. This species is characterized by absence of the preocular, the prefrontal and loreal entering the eye; internasals fused into a single shield (rarely double); sharply keeled scales in 17 rows; a single postocular; upper labials 5; ventrals 120-135; caudals 36-50.

Range.—Virginia to northern Florida, west to eastern Oklahoma and Texas.

A secretive species of woodland regions, found especially under bark and logs. It is particularly common in heavily wooded creek and river bottoms. This small snake is preyed upon by other snakes, such as the speckled king snake and the coral snake.

Size.—Average adult length about 10 inches; maximum recorded 12 inches.

Food.—Insect larvae, earthworms, and other invertebrates, and perhaps small lizards.

Breeding Habits.—Little is known beyond the fact that small broods of young (6-8) are born alive. They measure about four inches at birth.

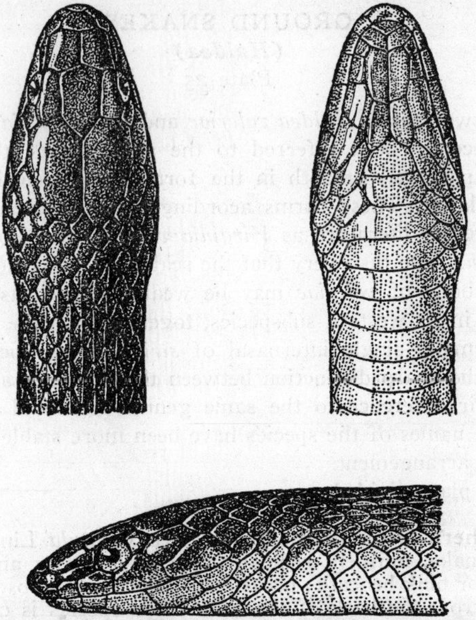

Fig. 75. Southern ground snake (*Haldea striatula*).

Strecker, J. K., 1927, Chapters from the Life-histories of Texas Reptiles and Amphibians. Part Two. *Contrib. Baylor Univ. Mus.*, No. 10, 14 pp.

Eastern Ground Snake.—*Haldea valeriae valeriae* Baird and Girard. General color gray or brown above, either uniform or with small black dots in 4 rows. Uniform whitish beneath. Agrees with *Haldea striatula* in the arrangement of the loreal and absence of the preocular. Differs in having smooth scales or only a few on the posterior part of the body weakly keeled; scales in 15 rows; upper labials 6; ventrals 115-127, caudals 25-37.

Range.—New Jersey to Georgia and west through northern Alabama, Tennessee, and southern Ohio.

Western Ground Snake.—*Haldea valeriae elegans* Kennicott. Well distinguished from the eastern ground snake in having scale rows 17, scales more usually and more extensively keeled, and a more reddish coloration. Ventrals 113-131, caudals 25-45. Distinguished from the southern ground snake (*striatula*) by its 6 upper labials.

Range.—Southern Indiana through western Kentucky and Tennessee to the Gulf of Mexico, westward to eastern Kansas and central Texas.

The two ground snakes of the species *valeriae* are secretive, usually found beneath stones, logs, or any surface trash-piles. They seem to prefer timbered regions. They are inoffensive creatures, occasionally flattening the fore part of the body when annoyed, but seldom attempting to bite.

Size.—The two subspecies are similar in size, although the western ground snake averages slightly larger. The average adult length is 8 or 9 inches. The longest authentic record

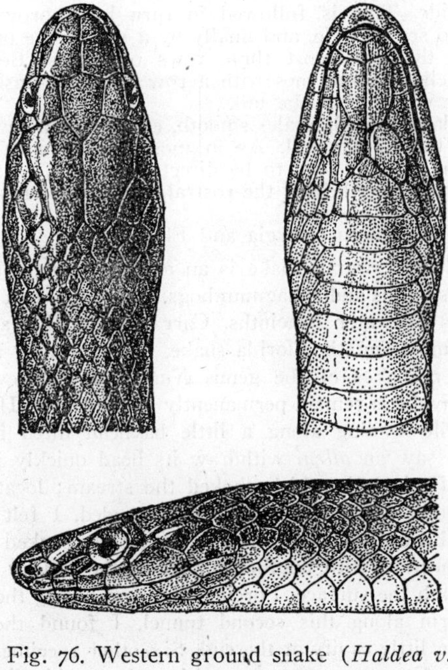

Fig. 76. Western ground snake (*Haldea v. elegans*).

is a specimen of the western form that measured 12½ inches (Blanchard).

Food.—Presumably insect larvae and small invertebrates. Captives feed well on earthworms.

Breeding Habits.—Living young are produced; otherwise unknown.

Blanchard, F. N., 1923, The Snakes of the Genus *Virginia. Papers Mich. Acad. Sci.*, Vol. 3, pp. 343-365, il.

FLORIDA SWAMP SNAKE

(*Liodytes alleni* Garman)

A moderate-sized striped snake, with a heavy body and very small head. There is a broad dark brown band about five or six scales wide down the center of the back, flanked on either side by a pale olive or yellowish stripe about two scales wide. This is followed in turn by a brown stripe about two scales wide, and finally by a wide olive or yellow band on the lowermost three rows of scales. Belly uniformly yellow, sometimes with a row of small dusky spots down the center near the tail.

Anal plate divided. Scales smooth, except for a few keeled ones on top of the tail. As in most snakes with aquatic habits, the nostrils tend to be directed upward, so that the nasal shields meet behind the rostral, and the internasals are fused into a single shield.

Range.—Southern Georgia and Florida.

The Florida swamp snake is an aquatic form, inhabiting marshes, sloughs and sphagnum bogs, where it is often found in masses of water hyacinths. Carr regards this as probably the most aquatic Florida snake, not excluding the several water snakes of the genus *Natrix,* and believes that many individuals remain permanently in the water. He states that "while wading along a little bayhead ditch in Lake County I saw an *alleni* withdraw its head quickly into the mass of *Utricularia* which choked the stream; locating the hole through which the head had protruded, I felt around and found a well-defined tunnel in the tightly packed vegetation, connecting with another tunnel in the mucky bank a foot beneath the surface. Forcing my hand nearly the length of my arm along this second tunnel, I found the snake coiled in a little cavity at the end. Six other specimens were taken on the same afternoon under almost identical conditions. They are frequently found in deep sphagnum bogs in winter."

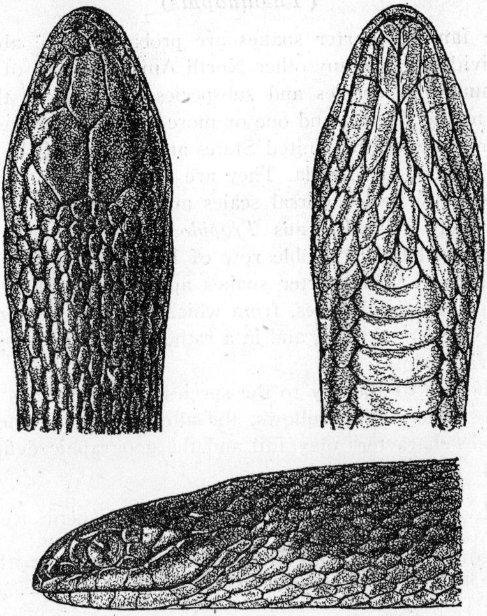

Fig. 77. Florida swamp snake (*Liodytes alleni*).

Size.—Adults average about 18 inches, with a maximum length of about two feet.

Food.—This snake feeds very largely on crayfish. Van Hyning examined 64 stomachs, only 9 of which contained food. Crayfish made up 73 per cent of the bulk of food, salamanders (*Pseudobranchus*) 14 per cent, and frogs 13 per cent. Carr found only crayfish in over a hundred stomachs that he examined.

Breeding Habits.—Living young are produced, the only recorded brood numbering 6.

Carr, A. F. Jr., 1940, A Contribution to the Herpetology of Florida. *Univ. Fla. Publ.,* Vol. 3, p. 92.

THE GARTER SNAKES
(*Thamnophis*)

The familiar garter snakes are probably more abundant in individuals than any other North American type of snake. The numerous species and subspecies range from the Atlantic to the Pacific, and one or more forms are to be found in every state of the United States and in each of the southern provinces of Canada. They are quite readily defined by their sharply keeled dorsal scales and undivided anal plate. The closely related genus *Tropidoclonion* is most readily distinguished by its double row of bold black spots on the ventral scales. The garter snakes appear to be directly related to the water snakes, from which they are distinguished by the single anal plate, and in a rather general way by more terrestrial habits.

In the use of the key to the species and subspecies of the garter snakes which follows, the alternatives of coloration and scale characters may fail and the geographic definitions must be used as controls.

Ruthven, A. G., 1908, Variations and Genetic Relationships of the Garter-snakes. *Bull. U. S. Nat. Mus.*, Vol. 61, pp. 1-201, 82 figs.; **Van Denburgh and Slevin**, 1918, The Garter-snakes of Western North America. *Proc. Calif. Acad. Sci.*, Ser. 4, Vol. 8, pp. 181-270, 11 pl.

KEY TO THE SPECIES AND SUBSPECIES OF *THAMNOPHIS*

1 a. Stripes usually entirely absent, or at most with a vestige on the neck, dark dorsal spots numerous and conspicuous, usually 2 or 3 preoculars (southern Arizona and southeastern New Mexico)
.....Spotted garter snake, *T. angustirostris*, p. 239

1 b. Lateral stripes present, dorsal stripe present or absent 2

2 a. Lateral stripes anteriorly on the third scale row only; a checkerboard pattern of spots very distinct between the stripes (Oklahoma and Texas to southeastern California)
......Marcy's garter snake, *T. marcianus*, p. 241

2 b. Lateral stripes on two or more scale rows........ 3

3 a. Lateral stripe anteriorly on the 2nd, 3rd, and 4th scale rows; upper labials frequently 6 (southern Michigan and Indiana to western Pennsylvania and New York)
......Butler's garter snake, *T. butleri,* p. 251

3 b. Lateral stripe on two scale rows only........... 4

4 a. Lateral stripe on the 3rd and 4th scale rows...... 5
4 b. Lateral stripe on the 2nd and 3rd scale rows...... 9

5 a. Tail usually more than 27% of the total length.... 6
5 b. Tail usually less than 27% of the total length.... 8

6 a. Upper labials usually 7 (Eastern United States, exclusive of Florida)
.....Eastern ribbon snake, *T. sauritus sauritus,* p. 255

6 b. Upper labials usually 8......................... 7

7 a. Dorsal stripe usually absent, at least posteriorly, tail 32 to 38% of the total length (Florida and coastal regions of Georgia and Alabama)
......Florida ribbon snake, *T. s. sackeni,* p. 255

7 b. Dorsal stripe always present, tail 25 to 35% of the total (eastern Illinois to western Nebraska and southward through the Great Plains into Mexico)
......Western ribbon snake, *T. s. proximus,* p. 256

8 a. Upper labials usually 8 or 9 (southern Arizona and southwestern New Mexico)
.......Mexican garter snake, *T. macrostemma megalops,* p. 241

8 b. Upper labials usually 7 or 8 (Southern Manitoba southward in the Great Plains and Prairie regions to Texas)
......Plains garter snake, *T. radix,* p. 250

9 a. A light crescentic mark on each side of the head behind the mouth, followed by a pair of large black spots usually united behind the head, succeeded by a series of large black spots on each side of the neck (western Texas to Arizona, southward on the Mexican Plateau)
......Brown garter snake, *T. eques,* p. 240

9 b. Nuchal pattern much less boldly marked........ 10

10 a. Upper labials usually 7........................ 11
10 b. Upper labials usually 8........................ 15

11 a. Dorsal scales usually 17 at mid-body (extreme northwestern California and Oregon, Washington and British Columbia, west of the Coast Range) ......Narrow-headed garter snake, *T. ordinoides ordinoides*, p. 248

11 b. Dorsal scales usually 19 or more at mid-body.... 12

12 a. Skin between the scales and light spaces between the dark spots not red, (with rare exceptions) (eastern United States) ......Common garter snake, *T. sirtalis sirtalis*, p. 252

12 b. Skin between scales and spaces between dark spots bright red.................................. 13

13 a. Dorsal stripe narrow, confined to a single scale row (Coastal region from British Columbia to San Francisco) Pacific red-sided garter snake, *T. s. concinnus*, p. 253

13 b. Dorsal stripe involving the scale rows adjacent to the middorsal row............................ 14

14 a. Ventrals and caudals more numerous, usually 163-169 and 83-90 (southern Oregon and northern two-thirds of California) ......California red-sided garter snake, *T. s. infernalis*, p. 253

14 b. Ventrals and caudals fewer, usually 156-166 and 76-85 (Great Plains region west of the Mississippi northward to Manitoba and Alberta, westward to Idaho and Nevada) ......Great Plains red-sided garter snake, *T. s. parietalis*, p. 253

15 a. Dorsal stripe very narrow or obscure, or absent, or present only on the neck......................... 16

15 b. Dorsal stripe always present and distinct........ 18

16 a. Lower labials 11 (Sierra Nevada and adjacent areas) .....Sierra Nevada garter snake, *T. o. couchii*, p. 246

16 b. Lower labials usually 10....................... 17

17 a. Usually a single preocular (southwestern Oregon and northwestern California south to San Francisco) ...Oregon gray garter snake, *T. o. hydrophila*, p. 246

17 b. Preoculars usually 2 on each side (southwestern California south of Monterey Bay and west of the Coast Range divide, southward into Lower California) ......Two-striped garter snake, *T. hammondii*, p. 249

18 a. Scale rows at mid-body usually 19 (coastal region of California north of Santa Barbara) ......Pacific Coast garter snake, *T. o. atratus*, p. 248

18 b. Scale rows at mid-body usually 21.............. 19

19 a. Dorsal stripe sharply defined; ventral surface not much spotted with black...................... 20

19 b. Dorsal stripe invaded by spots, its sides not sharply defined 21

20 a. Preocular normally single; dorsal stripe bright (southwestern California in the Coast Range and Sierra Nevada, with an isolated population in the San Bernardino Mountains) ......Elegant garter snake, *T. o. elegans*, p. 245

20 b. Preoculars normally two; dorsal stripe dull (but with sharply defined edges). (Klamath Lakes Basin, upper Klamath River, and Warmer Lakes basin, in southern Oregon and adjacent California) ......Klamath garter snake, *T. o. biscutatus*, p. 244

21 a. Scale rows on the anterior part of the body 23; ventral surface brownish (interior valley of California, from Sacramento south to Buena Vista Lake) ......Giant garter snake, *T. o. gigas*, p. 246

21 b. Scale rows on anterior part of body 21, ventral surface with extensive black markings (Rocky Mountain Region, northwestern United States, and adjacent parts of Canada) ......Great Basin garter snake, *T. o. vagrans*, p. 244

Spotted Garter Snake.—*Thamnophis angustirostris* Kennicott. A very distinct form, with numerous and prominent dark dorsal spots and the longitudinal stripes rarely distinguishable; the lateral stripes may be faintly visible, on the second and third scale rows; the dorsal stripe may be present on the neck. Preoculars usually 2 or 3; usually only one labial entering the eye. The rather high and narrow snout gives the species its name. There is occasionally a median scale between the internasals.

Range.—Southern Arizona and southwestern New Mexico, southward on the Mexican Plateau.

The spotted garter snake is perhaps the least garter snakelike of the garter snakes, and has been distinguished as a separate genus. It is much better to retain it in *Thamnophis*, which classifies it with its nearest relatives. It appears to be aquatic in its habits.

Size.—The few measurements available indicate a relatively small species, probably not exceeding 28 inches.

Food.—Unknown, presumably frogs, salamanders, and fishes.

Breeding Habits.—Unknown.

Brown Garter Snake.—*Thamnophis eques* Reuss. Pattern of three stripes very distinct, the dorsal stripe usually orange yellow, confined to the median scale row except on the neck, the lateral stripes on the second and third scale rows. Ground color of the scales between the stripes normally brown, the keels often reddish. A pair of crescentic white

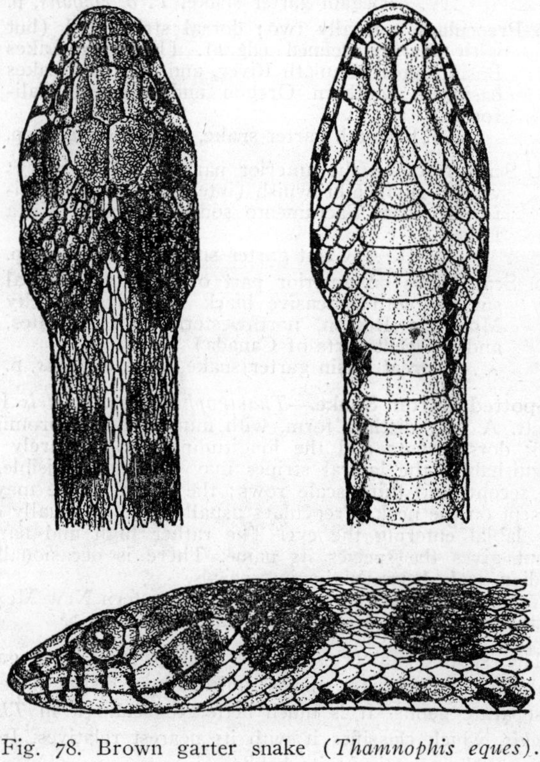

Fig. 78. Brown garter snake (*Thamnophis eques*).

markings behind the angle of the mouth, followed by a pair of black blotches behind the head which often unite; the labials boldly margined with black; preoculars white. Belly grayish-white to light greenish-yellow, marked with small black spots mostly concealed beneath the preceding plate. The dorsal scale rows are usually 19-19-17; ventrals 166-175 in males, 164-171 in females; caudals in males 85-97, in females 77-88.

Range.—Southern Arizona to western Texas, southward on the adjacent Mexican Plateau.

This snake is usually found in the vicinity of water, and according to Ruthven it takes to the water when frightened. It is by no means confined to this situation, and at least during the rainy season may be found almost anywhere. Berry Campbell found it to be by far the most abundant snake in the vicinity of Peña Blanca Springs, near Nogales, Arizona.

Size.—Adults average about 20 inches. Large individuals may exceed two feet in length.

Food.—A specimen with a tree toad in its stomach also had a toad in its mouth when it was found.

Breeding Habits.—Young are born alive. Breeding habits are otherwise unknown.

Arizona Garter Snake.—*Thamnophis macrostemma megalops* Kennicott.* Stripes on third and fourth scale rows on the sides; two rows of black spots (when discernible) between the dorsal and lateral stripe; tail long, nearly one-fourth of the total length; upper labials 8 or 9; ventrals, in both sexes, 149-169; caudals 69-89.

Range.—Southern Arizona and New Mexico, and western Texas, southward on the Mexican Plateau.

Although it inhabits an arid and semi-arid area, the Arizona garter snake appears to prefer the vicinity of water. A closely related form in Mexico, which is better known, is almost as aquatic as the true water snakes.

Size.—Adults average about two feet in length.

Food.—Unknown; probably chiefly frogs.

Breeding Habits.—Unknown.

Marcy's Garter Snake.—*Thamnophis marcianus* Baird and Girard. A very pallid garter snake. Three rows of

* *T. m. macrostemma* is the related form at the southern border of the Mexican Plateau, (Smith, H. M., 1939, *Zool. Ser. Field Mus. Nat. Hist.*, Vol. 24, p. 30).

square black spots between the stripes are distinct, so that the course of the lateral stripe may be somewhat obscured; on the anterior part of the body the lateral stripe is confined to the third scale row on each side. There is a *characteristic yellowish half-moon, followed by a large dark blotch,* on each side of the head behind the mouth. Belly light, with a row of dark spots on the ends of the ventrals. The dorsal scales are in 21 rows at mid-body; ventrals 157-163 in males, 149-159 in females; caudals in males 77-79, in females 63-67.

Range.—Kansas, Oklahoma and Texas to southeastern California, and adjacent parts of Mexico. (Fig. 79).

Marcy's garter snake inhabits the desert regions of the southwest, but is rarely found far from water. Banks of rivers, marshy ponds, and mud puddles in the desert are favored habitats.

Size.—Adults average about two feet in length.

Food.—Unknown, but probably largely frogs, toads, and earthworms.

Breeding Habits.—Young are born alive; there is one record of a brood of 14.

WESTERN GARTER SNAKES
(*Thamnophis ordinoides*)

The western garter snakes form a group of nine closely related forms occupying the region west of the Great Plains, most of them confined to the Pacific Coast region. There are two additional members in Lower California.

These snakes have recently been divided by Fitch into three main groups: (1) the Elegans group (*vagrans, biscutatus,* and *elegans*), with a distinct yellow dorsal stripe, a broad flat head, and of generalized, partly aquatic habits or adapted to a dry terrestrial habitat; (2) the Hydrophila group (*hydrophila, couchii, gigas,* and *hammondii*), with dull colors and a checkered or monotone pattern, a narrow pointed head, and decidedly aquatic habits; and (3) the Ordinoides group (*atratus* and *ordinoides*), with bright colors, of medium or small size, and with terrestrial tendencies.

It is noteworthy that many of these snakes are much more aquatic than the garter snakes of the Middle West, resembling the true water snakes (*Natrix*) in habits and behavior.

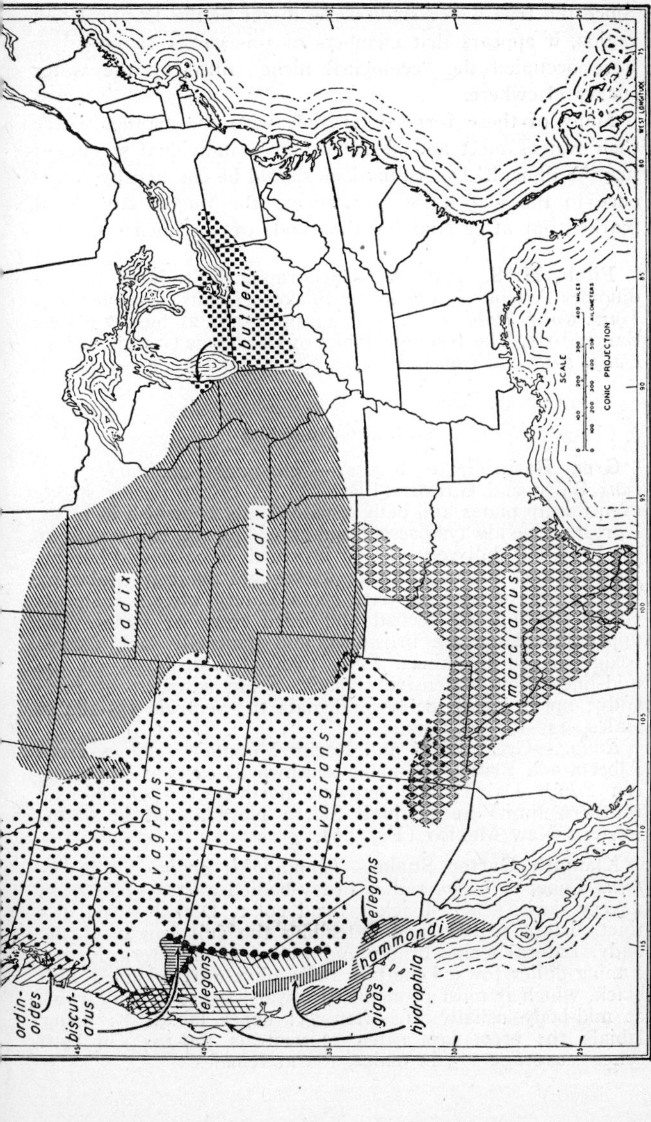

Fig. 79. Distribution of garter snakes of the *ordinoides* and *radix* groups (after Fitch and Ruthven). *T. o. atratus* and *T. o. couchii* have been omitted from the West Coast region.

Since the true water snakes are absent in the Pacific Coast region, it appears that members of this garter snake group have occupied the "ecological niche" filled by the water snakes elsewhere.

Many of these forms intergrade with one another where their ranges meet and identification of individual specimens may be difficult. Determinations should be checked by reference to the map (Fig. 79), where the ranges have been marked out after studying thousands of specimens.

Fitch, H. S., 1940, A Biogeographical Study of the ordinoides Artenkreis of Garter Snakes (Genus *Thamnophis*). *Univ. Calif. Publ. Zool.,* Vol. 44, pp. 1-150, 21 figs., 7 plates.
Same, 1941, The feeding Habits of California Garter Snakes. *Calif. Fish and Game,* Vol. 27, No. 2, pp. 1-32.

THE ELEGANS GROUP

Great Basin Garter Snake.—*Thamnophis ordinoides vagrans* Baird and Girard. (Plate 27). A brown garter snake, even the lip plates and belly usually being brownish in color. Dorsal stripe always present and extending the full length of the body, but dull yellowish or brownish in color and becoming indistinct toward the tail, its borders made irregular by invasion of the adjacent dark spots. Lateral stripes are present, occupying the second and third rows of scales. The upper lip plates are brownish, and generally lack darker wedge-shaped markings. Belly marked with black on the mid-line, often extensively black. Scale rows 21 at mid-body; upper labials 8; lower labials 10; ventrals 155-184 in males, 147-177 in females.

Range.—Great Basin and Rocky Mountain regions, from Alberta and British Columbia southward; eastward to western South Dakota and extreme northwestern Oklahoma; southern limits in the high Sierra Nevada and in southwestern New Mexico (Fig. 79).

Klamath Garter Snake.—*Thamnophis ordinoides biscutatus* Cope. A large, rather heavy-bodied garter snake with a very dark, nearly black ground color. Dorsal stripe distinct, bright yellow, and extending the full length of the body. Lateral stripe bright and well defined anteriorly, becoming duller toward the tail. Belly olive-gray, clouded with black, which is most pronounced toward the tail. Scale rows at mid-body usually 21, often 23; upper labials 8; lower labials 10; preoculars often 2; ventrals 160-184 (in both sexes), average 173 in males, 166 in females.

Range.—Klamath Lakes basin, upper Klamath River, and Warmer Lakes basin in south central Oregon and northeastern California (Fig. 79).

Elegant Garter Snake.—*Thamnophis ordinoides elegans* Baird and Girard. A brightly colored garter snake, with the stripes standing out prominently against a black or nearly black ground color. Dorsal stripe distinct, bright yellow, and extending the full length of the body. Lateral stripe dull yellow and distinct. The upper lip plates are pale, contrasting sharply with the dark ground color of the body, and are marked with triangular black wedge marks. Belly pale and unmarked, or but slightly spotted with black. Scale rows at mid-body usually 19; upper labials 8; lower labials 10; ventrals 159-173 in males, 151-177 in females.

Range.—Southern Oregon between the coast ranges and the divide of the Cascade Mountains from the southern end of the Willamette Valley; northern California, and adjacent Nevada; an isolated population at higher altitudes in the San Bernardino Mountains (Fig. 79).

The three garter snakes of the Elegans group are partial to the vicinity of water. The Great Basin form (*vagrans*) is more widely distributed than any other member of the western garter snake group, and much of its range is in arid or semi-arid country. Nevertheless it is limited to regions with a permanent water supply and usually remains near the water's edge along rivers and creeks. It retreats into the water when alarmed. The Klamath garter snake (*biscutatus*) is very aquatic, most individuals being found within ten feet of water. Its usual haunt is along boulder-strewn stream edges in canyon bottoms, individuals taking refuge in the water when alarmed, concealing themselves among rocks at the bottom. The elegant garter snake (*elegans*) is generally found along streams, but often along those that dry up during part of the year. It is seldom found in the water.

Size.—Adults average about two feet in length. *T. biscutatus* is the largest form, with a maximum length of about 39 inches.

Food.—Stomach analyses of these snakes reveals that food is quite varied, but corresponds quite closely with the habits of each form. Stomach contents of 69 *vagrans* was about evenly divided between aquatic animals (fish, tadpoles, leeches, etc.) and terrestrial animals (mice, frogs and toads, lizards, etc.); but all the terrestrial animals were kinds that prefer river banks.

Stomach contents of 20 *biscutatus* revealed only aquatic animals. Fishes (all economically unimportant) were oftenest eaten, although leeches, lampreys, tadpoles, and frogs were also found.

Stomachs of 33 *elegans* contained terrestrial animals almost exclusively. Mice, shrews, lizards, frogs and toads, slugs, and earthworms had been eaten. Fishes are eaten in certain restricted localities where other aquatic snakes are absent.

Breeding Habits.—Young are born alive in August and September. The number of young in a brood appears to be small; Ruthven and Gaige recorded three broods of *vagrans* that numbered 8, 10, and 12, respectively.

Fitch, H. S., 1940, *Univ. Calif. Publ. Zool.,* Vol. 44, pp. 16-50 (summaries of habitats, habits, food, etc.).

THE HYDROPHILA GROUP

Oregon Gray Garter Snake.—*Thamnophis ordinoides hydrophila* Fitch. A checkered garter snake, the area between the stripes bluish-gray to brownish-gray and prominently checkered with two alternating rows of black blotches. Dorsal stripe dull yellow, sometimes entirely absent; lateral stripes pale gray with some orange scales. Belly immaculate or nearly so, with a pink or purplish suffusion toward the tail. Maximum scale rows at mid-body 21, often reduced to 19; upper labials 8; lower labials 10; preocular single, rarely divided; ventrals 150-171 in males, 140-168 in females.

Range.—Southwestern Oregon and northwestern California. (Fig. 79).

Sierra Nevada Garter Snake.—*Thamnophis ordinoides couchii* Kennicott. Ground color brown, with two alternating rows of large squarish black blotches producing a checkerboard pattern. Dorsal stripe dull yellow and usually absent on the posterior part of the body and the tail. The lateral stripes are distinct and dull yellow in color. Belly yellowish, often heavily marked with black. Scale rows at mid-body 21; upper labials 8; lower labials 11 (rarely 10); preocular often divided; ventrals 170-183 in males, 163-180 in females.

Range.—Middle altitudes in the Sierra Nevada, eastward into the adjacent angle of Nevada.

Giant Garter Snake.—*Thamnophis ordinoides gigas* Fitch. A large brown garter snake, adults often exceeding 28 inches and occasionally more than a yard in length. Ground color dull brown, with small and well-separated black spots. Dorsal stripe dull yellow, but uniformly present; lateral stripes often absent. Upper lip plates brown and without darker markings. Belly brown. Dorsal scale rows 21 at mid-body; upper labials 8; lower labials 10 (rarely 11); ventrals 160-168 in males, 155-170 in females.

Range.—Floor of the Great Valley of California, from Sacramento and Antioch south to Buena Vista Lake. (Fig. 79).

The garter snakes of the Hydrophila group are almost as water-loving as are the true water snakes (*Natrix*) of the area east of the Rocky Mountains. Individuals are rarely found more than a few feet from water, and they seek refuge from danger and forage for food in the water. The Oregon and Sierra Nevada forms are associated with swift, clear streams with rock beds, where they are usually seen coiled on boulders. The giant garter snake lives in streams having mud bottoms; it is an alert and timid snake.

Size.—*T. hydrophila* is the smallest of this group, averaging about 18 inches in length. *T. couchii* averages about 2 feet and *T. gigas* about 30 inches. The giant garter snake reaches a maximum of about 5 feet (Fitch), and Van Denburgh records a specimen of *couchii* 55½ inches long.

Food.—These snakes feed almost exclusively on aquatic animals, as their habits would indicate. Stomachs of 96 *hydrophila* contained fish, fish eggs, tadpoles, salamander larvae, and occasional frogs. Stomachs of 18 *couchii* contained little but fish and tadpoles. One specimen of *gigas* contained a fish.

Breeding Habits.—Young are produced alive. Breeding habits are otherwise unknown.

Fitch, H. S., 1940, *Univ. Calif. Publ. Zool.*, Vol. 44, pp. 50-73 (summaries of habitats, habits, food, etc.).

THE ORDINOIDES GROUP

Pacific Coast Garter Snake.—*Thamnophis ordinoides atratus* Kennicott. (Plate 27). A brightly colored garter snake, often with red in the markings. Dorsal stripe distinct, dull yellow in color, and often 3 scale rows wide. Lateral stripes dull yellow or red, sometimes entirely absent. The ground color between the stripes is dark gray or brown; specimens from the vicinity of San Francisco usually have the ground color largely bright red. Belly blotched with yellow or pink down the center. Scale rows at mid-body 19; upper labials 8; lower labials 10; preocular single; ventrals 146-172 in males, 140-169 in females.

Range.—Coastal region of California from Humboldt County south to Santa Barbara County.

Narrow-headed Garter Snake.—*Thamnophis ordinoides ordinoides* Baird and Girard. A garter snake with three distinct light stripes. Dorsal stripe red, orange, or yellow. Ground color between stripes black, brown, greenish, or bluish. Belly often spotted with bright red, sometimes heavily marked with black. Scale rows at mid-body 19, often reduced to 17; upper labials usually 7; lower labials 8 or 9; preocular sometimes divided; ventrals 138-162 in males, 137-162 in females; caudals fewer than 85.

Range.—Southern Vancouver Island and opposite mainland of British Columbia, southward west of the Cascade Range to western Del Norte County, California. (Fig. 79).

The two garter snakes of the Ordinoides group are somewhat dwarfed forms that inhabit the humid fog belt along the Pacific coast. They are usually found in meadows and forest clearings rather than in aquatic situations, and do not voluntarily take to water when pursued, as many other western garter snakes do. These snakes are retiring and docile compared with their other western relatives, relying on concealment and the offensive secretion of their anal scent glands to escape from their enemies.

Size.—These are small snakes, *ordinoides* averaging about 18 inches and *atratus* about 2 feet.

Food.—Quite varied, but consisting largely of animals caught on land. In the stomachs of 59 *atratus,* slugs were most common (66 per cent had eaten them), but earthworms, fish, fish eggs, salamanders, lizards, snakes, birds, and small mammals were also found. Stomachs of 48 *ordinoides* also contained many slugs (66 per cent had eaten them), with salamanders, frogs, and earthworms also represented.

Breeding Habits.—Young are produced alive. Breeding habits are otherwise unknown.

Fitch, H. S., 1940, *Univ. Calif. Publ. Zool.,* Vol. 44, pp. 97-110 (summaries of habitats, habits, food, etc.).

TWO-STRIPED GARTER SNAKE
(*Thamnophis hammondii* Kennicott)
Plate 28

A brown garter snake usually lacking the middle stripe. This stripe may be present, usually rather faintly, in the neck region. The lateral stripes are distinct and yellowish in color. Ground color above brownish gray with four rows of alternately placed black spots, which are small and well separated. Belly pinkish, either unmarked or slightly marked with black. Scales at mid-body 21; upper labials 8, lower labials 10; preoculars usually 2; ventrals 159-178 in males, 150-171 in females.

Range.—Southwestern California, west of the Coast Range divide and south of Monterey, southward into Lower California. (Fig. 79).

This snake looks quite different from other garter snakes because the middle stripe, usually so conspicuous in these snakes, is lacking. Actually it is closely related to the garter snakes of the Elegans group, and like them it is usually found in the vicinity of water. It is most common along streams having rocky beds and bordered by dense vegetation. If molested it usually escapes by diving into the water and hiding in inaccessible places.

Size.—Adults average about 2 feet in length, with a maximum of about 38 inches.

Food.—This snake, like other garter snakes, is a voracious feeder. Klauber fed 30 tree frogs to a freshly captured individual, which it ate as rapidly as they were handed in. Tadpoles, toads, tree frogs and worms have been found in the stomachs of captured specimens.

Breeding Habits.—A brood of 25 young was born in captivity on Oct. 30.

PLAINS GARTER SNAKE

(*Thamnophis radix* Baird and Girard)
Plate 26

A moderate-sized garter snake with three distinct light stripes, the middle one usually bright orange-yellow. The lateral stripes are light yellow, and are on the *third and fourth rows* of scales.* The ground color between the stripes is brownish or black with two rows of squarish black spots. Belly bluish-green, usually with black markings near the ends of the belly plates. Scales at mid-body usually 19; upper labials 7, sometimes 8; ventrals, in both sexes, 142 to 176; caudals 57 to 87.

Range.—Eastern Illinois westward and northward through the Prairie and Plains regions; south to Missouri and Kansas (Fig. 79).

The plains garter snake is a very distinct plains and prairie form that thrives in a variety of habitats. It is by no means restricted to the vicinity of water, and rarely takes

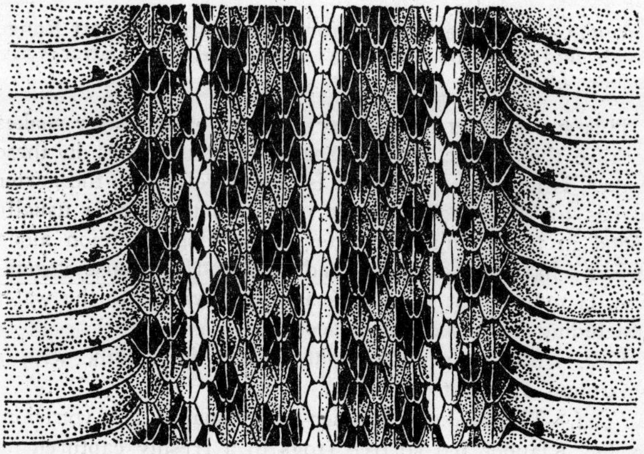

Fig. 80. Pattern of the Plains garter snake (*Thamnophis radix*).

* The common garter snake (*T. sirtalis*) is found in the same area as the plains garter snake, and is easily confused with it. The common garter snake is readily distinguished, however, by the fact that the lateral stripes are on the *second and third* scale rows.

refuge in water when pursued. In the Chicago region, where it is by far the commonest snake, individuals may be found almost everywhere, even in storm sewers near the business districts of populous suburbs. This snake has been found hibernating in small groups in post holes, and evidently finds hibernating situations beneath concrete sidewalks, especially those of defunct real estate "subdivisions." A hibernating aggregation has been reported from an ant hill in Manitoba, in which eight individuals were associated with large numbers of red-bellied snakes and green snakes.

These snakes defend themselves by biting when first captured, and almost invariably pour out the foul-smelling contents of their anal scent glands. Occasional individuals flatten the body when annoyed, and some even roll into a ball with the head hidden in the center. They soon become tame in captivity, and will flourish on a diet of frogs or earthworms, which they devour greedily.

Size.—Adults average about 2 feet in length. The maximum length, according to Conant, is 3 feet.

Food.—Quite varied. In the Chicago region this snake subsists very largely on earthworms, while farther west leopard frogs seem to form the staple diet. Insects (especially grasshoppers), tadpoles and fish are also eaten. Small mammals and birds, found as carrion by the snakes, are occasionally taken.

Breeding Habits.—There is surprisingly little exact information on the breeding habits of this common snake. Mating has been observed in April and May, and young are born in late July and through August and September. Broods number from 13 to 40 and the young measure about 7 inches at birth.

BUTLER'S GARTER SNAKE
(*Thamnophis butleri* Cope)

A small garter snake with a small head and very slight neck constriction and with the lateral stripes on the *second, third, and fourth scale rows* at least on the fore part of the body. Ground color olive-brown to deep brown, with three yellow stripes, the side stripes sometimes orange. Belly pale greenish, marked with black or gray. Scales at mid-body 19;

upper labials 6 or 7, lower labials usually 8; ventrals 138 to 148 in males, 130 to 143 in females; caudals 53 to 72.

Range.—Southern Michigan, Indiana, Ohio, southwestern Ontario, and western Pennsylvania and New York. An isolated population in southeastern Wisconsin. (Fig. 79).

Butler's garter snake appears to be a dwarfed relative of the plains garter snake (*radix*). Like many small snakes, it is inclined to be spotty in its distribution, forming large isolated colonies. This snake is usually found in open places near water—in low, wet meadows, or along streams, ponds and lakes—but it has been found in dry grass far removed from any water in Ontario.

Butler's garter snake is very awkward in its movements. On bare ground, when it is excited, it wriggles violently from side to side without making much forward headway. This locomotion is much more efficient in grass, where it moves with comparative ease and swiftness. This snake is mild-tempered, never attempting to bite when handled. Most specimens cling to the fingers with perceptible pressure.

Size.—Adults average about 18 inches in length. The longest authentic record is a female from Ohio that measured 25 inches (Conant).

Food.—Earthworms and leeches have been found in the stomachs of captured individuals. Captives thrive on a diet of small frogs, earthworms, and fishes.

Breeding Habits.—Mating takes place in late March and early April, and young are born in June and July. Four broods numbered from 4 to 14, with an average of 8. The young measure about 6 inches at birth.

Conant, R., 1938, The Reptiles of Ohio. *Amer. Midland Nat.*, Vol. 20, pp. 96-99. (habitat and habits; photo).

COMMON GARTER SNAKES

Plate 26

Common Garter Snake.—*Thamnophis sirtalis sirtalis* Linnaeus. A garter snake with three distinct light stripes, the middle stripe usually yellow, *never orange* as in the plains garter snake. The lateral stripes are on the *second and third* rows of scales. The ground color between the stripes is brownish or black, with two rows of black spots.

Belly greenish-white or yellow, with small black markings near the ends of the belly plates. Scales at mid-body 19; upper labials 7, lower labials 10; ventrals 137 to 167 (in both sexes); caudals 54 to 84.

Range.—Southern Canada, north of Lake Superior to New Brunswick and Nova Scotia; southward throughout the eastern United States, east of the Mississippi River.

Red-sided Garter Snake.—*Thamnophis sirtalis parietalis* Say. Differs from the common garter snake in having the ground color usually broken up by a series of red or orange bars, with the skin between the scales red. Often there is also red on the edges of the scales. Ventrals 150 to 178; caudals 65 to 95.

Range.—From the Mississippi River westward to Utah, and eastern Nevada and southern Idaho; southern Alberta, Saskatchewan and Manitoba, southward through the Great Plains to Oklahoma.

Pacific Red-sided Garter Snake.—*Thamnophis sirtalis concinnus* Hallowell. Differs from the red-sided garter snake (*parietalis*) in its darker color, smaller size or absence of the red areas, and in having the middle stripe narrower and sometimes fading out toward the tail.

Range.—Puget Sound region, Vancouver Island, and west of the Cascades to the Rogue River in Oregon.

California Red-sided Garter Snake.—*Thamnophis sirtalis infernalis* Blainville. Differs from the Pacific red-sided garter snake (*concinnus*) in having broader light stripes and a generally lighter coloration. Ventrals 161 to 175 (av. 169) in males, 156 to 174 (av. 164) in females. Caudals 82 to 97 (av. 90) in males, 74 to 93 (av. 83) in females.

Range.—Klamath Lake region of Oregon to the coast in northern California, south to San Bernardino County, and east to Modoc County and Lake Tahoe, California.

The common garter snake and its western relatives are perhaps the best-known snakes in the United States. Not only are they abundant in individuals, but also they are the first snakes to appear in the spring, often before the snow is entirely gone, and the last to disappear in the fall. These snakes are found in almost every environment, although the common eastern form is rarely found in forests and the western ones are absent in the desert. All show a preference for moist situations, such as bogs, marshes, and the edges of streams. Like other snakes, they are more in evidence in the spring than during the heat of summer.

All these snakes exhibit great variability in coloration, although scale characters are fairly constant. It is quite certain that careful studies will distinguish additional subspecies in this group. Melanism is common, and a melanistic strain is somewhat localized in southern Ontario. Shedding of the skin is said to take place at intervals of about six weeks (Stabler, *Copeia,* 1939, p. 228).

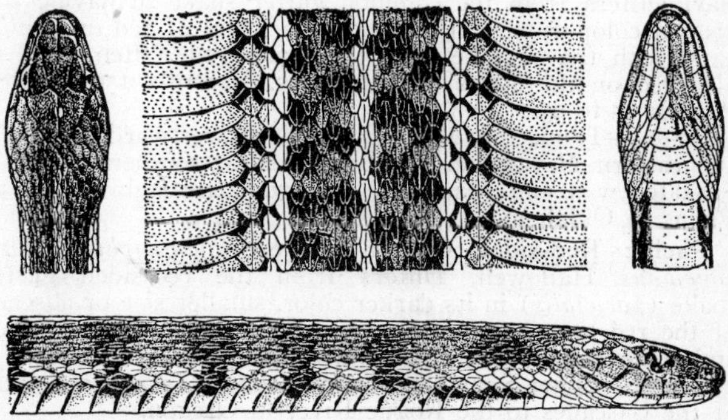

Fig. 81. Common garter snake (*Thamnophis s. sirtalis*).

The common garter snake seems to be one of the more aggressive garter snake species. Captured individuals usually defend themselves actively by biting, and invariably discharge a strong and characteristic scent from their anal glands. The body is often strongly flattened when one of these snakes is molested, displaying the pattern of spots between the stripes much more vividly.

Size.—Adults average about 2 feet in length. The longest authentic record is an Ohio specimen that measured 3 feet, 8 inches (Conant).

Food.—These snakes feed very largely on earthworms and amphibians. Uhler, Cottam, and Clarke recently analyzed the contents of 24 stomachs, finding that earthworms made up 37 per cent of the diet, salamanders 31 per cent, and toads 25 per cent. Fitch studied the contents of 48 stomachs of the Pacific Coast forms. He found that toads made up 30 per cent of the diet, tree toads 21 per cent, earthworms

24 per cent, and tadpoles 10 per cent. Small birds and mammals (usually only when found dead) are sometimes eaten by the common garter snake.

Breeding Habits.—Mating takes place in April and May, and young are born in July and early August. These snakes are very prolific, one brood of 78 young and another of 73 having been reported. Such numbers are abnormally high, however, the young usually numbering from 14 to 40. Nine recorded broods give an average of 28. The young measure about 7 inches at birth.

RIBBON SNAKES

Plate 28

The ribbon snakes differ from other garter snakes in their very slender bodies, very long tails, (from one-fourth to one-third the total length), and unmarked bellies. The stripes are brilliant and sharply defined, the lateral ones always on the third and fourth scale rows. The upper lip plates are unmarked and light in color in ribbon snakes (Fig. 82), and consequently stand out strikingly against the darker top and sides of the head.

Eastern Ribbon Snake.—*Thamnophis sauritus sauritus* Linnaeus. A slender snake with three bright yellow stripes standing out prominently against a dark brown or black ground color. The middle stripe sometimes has an orange or greenish tinge. Belly pale greenish and usually unmarked. The tail is very long, about one-third the total length. Upper labials usually 7; ventrals, in both sexes, 150 to 172; caudals very variable, 87 to 137.

Range.—Eastern United States, from Michigan and southern Ontario to southern Maine, and south to Georgia, Alabama, and Mississippi.

Southern Ribbon Snake.—*Thamnophis sauritus sackeni* Kennicott. A very slender snake with two bright yellow stripes, the middle stripe found in other ribbon snakes being indistinct, entirely absent, or present only on the neck. The ground color between the stripes is brown or olive. Belly yellowish-white, either unmarked or with the edges of the plates tinged with brown. Tail very long, up to 38 per cent of the total length. Upper labials 8; ventrals, in both sexes, 154 to 171; caudals 109 to 134.

Range.—Florida and the adjacent coastal regions, from Charleston, South Carolina, west to the Mississippi River.

Western Ribbon Snake.—*Thamnophis sauritus proximus* Say. A slender snake with three light stripes on a ground color of olive, brown or black. The middle stripe is usually yellow, but may be orange, reddish, or brownish. Belly yellowish-white or greenish-white, usually unmarked. The tail is very long, about one-third the total length. Upper labials 8; ventrals, in both sexes, 158 to 179; caudals 75 to 125.

Range.—Southern Wisconsin and Minnesota, southward west of the Wabash and Mississippi Rivers to the Gulf of Mexico and into eastern Mexico; westward into the Great Plains along water courses.

The ribbon snakes are much more partial to the vicinity of water than are the other garter snakes of the eastern and central United States. They are rarely seen far from some body of water. Bogs, small lakes or ponds, swampy regions, and the banks of creeks and rivers are their usual habitats.

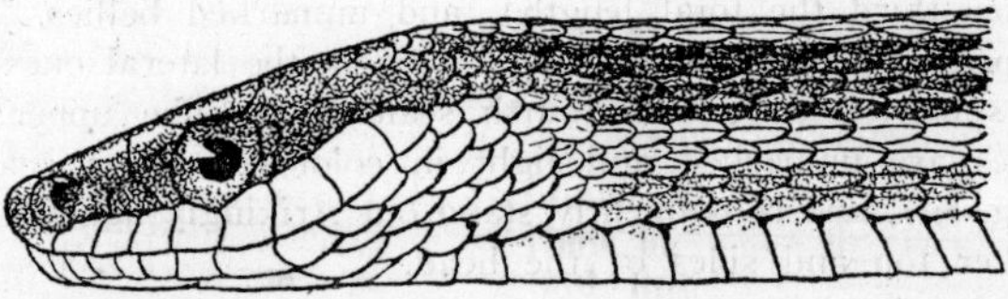

Fig. 82. Western ribbon snake (*Thamnophis s. proximus*). Note the absence of markings on the lip plates.

When pursued they usually enter the water, but conceal themselves among water plants or swim away on the surface, instead of diving to the bottom as water snakes (*Natrix*) do. These snakes occasionally climb into bushes several feet above the ground, and their speed and agility in threading their way through vegetation on the ground is astonishing.

Captured individuals usually strike repeatedly, although occasional specimens are docile. The sweetish-smelling contents of the anal glands is discharged freely. Captives remain alert and nervous, but feed readily on frogs and fishes.

Size.—Adults average about 2 feet in length. The western ribbon snake appears to be the largest form, especially in the region of the Lower Rio Grande. According to Conant and Bridges it reaches a maximum length of 3 feet 8 inches.

Food.—In spite of their aquatic habits, there does not appear to be a single authentic record of these snakes eating fishes. Salamanders and frogs form almost the sole diet; and perhaps because of the slender proportions of the ribbon snakes the smaller tree frogs are eaten much more regularly than are the larger frogs.

Breeding Habits.—Broods of young are very small in ribbon snakes compared with other garter snakes. Young are born during the latter half of July and through August, earlier in the southern form and later farther north. Thirteen recorded broods numbered from 5 to 20, with an average of 10. The young of the eastern ribbon snake average about 8½ inches at birth. Those of the western form are larger, averaging 9½ inches.

LINED SNAKE

(*Tropidoclonion lineatum* Hallowell)

Plate 29

A rather small, moderately stout three-striped snake with the belly conspicuously marked with a double row of black spots. The ground color above is grayish-brown, with a whitish or yellowish stripe down the midline and a similar but fainter stripe on each side on the second and third scale rows. Belly white or yellow, with two regular rows of large, clean-cut black spots.

Scales keeled. Anal plate single.

Range.—Southern half of Illinois, west to southeastern South Dakota, southward through Kansas to the Gulf of Mexico.

From above this snake looks very much like a garter snake, but may easily be distinguished by the double row of black spots on the belly. Garter snakes often have dark spots on the belly, but these are never as large, dark or uniform as in the lined snake.

This snake is inclined to be secretive, and is usually found beneath logs and stones, or under trash of all kinds in urban areas. Like the garter snakes, it thrives in thickly inhabited regions, and may be abundant in parks and vacant city lots.

It appears to be nocturnal, coming out of hiding at night to forage for food.

The lined snake is harmless and inoffensive when handled. When picked up it discharges the contents of its anal glands and thrashes about, but rarely attempts to bite.

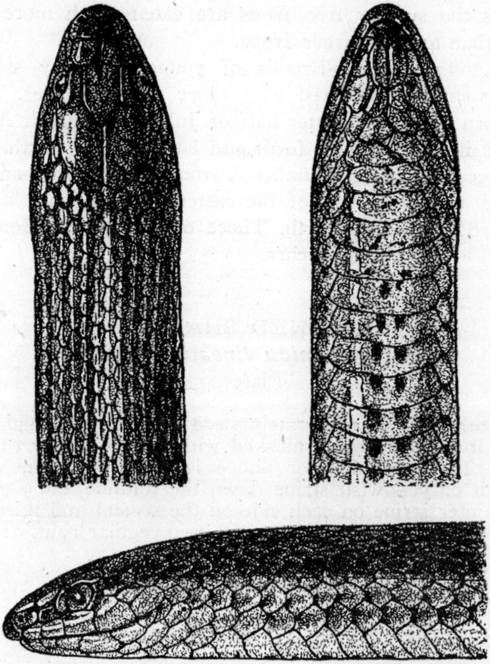

Fig. 83. Lined snake (*Tropidoclonion lineatum*).

Size.—Adults average about 12 inches in length. The longest authentic record is 20 inches (Force).

Food.—Individuals "have been found eating earthworms" (Force). Earthworms are taken readily in captivity.

Breeding Habits.—Young are born during August. Twenty-three broods born in captivity numbered from 2 to 12 young, with an average of 7 or 8. The young measure about 8 inches (120 mm.) at birth.

Force, Edith R., 1931, Habits and Birth of Young of the Lined Snake, *Tropidoclonion lineatum* (Hallowell). *Copeia,* 1931, pp. 51-53.

SPOTTED NIGHT SNAKE
(Hypsiglena ochrorhyncha Cope*)*
Plate 29

The spotted night snake appears to be closely related to the cat-eyed snakes, with a similar pattern and a similarly vertically elliptic pupil of the eye. It is distinguished by the fact that the enlarged teeth at the rear of the upper jaw

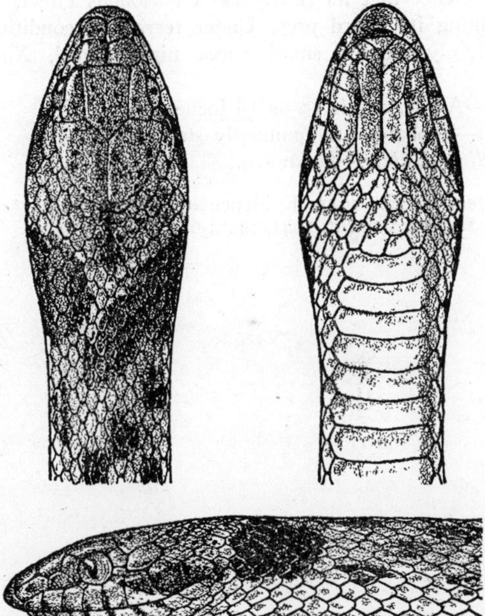

Fig. 84. Spotted night snake (*Hypsiglena ochrorhyncha*).

are not grooved; externally it is most readily distinguished by its color pattern of much more numerous spots on a gray or yellowish ground color. In this pattern there is a mid-dorsal row of larger spots, with an alternating series of smaller ones on each side, and a second alternating series of still smaller spots below this. Ventrals number about 180 and caudals about 50.

Range.—Southern Idaho and western Washington southward through Utah and Nevada to Arizona and California, and into Lower California; in the Great Plains from southern Kansas through western Texas and into adjacent northern Mexico.

The spotted night snake appears to be an inhabitant of rocky situations, as is the case with the lyre snakes. Its apparent relations to the back-fanged snakes is supported by some evidence that its saliva has a poisonous effect, useful in subduing its lizard prey. Under terrarium conditions, it feeds freely on the small yucca night lizard, *Xantusia vigilis.*

Size.—Adult length 15 or 16 inches.

Food.—Probably predominantly small lizards.

Breeding Habits.—Unknown.

Cowles, R. B., 1941, Evidence of Venom in *Hypsiglena ochrorhynchus. Copeia,* 1941, pp. 4-6.

THE REAR-FANGED SNAKES

Family BOIGIDAE

Enlarged fangs at the back of the upper jaw, with deep grooves on the front side of each of the enlarged teeth, appear to have developed independently in several different lines of evolution, as was mentioned in the introductory chapters. This means that the family name Boigidae as here used is only a convenience, pending a more natural subdivision of the family Colubridae. The snakes in question in our list exhibit no characters in common except the presence of grooved teeth. The genera in question are *Leptodeira, Trimorphodon, Coniophanes, Oxybelis,* and *Tantilla.* The genus *Hypsiglena,* without grooved fangs, appears to be closely related to *Leptodeira.* It is possible that *Sonora* (p. 197) should be listed with the Boigidae.

There are many more types of rear-fanged snakes in tropical America and in the Old World, and these include terrestrial, arboreal, and subterranean forms.

NORTHERN CAT-EYED SNAKE

(*Leptodeira septentrionalis* Kennicott)

Moderately slender snakes, with the head conspicuously wider than the neck. The vertical pupil of the eye gives them their common name. The large dark blotches of the back extend downward nearly to the first scale row, and the ventral scales usually have dark posterior borders. The species is further distinguished by having three preoculars; ventrals 186-197, caudals 63-89.

Scales smooth. Anal plate divided.

Range.—Extreme southern Texas to the Mexican state of Vera Cruz.

The cat-eyed snake, like the speckled ground snake (*Drymobius*), the black-banded snake (*Coniophanes*), and vari-

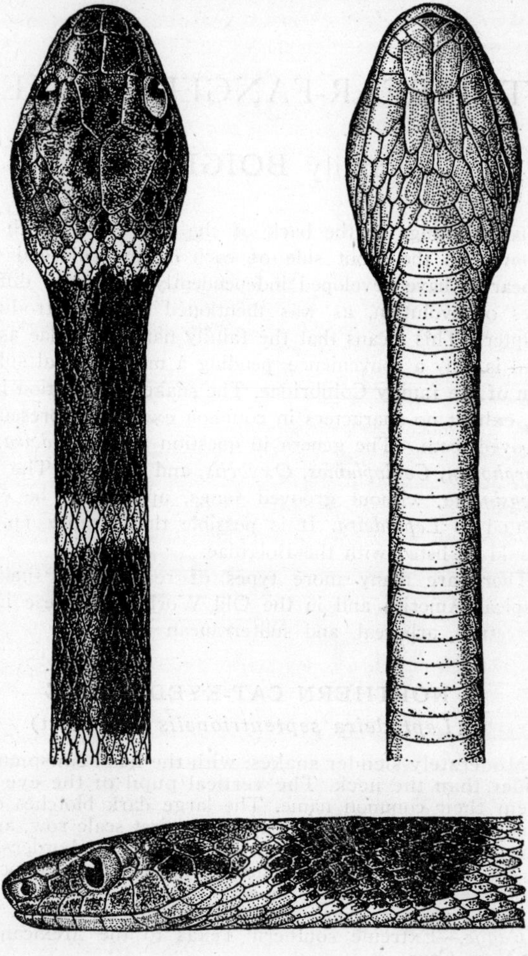

Fig. 85. Northern cat-eyed snake (*Leptodeira septentrionalis*).

ous other forms, reaches the United States only in extreme southern Texas. These snakes may be found climbing in trees and bushes at night.

Size.—Average adult length about 30 inches.

Food.—Small birds and mammals as well as lizards are eaten by the related tropical forms.

Breeding Habits.—Unknown.

LYRE SNAKES
(Trimorphodon)
Plate 29

The lyre snakes have broad heads and vertically elliptic pupils like the cat-eyed snake, and like it they are typical members of the rear-fanged sub-family of snakes, with enlarged and grooved fangs at the back of the upper jaw. They are most easily distinguished by the presence of two or three loreal plates. A pattern of dark markings on the head in some species is referred to by the name "lyre snakes."

Scales smooth. Anal plate divided or entire.

KEY TO THE LYRE SNAKES OF THE UNITED STATES

1 a. Blotches on body (without tail) much narrower than the spaces between them, usually fewer than 23 ......Texas lyre snake (*T. vilkinsonii*)

1 b. Blotches equaling or exceeding the spaces between them; usually more than 22.................... 2

2 a. Anal plate usually entire ......California lyre snake (*T. vandenburghi*)

2 b. Anal plate normally divided ......Arizona lyre snake (*T. lyrophanes*)

Arizona Lyre Snake.—*Trimorphodon lyrophanes* Cope. About 28 large dark blotches on the body, each of which is split by a light cross-line. The blotches are fewer than in the next species, and more numerous than in the Texas lyre snake. The anal plate may be entire as a rare anomaly.

Range.—Western Arizona, southward into Sonora and Lower California.

California Lyre Snake.—*Trimorphodon vandenburghi* Klauber. About 35 large dark blotches on the body (without tail), with light cross-lines as in the Arizona species; the anal plate is usually entire, but may be divided in a small percentage of specimens.

Range.—Southern California from Los Angeles County and central Inyo County south into northwestern Lower California.

Texas Lyre Snake.—*Trimorphodon vilkinsonii* Cope. The dark cross-bands are fewer and narrower than in the other species of *Trimorphodon,* with scarcely a trace of the light cross-line, and the pattern on the head is obscure.

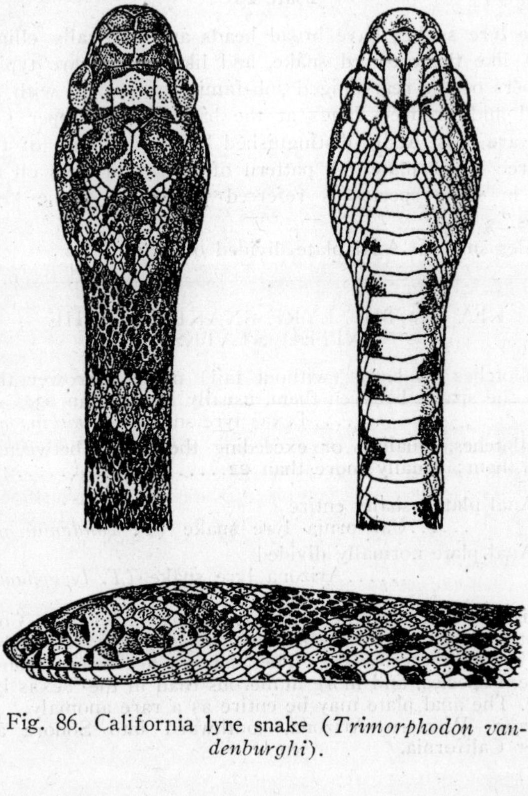

Fig. 86. California lyre snake (*Trimorphodon vandenburghi*).

Range.—Extreme western Texas and adjacent Mexico (known from only three specimens).

Our knowledge of the habits of the lyre snakes is based mainly on the California species, and is summarized by Klauber. These snakes are found especially in rocky localities, and are abroad at night.

Size.—Adults measure about 36 inches in length; the longest known specimen (*vandenburghi*) measures 41½ inches.

Food.—The California lyre snake is mainly a lizard eater; the other species presumably have similar habits. A captive ate a mouse, which it first killed by constriction (Rodman). The mouse had previously been held in the snake's jaws for 15 minutes, and although the effect of the venom was apparent, it had not been fatal.

Breeding Habits.—About a dozen eggs are produced, apparently late in the season.

Klauber, L. M., 1940, *Trans. San Diego Soc. Nat. Hist.,* Vol. 9, pp. 163-194 (review of the species in the United States, notes on habits); **Rodman, G. B.,** 1939, Habits of *Trimorphodon vandenburghi* in Captivity. *Copeia,* 1939, p. 50.

BLACK-BANDED SNAKE
(*Coniophanes imperialis imperialis* Baird)

A small moderately slender snake, brown in general color, with a blackish vertebral stripe, with another dark stripe on each side. A sharply defined yellow line extends on each side of the head from the nostrils to the temporals; upper labials white with black dots, belly reddish. (Fig. 87).

Scales smooth. Anal plate divided.

Range.—Brownsville region of Mexico southward to southern Mexico and northern Central America.

The black-banded snakes have their headquarters, with several distinct species, in Central America, and our only representative is found in extreme southern Texas.

There is an account of a bite from this snake on a man's finger by Bryce C. Brown (*Copeia,* 1939:109); the symptoms reported indicate that a true venom is present, but that it can not be regarded as in any way dangerous to man.

Size.—Length about 16 inches.

Food.—Probably lizards.

Breeding Habits.—Unknown.

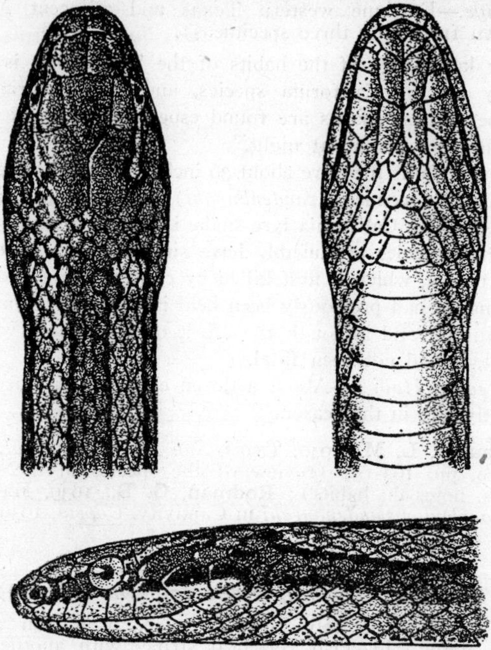

Fig. 87. Black-banded snake (*Coniophanes i. imperialis*).

ARIZONA VINE SNAKE

(*Oxybelis microphthalmus* Barbour and Amaral)

The tropical relatives of this snake live in trees and bushes in a climate quite different from that of Arizona. The extreme elongation of the head is paralleled in other long-headed tropical snakes in Africa and in southeastern Asia.

A snake characterized by extreme slenderness of body and tail, and by remarkable elongation of the head, which is unique among North American snakes north of the tropics. Snout four times as long as eye. General color brown, reddish above, mottled with darker spots. Belly reddish with a white line down the middle of the belly and white lateral lines along the outer ends of the ventrals.

Scales smooth, anal plate divided.

Range.—Known only from the bush desert of southern Arizona.

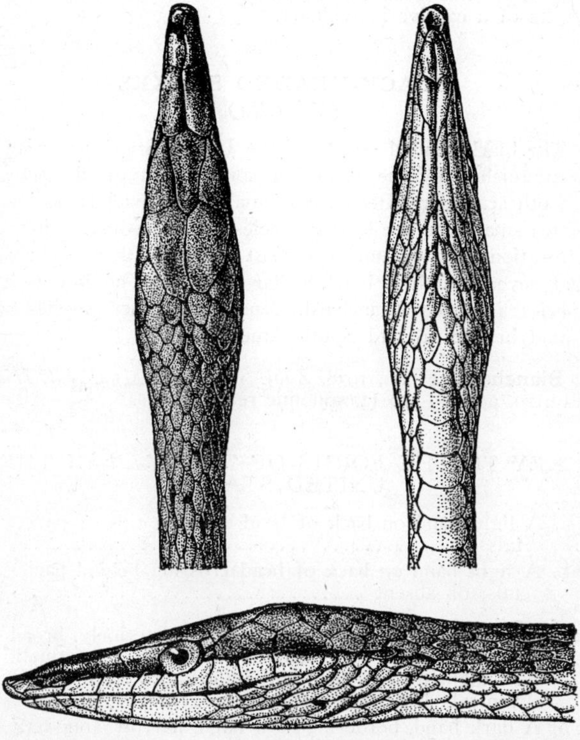

Fig. 88. Arizona vine snake (*Oxybelis microphthalmus*).

Size.—Total length of type specimen 52½ inches (1350 mm.), of which the tail amounts to 21¾ inches (550 mm.).

Food.—Presumably a lizard eater. A captive kept by Mr. Charles T. Vorhies ate small lizards, which it killed "by gripping them tightly well back in the mouth until the poison has done its work."

Breeding Habits.—Unknown.

Vorhies, C. T., 1926, *Copeia,* No. 157, pp. 156-157. (First record of this remarkable snake, with brief notes on the habits of a captive individual).

BLACK-HEADED SNAKES
(Tantilla)

The black-headed snakes of the United States are readily distinguished by the following combination of characters: smooth scales, in fifteen rows; anal plate divided; no loreal plate; small size, the largest species not exceeding 16 inches; coloration of body uniform, most species with a black cap, and several with a black collar as well. The key to the species is from Blanchard. Numerous other species are found in Central and South America.

Blanchard, F. N., 1938, *Zool. Ser. Field Mus. Nat. Hist.*, Vol. 20, pp. 369-376 (taxonomic review).

KEY TO THE FORMS OF *TANTILLA* IN THE UNITED STATES

1 a. A light band on back of head crossing tips of parietals 2

1 b. A light band on back of head crossing behind parietals, or absent 4

2 a. A dark band, bordering light band posteriorly, broad (two to four scale lengths in width); eye small, its diameter less than half its distance from snout; ventrals less than 150 3

2 b. A dark band, bordering light band, narrow (one-half to one and one-half scale lengths in width); eye large, its diameter more than half its distance from snout; ventrals 149-157 ....*T. wilcoxi*

3 a. Ventrals in males 131 to 141, average 135; in females 139 to 148 average 143; caudals in males 42 to 51, average 46; in females 41 to 46, average 44; light band on back of head well defined although often interrupted on the mid-line ....*T. coronata coronata*

3 b. Ventrals in males 119 to 129, average 127; in females 123 to 145 average 131; caudals in males 50 to 67, average 57, in females 41 to 59, average 51; light band on back of head usually more or less obliterated ....*T. coronata wagneri*

4 a. Upper labials usually seven (the sixth approximately as long as the fifth); postoculars usually two, rarely single; head black or dark brown above, contrasting with the general dorsal color; ventrals 123 to 190 5

4 b. Upper labials usually six (when seven, the sixth usually much shorter than the fifth); rarely more than one postocular; head usually but little darker than the body color above; ventrals 115 to 138 ......*T. gracilis*

5 a. Black of head extending three to five scale lengths behind parietal suture, not bordered behind with a narrow white band, nor extended behind or below angle of mouth; mental plates usually separated from chin shields by first lower labials.... 6

5 b. Black of head usually extending only one or two scale lengths behind parietal suture, usually bordered behind with a narrow white band and in some species extending behind and below angle of mouth; mental plate usually in contact with chin shields 8

6 a. Black of head very convex or even pointed behind in the median line, not extending laterally on the last two upper labials nor reaching nearly or quite to the mouth line below the eyes; ventrals 130 to 150 in males and 141 to 161 in females 7

6 b. Black of head transverse to body length posteriorly, extending laterally on one or both last two upper labials, and reaching nearly or quite to the mouth line below the eyes; ventrals 119 to 129 in males and about 123 to 145 in females ......*T. coronata wagneri*

7 a. Ventrals 141 or less (both sexes) ....*T. kirnia*

7 b. Ventrals 145 or more (both sexes) ....*T. nigriceps*

8 a. Black of head extending below angle of mouth onto gular scales ....*T. eiseni*

8 b. Black of head not extending below angle of mouth onto gular scales 9

9a. Ventrals in males 130 to 147, in females 145 to 157 ......*T. atriceps*

9b. Ventrals in males 153 to 160, in females 163 to 172 ......*T. utahensis*

Huachuca Black-headed Snake.—*Tantilla wilcoxi* Stejneger. A light cross-band behind the dark cap is bordered by a dotted dark line. Ventrals (in both sexes) 149-157, caudals 58-69. Maximum length known 14 inches.

Range.—Huachuca Mountains, southeastern Arizona.

Crowned Snake.—*Tantilla coronata coronata* Baird and Girard. A light band behind the dark cap crosses the tips of the parietals and is bordered behind by a black band on the nape. Ventrals 131-148, caudals 41 to 51. Maximum length known 13 inches.

Range.—Atlantic and Gulf coastal plain from Virginia to southeastern Louisiana, north in the Mississippi Valley to western Kentucky, except for peninsular Florida.

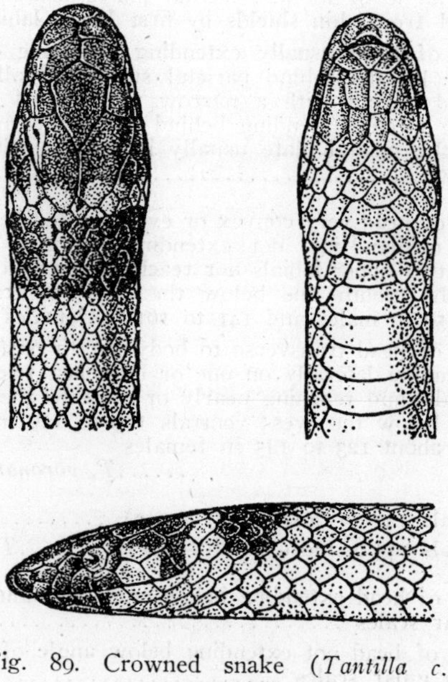

Fig. 89. Crowned snake (*Tantilla c. coronata*).

Florida Crowned Snake.—*Tantilla coronata wagneri* Jan. The light cross-band behind the head is more or less obscure, and the black band of the nape is narrower than in the crowned snake. Ventrals 119-145, caudals 41-67. Maximum length known 10 inches.

Range.—Peninsular Florida.

California Black-headed Snake.—*Tantilla eiseni* Stejneger. The light cross-band is behind the tips of the parietals, bordered behind with a few black dots, but with no black band on the nape. Ventrals 165-190, caudals 53-69. The largest species, maximum length known 15 inches.

Range.—Fresno County, California, to northern Lower California.

Slender Tantilla.—*Tantilla gracilis* Baird and Girard. This is the only species without a black cap; the head is usually brown and little if at all darker than the body. Upper labials usually 6; postoculars usually 1; ventrals 115-138, caudals 36-57. Maximum size in 85 specimens 9 inches.

Range.—Missouri and southeastern Kansas to extreme southern Texas.

Mexican Black-headed Snake.—*Tantilla atriceps* Günther. A species closely similar to the following, but distinguished by a number of characters: black cap extending only one or two scales behind parietals; mental plate usually separating the first pair of chin shields; caudals more numerous; and size much smaller. Ventrals 130-157, caudals 51-70. Maximum length known a little over 9 inches.

Range.—Oklahoma and western Texas to southeastern Arizona, southward into Mexico.

Great Plains Black-headed Snake.—*Tantilla nigriceps* Kennicott. Black cap extending three or four scales behind the parietals, its posterior border convex or pointed, not reaching the last two upper labials on the sides. First lower labials in contact behind the mental. Maximum size 14 inches.

Range.—Western Kansas and eastern Colorado southward through Oklahoma and Texas to New Mexico and Arizona.

Utah Black-headed Snake.—*Tantilla utahensis* Blanchard. Top of head dark brown, extending backward to the scales bordering the parietals and downward to the upper labials. Mental in contact with the anterior chin shields as in *atriceps*. Ventrals 153 to 172, the number of ventrals much higher in females than in males. Maximum length known 12 inches.

Range.—Southwestern Utah, southwest to the Sierra Nevada in California.

Texas Black-headed Snake.—*Tantilla kirnia* Blanchard. Allied to the Great Plains black-headed snake, but smaller in size, and with a lower number of ventrals and caudals in both sexes. Ventrals in males 130-138, caudals 43-48; 141 and 39 in the single female specimen known. Top of head dark brown, extending backward to the third scale behind the parietals. Maximum length known 9 inches.

Range.—Comanche County, Oklahoma, southward in Texas nearly to Brownsville and westward to San Antonio.

The black-headed snakes are all small and secretive forms, found beneath stones and logs or other debris. The Mexican black-headed snake, for example, is especially abundant under the large dried heads of dead sotol plants in western Texas. That they may be extremely abundant is shown by a collection of several hundred specimens of the slender black-headed snake from rocky hillsides in a limited area in Oklahoma.

All the species have the cylindrical bodies, small heads, and smooth scales characteristic of secretive or burrowing species, but the tail is not especially short. They do not attempt to bite when handled, but try to hide in the palm of the hand and burrow between the fingers. They usually remain hidden in captivity.

Size.—The various species of black-headed snakes, though all small, differ so considerably in length that this has been stated for each form.

Food.—Stomach contents of 63 specimens of *gracilis* consisted of "centipedes and earth-dwelling insect larvae such as cutworms, wireworms, and leatherjackets (larvae of Tipulidae or crane-flies)." (Force.)

Breeding Habits.—The slender tantilla (*T. gracilis*) lays from one to four eggs in June and early July. These measure from one-half to 1⅜ inches (13-36 mm.) in length and about a quarter of an inch (4-6.5 mm.) in diameter. Hatching takes place during the first half of September.

Force, Edith R., 1935, A local study of the opisthoglyph snake, *Tantilla gracilis* Baird and Girard. *Papers Mich. Acad. Sci.,* Vol. 20, pp. 645-659. (Habits, food, breeding habits).

THE CORAL SNAKES

Family ELAPIDAE

The elapid snakes are abundant in Africa, tropical Asia, and especially in Australia, where they are found in great variety. In the Americas they are represented by only three genera, *Micrurus,* mainly in tropical America, *Micruroides,* the Arizona coral snake, and the tropical *Leptomicrurus.* The family is characterized by having fixed poison fangs at the front of the jaw, i.e., the proteroglyph condition, and is thus allied to the sea snakes.

Though some of the smaller Australian forms of this family have only a weak venom, the venom of the larger cobras, mambas, and kraits is extremely potent. There are only few records of human beings being bitten by coral snakes, but these include a higher percentage of fatalities than is the case with the bites from the rattlesnakes; as the coral snakes are relatively small forms, this indicates that they must have a remarkably effective venom (see Poison Apparatus and Venom, p. 36).

The coral snakes are almost all ringed with black, yellow, and red (sometimes only with black and red, or with black and yellow, in the tropical forms). The resemblance of certain similarly ringed harmless snakes to them has often been pointed to as mimicry of the poisonous forms by the non-poisonous, to the advantage of the latter. There are objections to this interpretation when the facts are critically considered.

Schmidt, K. P., 1928, Notes on American Coral Snakes, *Bull. Antiv. Inst. Amer.,* Vol. 2, pp. 63-64.

THE TRUE CORAL SNAKES
(Micrurus)
Plate 6

The true coral snakes include more than fifty distinct forms, ranging in size from the Brazilian Spix's coral snake, which reaches a length of five feet, to a diminutive Colombian form rarely more than a foot in length. The species in the southeastern United States is closely allied to the tropical forms.

In this genus the teeth on the maxillary bone are reduced to the single poison fang, an evident evolutionary advance from the primitive Australian elapids with numerous maxillary teeth.

Scales smooth. Anal plate divided.

Common Coral Snake.—*Micrurus fulvius fulvius* Linnaeus. The pattern is made up of broad black rings, each with a narrow yellow ring on each side, separated from the next black and yellow group by a broad red ring. The scales of the red zone are more or less marked with black, and this black pigment in the red zones is often grouped into a pair of black spots. A broad yellow ring crosses the back of the head, followed by a broad black ring on the neck.

Range.—Central Florida north and west to North Carolina and westward to the Mississippi River.

South Florida Coral Snake.—*Micrurus fulvius barbouri* Schmidt. Distinguished from the common coral snake by the reduction or entire absence of black spotting in the red zones.

Range.—Confined to the southern part of the Florida Peninsula.

Texas Coral Snake.—*Micrurus fulvius tenere* Baird and Girard. Distinguished from the common coral snake chiefly by the increased amount and irregular distribution of the black spotting in the red zones.

Range.—Arkansas to southern Texas and into northeastern Mexico.

The coral snakes of the species *Micrurus fulvius* agree in having a cylindrical body with fifteen scale rows, the head not wider than the neck, and the tail of moderate length.

The three subspecies defined above are not sharply distinguishable, and until further information about their areas of intergradation is available, some specimens will necessarily have to be assigned in accordance with geographic distribution.

The common coral snakes are sometimes also known as "harlequin snakes," but this appears to be only a book name. Though by no means rare in the southern portion of their range, coral snakes are not often encountered, evidently as a result of secretive and even burrowing habits. They are entirely inoffensive in behavior and rarely bite when handled. They are consequently often handled with impunity by reckless persons. In view of the potency of their venom and of

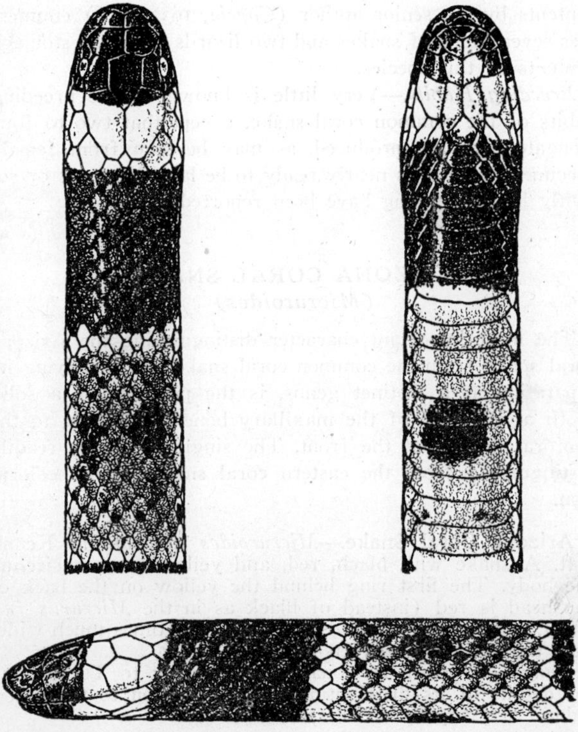

Fig. 90. Common coral snake (*Micrurus f. fulvius*).

the fact that no one knows why or when they *will* bite, they should *never* be handled with bare hands. Kipling's story "Rhinelander and the German Flag," based on the fact that the famous herpetologist Cope reported the coral snakes to be "not dangerous to man," should be read in this connection.

Size.—The largest specimen recorded is 39 inches long. Eight out of 66 Florida specimens and eight out of 43 Texas specimens measured more than 31 inches.

Food.—The venom appears to be especially adapted to the lizard and snake prey. A study of all known stomach contents by the senior author (*Copeia,* 1932, p. 6) enumerates seven kinds of snakes and two lizards from the stomach contents of this species.

Breeding Habits.—Very little is known of the breeding habits of the common coral snake, except that two to four elongate eggs are produced, as may be seen from female specimens with eggs nearly ready to be laid. No nests or recently hatched young have been reported.

ARIZONA CORAL SNAKE
(Micruroides)

The most important character distinguishing the Arizona coral snake from the common coral snake and justifying its separation as a distinct genus, is the presence of a solid tooth at the rear of the maxillary bone in addition to the perforated fang at the front. The single species is readily distinguished from the eastern coral snakes by its coloration.

Arizona Coral Snake.—*Micruroides euryxanthus* Kennicott. A snake with black, red, and yellow rings encircling the body. The first ring behind the yellow on the back of the head is red (instead of black as in the *Micrurus fulvius*), and the yellow bands are wide, sometimes much wider than the red zone between them.

Range.—Western Arizona, from Phoenix to Tucson, but the details of its distribution and its relation to the desert habitat are very little understood.

There seems to be no case of bite from *Micruroides eury-*

xanthus on record. Its venom may be presumed to be potent. Its habits are secretive and subterranean.

Size.—Maximum size known about 18 inches.

Food.—Primarily snakes (Vorhies, *Copeia,* 1929, p. 98).

Breeding Habits.—Unknown.

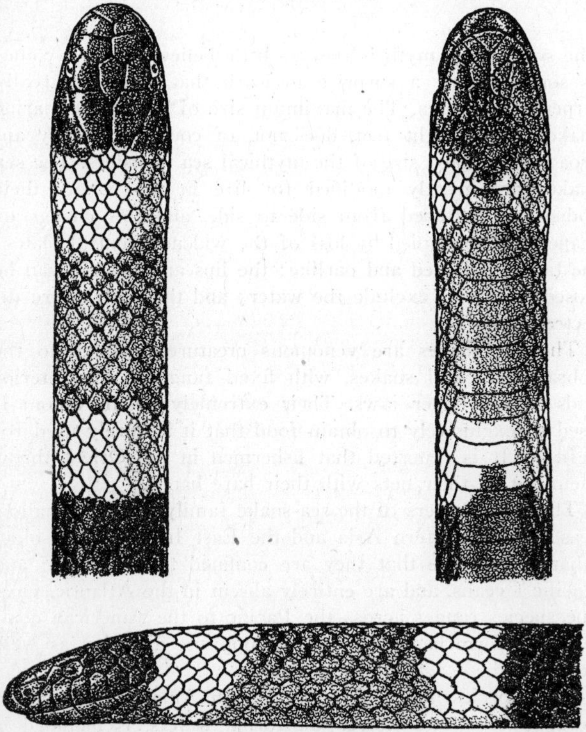

Fig. 91. Arizona coral snake (*Micruroides euryxanthus*).

THE SEA SNAKES

Family HYDROPHIDAE

The sea-serpent myth is now so little believed that it comes as something of a surprise to learn that there are really serpents in the sea. The maximum size of these true marine snakes, about eight feet, does not, of course, remotely approach the fabled size of the mythical sea monsters. The sea snakes are greatly modified for life in the water; their bodies are flattened from side to side, and this change of shape is accompanied by loss of the widened ventral plates; the tail is flattened and oarlike; the lips and nostrils can be closed tightly to exclude the water; and the nostrils are directed upward.

The sea snakes are venomous creatures, related to the cobras and coral snakes, with fixed fangs at the anterior ends of the upper jaws. Their extremely potent venom is used so exclusively to obtain food that it is rarely used for defense. It is reported that fishermen in the Orient throw them out of their nets with their bare hands.

The headquarters of the sea-snake family is in the shallow seas of southeastern Asia and the East Indies; it is somewhat remarkable that they are confined to the Indian and Pacific Oceans, and are entirely absent in the Atlantic. Only one species ranges across the Pacific to the American coast and this form has spread in the opposite direction as well, reaching the coast of Madagascar.

This species, included in the North American *Check-list* because it reaches Lower California waters, is included in the present book for its great biological interest. It affords a glimpse of the extraordinary nature of some of the adaptations of snakes to food and environment.

Yellow-bellied Sea Snake.—*Pelamydrus platurus* Linnaeus. Coloration remarkable, the dark brown or bluish black of the upper half of the body being sharply set off from the bright orange or yellow lower parts; tail yellow, with dark bars.

Range.—Madagascar to the coasts of India, eastward through the East Indies, and on the coasts of the Americas from Ecuador to the Gulf of California. Occasionally in great numbers in the Bay of Panama.

Size.—Maximum length about 3 feet.

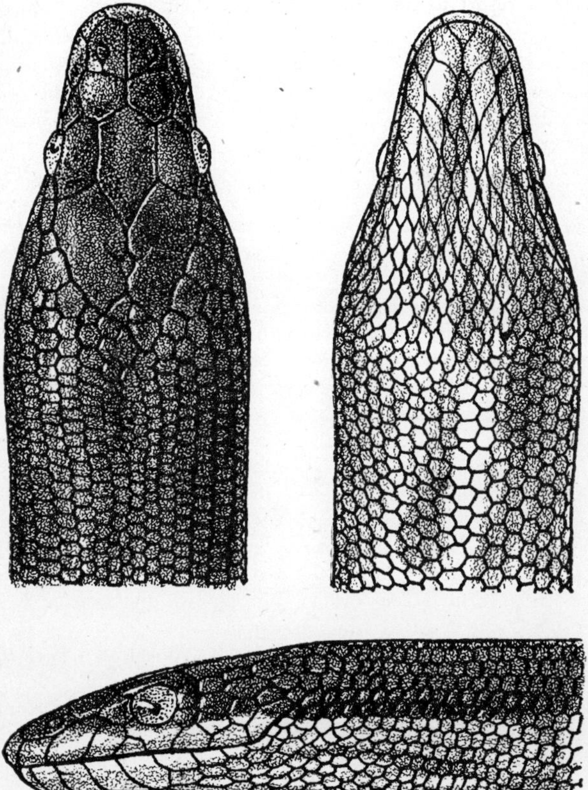

Fig. 92. Yellow-bellied sea snake (*Pelamydrus platurus*).

Food.—Fishes. Klauber (*Copeia,* 1935, p. 182) reports that these snakes have been observed to feed on small fishes that gather alongside them as they float at the surface of the sea. Such small fishes gather at every floating stick or bit of seaweed, and the snakes attract a regular food supply by their simulation of such objects.

Breeding Habits.—The young are born alive. Ditmars (1936, *Reptiles of North America,* p. 316) reports that the females resort to tidepools to produce their young.

THE PIT VIPERS

Family CROTALIDAE

This family of highly venomous snakes contains about 100 species and subspecies of which only 30 are found in the United States. It is predominantly American, although pit vipers of the genera *Trimeresurus* and *Agkistrodon* are found in southeastern Asia and the East Indian region, and one species of moccasin (*Agkistrodon halys*) reaches extreme eastern Europe. The Neotropical pit vipers, also of the genus *Trimeresurus,* of southern Mexico and Central and South America, and the bushmaster (*Lachesis*) of Central and South America, do not reach the United States.

The pit vipers differ from their nearest relatives, the Old World "true" vipers (*Viperidae*), in possessing a complex facial pit situated between the eye and the nostril. The two families agree in having long erectile fangs and a highly developed poison apparatus.

The facial or loreal pit, which is the most distinctive feature of the family, "is a rather complex organ consisting of two chambers separated from each other by a thin sheet of tissue, the 'pit membrane.' The outer chamber is widely open and is in free communication with the air; the inner chamber communicates with the exterior by a small pore situated near the anterior border of the orbit. The cuticle which covers the body extends into this inner chamber and there presents a much-tuberculated appearance" (1931, Lynn, *Amer. J. Anat.,* 49). The lining of the pit and the pit membrane are richly supplied with nerve endings. Experiments have shown that, like the labial pits of boas and pythons, it is capable of detecting the body heat of warm-blooded animals at some distance, and thus aid in directing the strike. The pit membrane, which is stretched between the chambers like a drumhead, seems to function in recording air vibrations.

The pupil of the eye is always vertically elliptical in the pit vipers. This feature, which is associated with nocturnal habits, is also found in some nonpoisonous snakes.

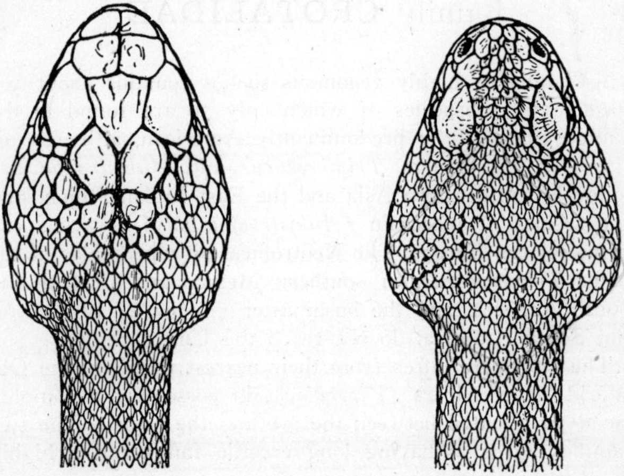

Fig. 93. Heads of moccasin (left) and rattler compared. Note the small scales on top of the head in the rattlesnake.

All North American pit vipers produce living young.

The moccasins (*Agkistrodon*) are readily distinguished from the rattlesnakes (*Crotalus*) and ground rattlers (*Sistrurus*) by the presence of a rattle on the end of the tail in the rattlers. Even if the rattle has been accidentally lost, the end of the tail will always be short and blunt (never pointed) in a rattlesnake.

Stejneger, L., 1895, The Poisonous Snakes of North America. *Rep. U. S. Nat. Mus.* for 1893, pp. 337-487, 70 figs., 19 pl.

KEY TO THE GENERA

A. A rattle on end of tail

a. Top of head covered to well back of eyes with large plates, usually 9 in number (Fig. 95).
......Pigmy rattlesnakes (*Sistrurus*) p. 287

b. Top of head covered with smaller scales of varying size. If large scales are present, they do not extend back of eyes (Fig. 97).
......Rattlesnakes (*Crotalus*) p. 290

B. No rattle on end of tail
......Moccasins (*Agkistrodon*) p. 283

THE COPPERHEADS
(*Agkistrodon mokasen*)
Plate 30

There are three subspecies of the copperhead, each occupying a particular range. These grade into one another, and specimens from the areas of intergradation probably cannot be named with certainty.

The copperheads are richly colored, heavy-bodied snakes. The pattern consists of a series of 15 to 25 chestnut-brown cross-bands, constricted toward the midline so that they look like triangles or inverted Y's when the snake is seen from the side, on a lighter ground color. The top of the head is without marking, and coppery-red in color as the common name implies.

Scales keeled. Anal plate single.

Southern Copperhead.—*Agkistrodon mokasen mokasen* Beauvois. Coloration pale, usually with a pinkish tinge in life. The pattern consists of a series of dark hourglass-shaped cross-bands. conspicuously narrow at the midline (rarely more than 2 or 3 scales wide); the cross-bands may fail to meet at the midline. Belly pale and not heavily marked.

Range.—Coastal plain of the Gulf States, from Victoria Co., Texas north to northeastern Texas, central Arkansas, southern Illinois, and east-central Alabama; the Atlantic coastal plain and lower Piedmont areas north to central Maryland, exclusive of peninsular Florida.

Northern Copperhead.—*Agkistrodon mokasen cupreus* Rafinesque. Coloration darker than in the southern copperhead, often reddish brown or chestnut; there may be little contrast between pattern and ground color. The cross-bands are wider at the midline (3 to 5 scales), and all of them usually meet at the midline. Belly darker and more or less mottled with gray or black.

Range.—Eastern Oklahoma and eastern Kansas; higher areas of west-central and northwestern Arkansas, Missouri (except southeastern part), north to central Illinois, central Indiana, southern and eastern Ohio, Pennsylvania, and southeastern New York; Appalachian highlands from the Tennessee River and northeastern Alabama to eastern Massachusetts.

Broad-banded Copperhead.—*Agkistrodon mokasen laticinctus* Gloyd and Conant. Coloration bright, with sharp contrast between pattern and ground color. The cross-bands are very broad at the midline (4 to 8 scales), all of them meeting at the midline. Belly still darker and mottled with gray or black.

Range.—Western and central Texas, from Jeff Davis, Reeves, and Brewster Counties eastward to Colorado Co.; north through central Oklahoma to Cowley Co., Kansas.

The copperheads are known by a variety of popular names: upland moccasin, chunk-head, deaf-adder, or pilot snake. They are partial to rocky or wooded areas and apparently are inclined to be gregarious, as individuals are usually numerous in localities where the species occur. In the fall they congregate to den up for the winter, often sharing dens with the banded rattlesnake.

These snakes are rather inoffensive, spending much time in hiding and usually lying quiet or trying to crawl away when discovered. When aroused or restrained they fight savagely, however, and the bite is decidedly dangerous. Excited copperheads often vibrate their tails, and in dry leaves this may produce a sound similar to that of a rattlesnake.

Size.—Adults average about 30 inches in length. Ditmars records a specimen that measured 4 feet, 5 inches.

Food.—Copperheads are not very discriminating in their diet. Although small mammals are most often taken, they also eat a variety of other vertebrates and insects. The fact that several have been found with their stomachs crammed with 17-year cicadas indicates that they are likely to feed on what is most available. A recent study of 72 stomachs from Virginia showed that mice, caterpillars, and shrews are the three most important items in the diet.

Breeding Habits.—Mating takes place in April and May. The young are born in August and September. Gloyd found 2-6 (av. 4) young in 20 females from eastern Kansas, while 32 females from eastern U. S. contained or gave birth to 3-10 (av. 6) young.

Gloyd, H. K., 1934, Studies on the Breeding Habits and Young of the Copperhead, *Agkistrodon mokasen* Beauvois. *Papers Mich. Acad. Sci.,* Vol. 19, pp. 587-604, 2 figs., 3 pl.; **Conant, R.,** 1938, *Amer. Midland Nat.,* Vol. 20, pp. 107-112 (general natural history in Ohio).

WATER MOCCASIN

(Agkistrodon piscivorus Lacépède)

Plate 30

This snake is semi-aquatic, and is most likely to be confused with various species of harmless water snakes. The presence of a loreal distinguishes it from its nearest relatives, the copperheads. The pattern consists of 10 to 15 wide dark cross-bands, slightly wider at the base, on an olive or brown ground color. The cross-bands are usually lighter in the center than at the edges. The pattern becomes obscure or disappears completely in large individuals, which become very dark, often almost uniformly black. The young, on the other hand, are brilliantly colored and may easily be confused with young copperheads. The belly is yellowish, blotched with darker markings. The underside of the tail, and for a short distance in front of it on the body, is usually black.

Range.—Dismal Swamp, Virginia, to Florida and the Gulf States, and Arkansas to Illinois.

The habits of the water moccasin are very similar to those of the larger water snakes. It is seldom found far from water, and is fond of basking on branches and logs along sluggish streams, bayous and swamps. In the fall, moccasins retreat to higher ground to hibernate. They are more sluggish than the water snakes, and frequently stand their ground when molested. Under these circumstances the mouth is widely opened in a threatening gesture, which exposes its white interior. This is the reason for two of its common names: "cottonmouth" and "gapper." Like many other snakes, it often vibrates its tail when cornered.

Size.—Adults average about 40 inches in length. The maximum recorded length is 4 feet, 10½ inches (Ditmars).

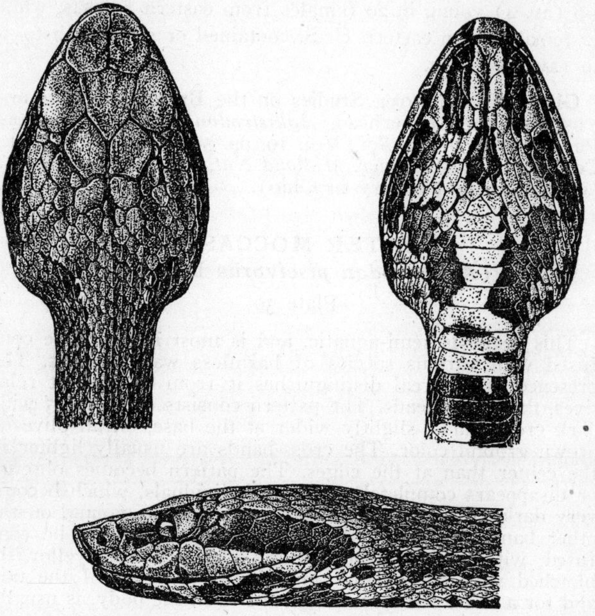

Fig. 94. Water moccasin (*Agkistrodon piscivorus*).

Food.—Because of the nature of their habits, water moccasins feed largely on fish, frogs, and other aquatic or semiaquatic vertebrates. They also eat small mammals, birds, lizards, etc., when these are available. The senior author found moccasins feeding on large numbers of juvenile turtles in Louisiana, with masses of horny plates of the turtle shells in their stomachs.

Breeding Habits.—Mating takes place in March (Beyer).

The young are born in late August and early September. Eight broods from various parts of the range of the species numbered from 5 to 15 young, with an average of 8. According to Beyer a brood of 9 young from Louisiana averaged 6⅜ inches in length at birth. Conant gives the length of one born to a female from Illinois as 10¾ inches.

THE PIGMY RATTLESNAKES
(*Sistrurus*)
Plate 31

The pigmy rattlesnakes, massasaugas, or ground rattlers, form a small and relatively compact group of snakes. They differ from the true rattlesnakes (*Crotalus*) chiefly in having the top of the head covered with nine large plates similar to those of typical harmless snakes. The rattle is also proportionately smaller in these snakes than in the true rattlesnakes. The pigmy rattlers are thus less highly specialized than the true rattlers.

The pigmy rattlers are divided into two species: *catenatus* (with two subspecies), in which the upper preocular is in contact with the postnasal, the tail relatively short, and the rattle of moderate size; and *miliarius* (with three subspecies), in which the upper preocular is not in contact with the postnasal, the tail is long and slender, and the rattle very small. There is a third species (*ravus*) in Mexico.

Eastern Massasauga.—*Sistrurus catenatus catenatus* Rafinesque. A series of 21 to 37 squarish blotches, red-brown or black in color and usually with a fine white border, along the midline of the back. Two alternating rows of similar but smaller markings along the side. Ground color gray-brown. Occasional individuals are almost black. Belly dark, heavily blotched with black. Scale rows usually 25.

Range.—From central New York and western Pennsylvania west through Ontario, lower Michigan, north and central Ohio and Indiana, Illinois, southern Wisconsin, eastern and southern Iowa, Missouri, extreme southeastern Nebraska, extreme eastern Kansas, and extreme northeastern Oklahoma. Intergrades with *S. c. tergeminus* in Kansas and Oklahoma.

Western Massasauga.—*Sistrurus catenatus tergeminus* Say. Similar to *S. c. catenatus,* but usually with more than

36 dorsal blotches. Belly mottled or spotted, the light areas being more extensive than the dark. Scales rows often 23.

Range.—Continues the range of *S. c. catenatus* west and south into the great plains: Kansas except northwestern and extreme eastern parts, extreme southeastern Colorado, central and western Oklahoma, Texas west of the Brazos River except extreme southwestern part, southeastern New Mexico, and extreme southeastern Arizona. Crosses Rio Grande into Tamaulipas, Mexico.

Massasaugas are partial to bogs and swamps, although during the summer they may move into drier situations. In

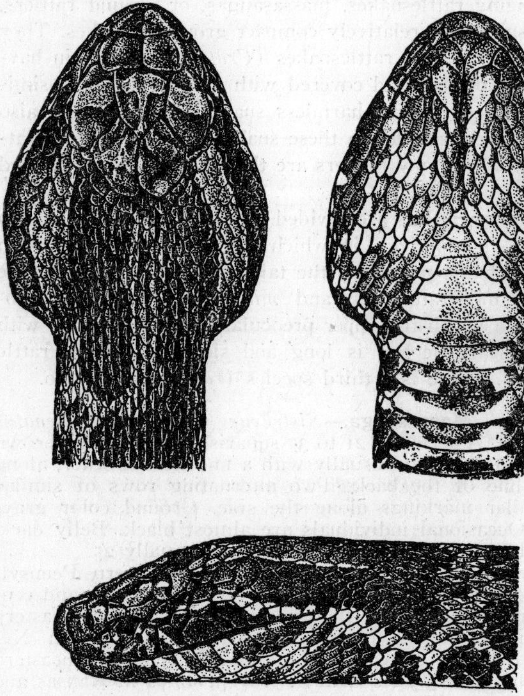

Fig. 95. Eastern massasauga (*Sistrurus c. catenatus*).

many parts of their range they are referred to as "black snapper" or "swamp rattler." They are rather mild-tempered snakes, sometimes refusing to strike unless annoyed repeatedly. Although there appear to be no records of deaths from their bites, they must be regarded as dangerous, since the venom has a high degree of toxicity.

Size.—Adults average about two feet; large individuals may slightly exceed three feet.

Food.—Mice form the bulk of the diet, although frogs are also frequently taken. Frogs are swallowed directly, while the fangs are used and the venom allowed to act on warm-blooded prey. Unlike copperheads, they do not eat insects.

Breeding Habits.—Young are born in August and September. Litters number up to 12, with an average of 8 or 9. The young measure from 8 to 9½ inches in length at birth.

Ground Rattlesnake.—*Sistrurus miliarius miliarius* Linnaeus. A series of 36 or more oval, well-separated black blotches along the midline of the back. Two or three rows of similar but smaller markings along the side. Ground color gray. There is often a distinctly reddish mid-dorsal stripe between the dorsal blotches. Belly cream, heavily spotted with black blotches usually occupying two adjacent scutes. Dorsal scale rows usually 21.

Range.—South Carolina except extreme southern part (where it intergrades with *S. m. barbouri*), north through southeastern North Carolina and west through central Georgia and Alabama.

Florida Ground Rattlesnake.—*Sistrurus miliarius barbouri* Gloyd. A series of about 35 black blotches along the midline of the back. Three rows of similar but smaller markings along the side. Ground color dark gray to black, which gives the snake a dark appearance compared with the other two subspecies. Head pattern obscure. Belly white, heavily blotched or distinctly spotted with black or very dark brown. Dorsal scale rows usually 25.

Range.—Florida, extreme southeastern South Carolina, southern Georgia and southern Alabama, and extreme southeastern Mississippi.

Western Ground Rattlesnake.—*Sistrurus miliarius streckeri* Gloyd. About 30 dark brown spots, wider than long and with irregular borders, along the midline of the back. One or two rows of spots, usually higher than wide, along the side. Ground color pale grayish brown. Belly cream, with diffuse dark blotches usually not more than one scute wide. Dorsal scale rows usually 21. (Plate 31).

Range.—From the Pearl River Valley of southeastern Louisiana and western Mississippi (where it intergrades with *S. m. barbouri*) west through Louisiana and eastern Texas, north through Arkansas and southeastern Oklahoma to southern Missouri and extreme southwestern Tennessee.

Ground rattlesnakes, often referred to as "pigmy rattlers," apparently prefer a drier environment than massasaugas do. They are also more aggressive, and their disposition is usually described as short-tempered or fiery. The tiny rattle makes a faint insectlike buzz that can be heard only a few feet away.

Size.—Adults average about 18 inches in length; large individuals may slightly exceed two feet.

Food.—Ground rattlesnakes appear to be more partial to small lizards and snakes than massasaugas are; otherwise their food and feeding habits are similar.

Breeding Habits.—Broods of young may number up to 18, but average 8 or 9. According to Beyer, a brood born to a Louisiana female averaged about 5½ inches in length at birth.

THE RATTLESNAKES
(Crotalus)

The rattlesnakes form one of the most characteristically American of all groups of snakes. Thirty-four forms, ranging in size from the formidable eastern diamond-back to the dwarf rock rattlesnakes, are recognized, and the ranges of only 8 of these do not touch the United States or Lower California. The headquarters of the rattlesnakes is in the arid regions of southwestern U. S., and only the two species *adamanteus* and *horridus* are found east of the Mississippi River.

THE RATTLE

The rattle is the most characteristic feature of the rattlesnakes, and is one of the most remarkable stuctures in nature Nothing remotely resembling the rattle is found in any other group of snakes. The astonishment and incredulity with which early travelers to America were greeted when they returned to Europe with stories of a snake with a "bell" on its tail may easily be imagined.

It is not surprising that so extraordinary a structure should have attracted the attention of naturalists from the time of its discovery. A long list of their writings on this subject is given by Klauber (1940), who has also carefully reviewed the many theories regarding the rattle and studied its development, structure, and method of functioning.

The rattle is made up of a number of segments that interlock loosely with one another to form a jointed string (Fig. 96). The rattle is higher than it is wide, and is vibrated

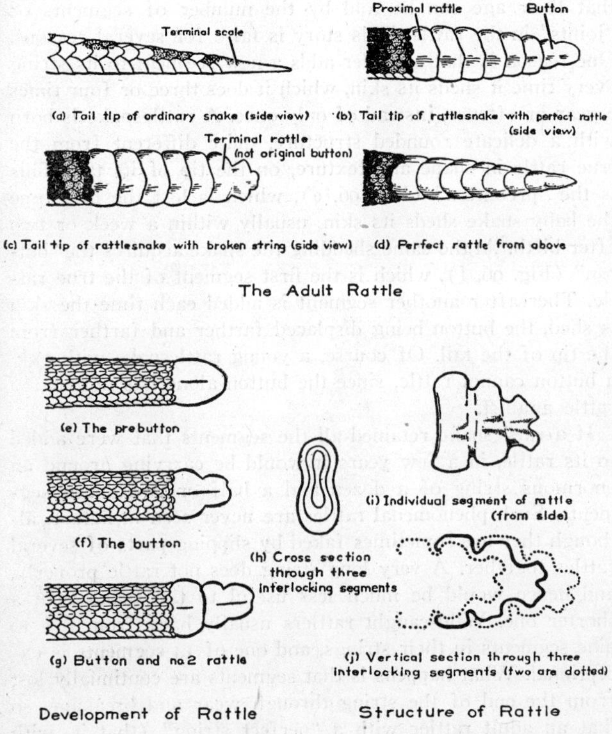

Fig. 96. The rattle of the rattlesnake, showing details of its structure and development. (Partly after Klauber).

sideways, not up and down. Each segment is composed of a thin shell of hornlike substance, and the several segments striking against each other when the tail is vibrated produce the "rattling" sound. Actually the sound is more like the buzz of a cicada or the hiss of escaping steam than like a true rattling sound. Klauber found by using a kymograph (the instrument used to record heart beats) that the rattle averages about 48 cycles per second, a speed that makes the rattle look blurred when it is in motion.

One of the most persistent stories about rattlesnakes is that their age can be told by the number of segments or "joints" in the rattle. This story is false for several reasons. One reason is that a rattler adds a new segment to its string every time it sheds its skin, which it does three or four times a year or oftener, instead of only once. A rattlesnake is born with a delicate rounded structure, quite different from the true rattle in shape and texture, on the tip of its tail. This is the "prebutton" (Fig. 96, e), which is lost the first time the baby snake sheds its skin, usually within a week or two after birth. At the same shedding the snake acquires the "button" (Fig. 96, f), which is the first segment of the true rattle. Thereafter another segment is added each time the skin is shed, the button being displaced farther and farther from the tip of the tail. Of course, a young rattlesnake with only a button cannot rattle, since the button alone has nothing to rattle against.

If a rattlesnake retained all the segments that were added to its rattle, in a few years it would be carrying around an enormous string of a dozen and a half or two dozen segments. Such phenomenal rattles are never seen in nature, although they are sometimes faked by slipping parts of several rattles together. A very long string does not rattle properly, and hence would be much less useful to the snake than a shorter one. Wild-caught rattlers usually have from five to nine segments in their strings, and one of 14 segments is exceptional. What happens is that segments are continually lost from the end of the string through wear and breakage, so that an adult rattler with a "perfect string" (that is, with the original button present at the tip [Fig. 96, b]) is very unusual; most of them have "broken strings" (Fig. 96, c).

The origin of the rattle is much easier to imagine when it is remembered that many harmless snakes vibrate their tails when they are nervous or angry, exactly as a rattler does. This is particularly characteristic of rat snakes and king snakes, for example. Many people have speculated on the purpose of the rattle, and it is now generally agreed that it is a warning to intruders who might injure the snake, like a skunk or badger intent on a meal or a bison that might crush the snake by stepping on it accidentally. It is all too easy to assume human purposive reasoning on the part of the snake, however, and hence to assume that it is consciously "warning" an intruder. Actually the snake vibrates its tail for the same reason that a harmless snake does—because it is nervous and angry; the fact that a startling noise results is incidental, and certainly unknown to the snake. Remember that a rattlesnake is deaf, and consequently cannot hear its own rattle!

Klauber, L. M., 1940, A statistical Study of the Rattlesnakes. VII, The Rattle. *Occ. Papers San Diego Soc. Nat. Hist.,* No. 6, 62 pp., il.

The 26 species and subspecies of North American rattlers are most satisfactorily identified by means of a key. In the following key, which is adapted from Klauber,* considerable use is made of the details of head scutellation. The special names used for scales, some of which are peculiar to rattlesnakes, are explained in Fig. 97. Tentative identifications made from the key should be checked by referring to the ranges and more detailed descriptions given on succeeding pages.

Gloyd, H. K., 1940, The Rattlesnakes, Genera *Sistrurus* and *Crotalus*. A Study in Zoogeography and Evolution. *Special Publ. Chicago Acad. Sci.,* No. 4, 266 pp., 10 figs., 31 plates (contains excellent photographs of all rattlesnakes of the U.S.); **Klauber, L. M.,** 1936-1940, A statistical Study of the Rattlesnakes, Parts I-VII. *Occ. Papers San Diego Soc. Nat. Hist.,* Nos. 1-6 (sex ratio, birth rate, growth, head dimensions, fangs, rattle).

* Klauber, L. M., "A key to the rattlesnakes with summary of characteristics." *Trans. San Diego Soc. Nat. Hist.,* Vol. 20, 1936.

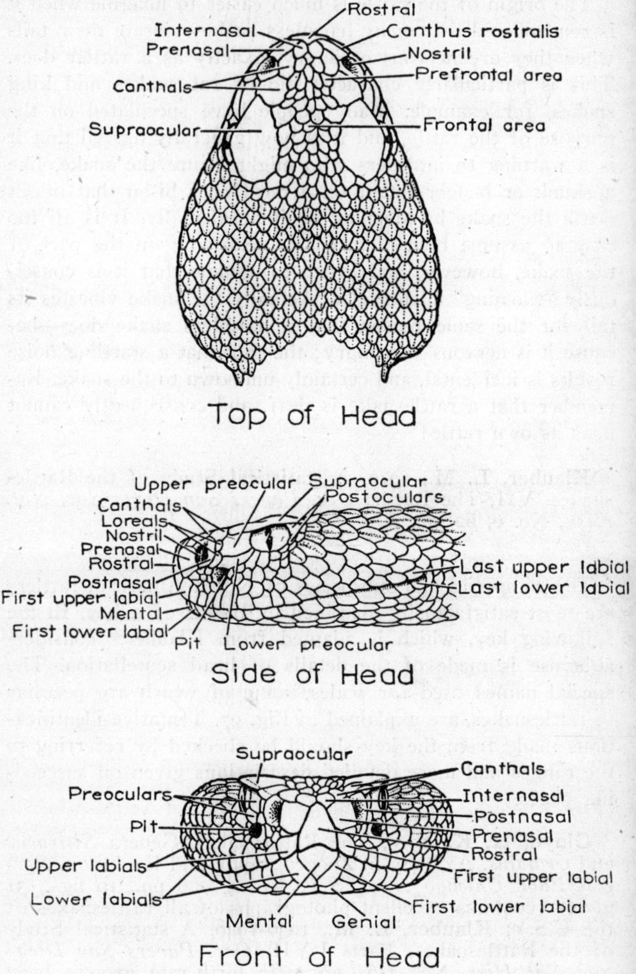

Fig. 97. Names of head scales of rattlesnakes (*Crotalus*). (After Klauber).

KEY TO SPECIES OF *CROTALUS*

1 a. Outer edges of supraoculars not extended into raised and flexible hornlike processes.......... 2

1 b. Outer edges of supraoculars extended into raised and flexible hornlike processes. (Fig. 99). ......Sidewinder (*C. cerastes*) p. 300

2 a. Tip of snout and canthus rostralis not raised into a sharp ridge; no central light line on rostral and mental 3

2 b. Tip of snout and canthus rostralis raised into a sharp ridge, by bending up of the outer edges of internasals and canthals; rostral and mental usually marked vertically by a narrow light line on a red-brown ground (Fig. 103) ......Willard's rattlesnake (*C. willardi*) p. 311

3 a. Upper preocular not split vertically, or if split the anterior section not conspicuously higher than the posterior and not curved over the canthus rostralis; prenasal not curved under postnasal; pattern not of widely separated crossbars or rings.. 4

3 b. Upper preocular split vertically, the anterior section being higher than the posterior and curved over the canthus rostralis in front of the supraocular; prenasal curved under postnasal; pattern usually consisting of widely separated crossbars. ......Rock rattlesnakes (*C. lepidus*) p. 302

4 a. Prenasals in contact with rostral; upper preoculars not divided, or if divided, loreal conspicuously longer than high.......................... 5

4 b. Prenasal separated from rostral by small scales; upper preoculars often sub-divided; rostral usually wider than high; a pattern of dorsal blotches made up by aggregation of punctations ......Southwestern speckled rattlesnake (*C. mitchellii pyrrhus*) p. 303

5 a. Tail with alternating black and light gray rings, both colors contrasting so sharply with the color of the hinder part of the body as to give the impression of the wrong tail being attached to the snake 6

5 b. Tail not of alternating black and light gray rings in sharp contrast to the body color immediately anterior to the tail.......................... 8

6 a. Dark tail rings narrower than light ones; postocular light stripe, if present, passing backward above angle of mouth; scales between supraoculars rarely more than two; lower half of proximal rattle light in color
......Mohave rattlesnake (*C. scutulatus*) p. 305

6 b. Dark and light tail rings of about equal width; postocular light stripe, if present, intersecting the supralabials one to three scales anterior to the angle of the mouth (Fig. 98); scales between supraoculars usually three or more; proximal rattle black
......Western diamond rattlesnake group 7

7 a. First lower labials not usually divided transversely; markings with dark punctations
......Western diamond rattlesnake (*C. atrox*) p. 298

7 b. First lower labials usually divided transversely; dark punctations weak or absent from markings
......Red diamond rattlesnake (*C. ruber*) p. 299

8 a. Two internasal scales.......................... 9

8 b. More than two internasals (i.e., three or more scales in contact with rostral and between nasals)
.,....Prairie rattlesnake group (*C. viridis*) p. 306

9 a. No vertical light line on the posterior edge of the prenasals and first upper labials................ 10

9 b. A well-defined light line on the posterior edge of the prenasals and first upper labials
......Eastern diamond rattlesnake (*C. adamanteus*) p. 297

10 a. Supraoculars not pitted, sutured, or with outer edges broken.............................. 11

10 b. Supraoculars pitted, sutured, or with outer edges broken
Panamint rattlesnake (*C. mitchellii stephensi*) p. 304

11 a. Head decidedly small for a rattlesnake; pattern a series of cross-bands or transverse blotches comprising brown punctations on a pink, buff, or gray background
......Tiger rattlesnake (*C. tigris*) p. 305

11 b. Head larger, head length in adult contained less than 25 times in body length; width of proximal rattle contained more than two and a half times in head length............................ 12

12 a. A definite division between the scales in the frontal and prefrontal areas; enlarged scales in anterior part of frontal area; front part of body not black and without chevron-shaped cross-bands........ 13

12 b. No definite division between the scales of the prefrontal and frontal area not distinctly enlarged; normal pattern consisting of chevron-shaped cross-bars, or all black
......Timber rattlesnakes (*C. horridus*) p. 301

13 a. Dorsal scale rows usually less than 24; scale rows at center of tail 11 or fewer; ventrals usually less than 168; usually a single loreal, longer than high; a pattern of numerous relatively small spots; size small, adults rarely exceeding two feet
......Arizona spotted rattlesnake (*C. triseriatus pricei*) p. 306

13 b. Dorsal scale rows usually more than 24; scale rows at center of tail 12 or more; ventrals usually more than 169; usually more than one loreal, but if single, loreal higher than long; size larger.... 14

14 a. Loreal usually single; tail rings sharply contrasting in color
......Mohave rattlesnake (*C. scutulatus*) p. 305

14 b. Usually two or more loreals; tail usually black; a pattern of diamonds in which the light scales are entirely light and with a pair of light spots in the dark ground color of each diamond
......Black-tailed rattlesnake (*C. molossus molossus*) p. 305

Eastern Diamond Rattlesnake.—*Crotalus adamanteus* Beauvois. A bold pattern of black or dark brown diamonds, with lighter centers, and with contrasting borders of yellow one scale in width. The pattern becomes less sharp toward the tail. Ground color olive to dark brown. A vertical light line on the posterior edge of the prenasals and first supralabials.

Range.—Florida with many of the adjacent keys, and the coastal plains north to Albemarle Sound in North Carolina, and west to extreme southeastern Louisiana.

The eastern diamond rattlesnake is the largest poisonous snake in North America. The fangs are correspondingly long, and may measure an inch in straight-line length in large individuals.

This snake inhabits the wild brush country of the southern lowlands. Those who have encountered it in its native haunts invariably speak of the experience with awe. There is considerable disagreement as to its temperament. Some claim that it is bold and aggressive, while others maintain that it is sluggish and slow to rattle. Individuals encountered in the field usually assume a defensive posture and hold their ground, however, rather than seeking safety in flight.

Size.—Adults average about 5 feet in length. The maximum appears to be an 8 foot 9 inch specimen recorded by Stejneger.

Food.—Adults feed largely on rabbits, although birds and other small mammals are also taken.

Breeding habits.—Broods average nine or ten, the young measuring about 14 inches at birth. Van Hyning found 14 new-born young in a gopher tortoise burrow on August 21.

Western Diamond Rattlesnake.—*Crotalus atrox* Baird and Girard. (Plate 32). A pattern of brown diamonds or rhombs, consisting of aggregations of minute dots, on a buff, gray or gray-brown background. The diamonds are edged with lighter-colored borders, often with a narrow black zone just inside the light border. The tail, which is marked with alternate black and white rings, contrasts sharply with the body.

Range.—Extreme southeastern Missouri and central Arkansas west through Oklahoma, Texas (except the Panhandle and east of Long. 95°), central and southern New Mexico and Arizona, southeastern California, extreme northeastern Lower California, and Tiburon Island in the Gulf of California. Introduced in Vernon Co., Wisconsin.

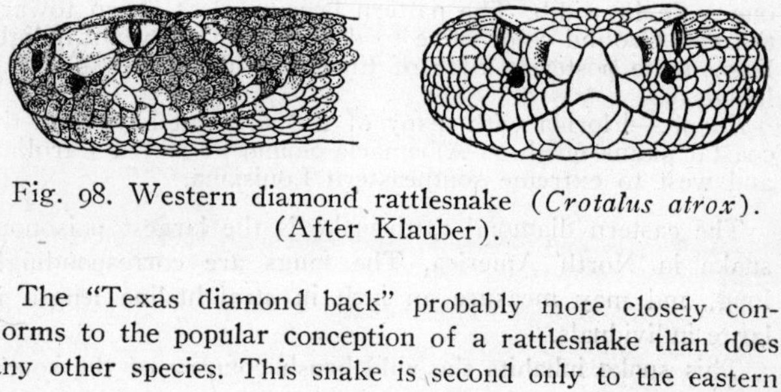

Fig. 98. Western diamond rattlesnake (*Crotalus atrox*). (After Klauber).

The "Texas diamond back" probably more closely conforms to the popular conception of a rattlesnake than does any other species. This snake is second only to the eastern diamond-back in size, and because of its wide distribution and aggressive nature it accounts for more fatalities than any other North American snake.

The habitat of this snake is the arid southwest, where it is at home in a variety of environments ranging through prairie and desert flats to the rough foothills of mountains. At altitudes above one or two thousand feet it is usually replaced by other species. It is a bold and aggressive snake, and when disturbed almost invariably throws itself into a defensive coil, rattling persistently, from which it will strike viciously.

Size.—Adults average about 4½ feet in length. Occasional individuals may exceed 7 feet.

Food.—Consists chiefly of rodents, apparently predominently of rabbits. Birds are also taken occasionally.

Breeding Habits.—Mating takes place in early spring. Few records of number of young are available, but broods apparently average about 10, occasionally numbering 20 or more. Young are about a foot in length at birth.

Red Diamond Rattlesnake.—*Crotalus ruber* Cope. (Plate 32). The red rattlesnake is so much like the western diamond-back rattlesnake in pattern and so well distinguished by its reddish general color from the usual coloration of the diamond-back, that its recognition offers little difficulty. It is distinguished also by the division of the first pair of lower labials, a scale character, forming a pair of anterior chin shields.

Range.—Southeastern Los Angeles County southward (west of the desert) into Lower California.

This large rattlesnake, much like *atrox* in general appearance, is said to be much more sluggish in disposition. It is most plentiful in the rock and chaparral area of the western foothills of the Coast Ranges.

Size.—Reaches a length of 6 feet, adults averaging about 4½ feet.

Food.—Largely rodents, and especially ground squirrels and young rabbits.

Breeding Habits.—Presumably similar to those of the western diamond rattlesnake. Broods of young average 8 (Klauber).

Sidewinder.—*Crotalus cerastes* Hallowell. (Plate 33). The conspicuous hornlike processes over each eye distinguish this species from all other rattlesnakes. Dorsal scales strongly keeled and with posterior bosses. Ground color cream to light gray, with a series of 31 to 34 square brownish blotches along the midline; often yellow or orange on the midline between the blotches.

Range.—The sandy deserts of northwestern Lower California, southern California, southern Nevada, southwestern Utah, and south and western Arizona.

The sidewinder, often called the horned rattlesnake, is in many ways the most remarkable of the rattlesnakes. Its habitat is the loose desert sand, and it is curiously adapted to this environment. It often lies almost buried in the sand,

Fig. 99. Head of sidewinder (*Crotalus cerastes*), front and side views. Note the hornlike process over each eye. (After Klauber).

and Klauber has pointed out that the "horn" over the eye would form a small cliff in the drifting sand that would leave the eye uncovered, or that it would form a partial shade for the eye from the intense glare and heat of the desert sun. The most extraordinary feature, however, is the sidewinder's locomotion. This looping, sidewise locomotion enables it to travel with ease over loose sand where other snakes are greatly handicapped. Mosauer has compared its locomotion to the rolling of a coil spring, although the snake of course, does not actually roll. The head, with the neck sharply bent, is brought forward through the air and set down. Then the body is brought forward through the air in a rolling motion, and laid down in front of the head. Thus the body is never dragged as it is in other snakes, and good tracks in sand will show a perfect outline of every belly scale. The looping motion is repeated continually, so that the trail of one of these snakes looks like a series of J's lying parallel to one another, and going off at an oblique angle to the direction in which the snake is pointing. The hook of each J is formed by the head and neck, and the transverse cross-bar by the tail. As these snakes are almost entirely nocturnal, their presence is often shown only by these peculiar tracks.

The sidewinder is the only rattlesnake of the United States in which females exceed the males in average size.

Size.—Adults average about 18 inches in length. Large individuals will exceed 2½ feet.

Food.—The few available records show that small desert rodents and lizards are eaten.

Breeding Habits.—Mating takes place in late April and early May. No information is available on the number of young.

Timber Rattlesnake.—*Crotalus horridus horridus* Linnaeus. (Plate 33). A series of V-shaped cross-bands, dark brown or black in color and occasionally broken, on a yellow or brown ground color. Often a reddish-brown dorsal stripe on the posterior part of the body. Occasional individuals are very dark, sometimes almost black.

Range.—Southern Maine to northern Alabama and Georgia; west through Illinois to northeastern Texas, eastern halves of Oklahoma, Kansas, and Iowa to extreme southeastern Minnesota. Intergrades with *C. h. atricaudatus* on the south. (Fig. 102).

This snake, often called the banded rattlesnake, is widely distributed through the most densely populated areas of the U. S. It prefers timbered areas where rocks, such as limestone outcroppings, are abundant. This, together with the fact that it has been persistently persecuted for generations, has resulted in a very spotty distribution over most of its range. In the fall great numbers gather to den up for the winter, in limestone crevices or similar situations, often in company with copperheads and blacksnakes. Hundreds are sometimes killed in a raid on a single den.

The disposition of the timber rattlesnake is rather gentle, although it will often stand its ground if cornered.

Size.—The average length is about 3½ feet. Ditmars records an individual that measured 6 feet, 2 inches.

Food.—The diet of this snake consists almost exclusively of small mammals, chiefly mice. Uhler, Cottam, and Clarke recently analyzed the contents of 141 food-containing stomachs of this snake from the George Washington National Forest, Virginia. They found that mice made up 38 per cent of the diet, squirrels and chipmunks 25 per cent, rabbits 18 per cent, shrews 5 per cent, and birds (chiefly song birds) 13 per cent.

Breeding Habits.—Remarkably little is known of the breeding habits of this relatively abundant species.

Canebrake Rattlesnake.—*Crotalus horridus atricaudatus* Latreille. Distinguished from the northern timber rattlesnake by having a postocular dark stripe distinct and contrasting with the ground color; a mid-dorsal brown or reddish-brown stripe anteriorly; and ground color generally pale. Dorsal scales 25 (23 in *C. horridus horridus*).

Range.—Coastal plain of the South Atlantic and Gulf states, from North Carolina to eastern Texas; northward in the Mississippi lowland to the southern tip of Illinois. (Fig. 102).

This relative of the more familiar banded or timber rattler of the northeastern states is a larger and apparently somewhat more stocky form. It inhabits the canebrake bottomlands of the larger southern rivers.

Size.—Average length more than four feet, maximum more than six feet.

Food.—Small mammals.

Breeding Habits.—No actual records of the courtship, birth of young, or number in a brood are available for this species.

Eastern Rock Rattlesnake.—*Crotalus lepidus lepidus* Kennicott. A distinctive pattern of widely separated cross-bands, together with the scale characters mentioned in the key, serve to distinguish the rock rattlesnakes. The eastern subspecies is distinguished from the Arizona form by a more mottled and more pinkish ground color between the cross-bands, which are also somewhat less sharply defined, and by the presence of a dark stripe from the eye to the angle of the mouth.

Range.—Western Texas in the Big Bend region and along the Rio Grande as far as Presidio Co., southward into Mexico in the mountains.

Green Rock Rattlesnake.—*Crotalus lepidus klauberi* Gloyd. Distinguished by the greenish-gray ground color on which the dark brown or black cross-bands are sharply set off; absence of the stripe from eye to angle of mouth; and the lighter color of the belly.

Range.—Mountains of southeastern Arizona, western New Mexico, and the El Paso region in western Texas, southward into Mexico.

The rock rattlesnakes are inhabitants of the mountain ranges of western Texas and Arizona, where they are found mostly at high levels and especially in the rock slides which provide shelter for both the snakes and their small rodent prey. They are not especially aggressive and there seems to be no record of a human being being bitten by this species. It is noteworthy that the rattle is relatively large in proportion to the size of the snake.

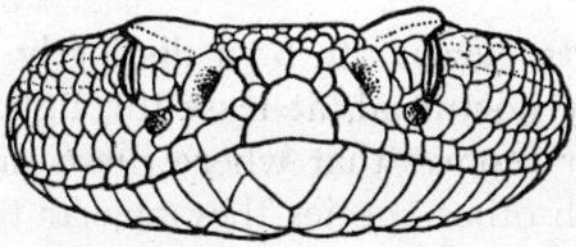

Fig. 100. California speckled rattlesnake (*Crotalus mitchellii pyrrhus*), to show small scales between nasal and rostral. (After Klauber).

Size.—Adult specimens measure about 2 feet in total length; newly born young average less than eight inches.

Food.—The food doubtless consists mainly of small rodents of the rocky terrain in which these snakes live. A captive specimen is reported to have fed freely on house mice (Falck, *Copeia,* 1940:135) but accepted some frogs and salamanders.

Breeding Habits.—The young are born alive and average only four in number (Klauber). Further details are not available for this species.

Southwestern Speckled Rattlesnake.—*Crotalus mitchellii pyrrhus* Cope.* Coloration highly variable, but usually read-

* *Crotalus mitchellii mitchellii* is confined to southern Lower California.

ily distinguishable by the sandy speckled appearance; differs from all other rattlesnakes in the United States by the row of small scales between the rostral and the nasal shields. (Fig. 100).

Range.—Central and southwestern Arizona and adjacent California to San Bernardino County; southward into northern Lower California.

Panamint Rattlesnake.—*Crotalus mitchellii stephensi* Klauber. Characterized by a pattern of transverse blotches on body and tail, on a generally sandy ground color, which is highly variable in tone—gray, yellow, or reddish brown, with the blotches similarly variable in color from gray or buff to deep reddish brown. The anterior nasal shield is in contact with the rostral. Traces of sutures on the anterior nasal appear to represent a rudimentary stage of the development of the separate row of scales of *C. m. pyrrhus.*

Range.—East of the Sierra Nevada in Inyo County, California south to central San Bernardino County, and the adjacent part of Nevada.

Klauber reports *pyrrhus* to be a distinctly nervous species. It is distinctively nocturnal, at least throughout the summer. The same author reports that where these rattlesnakes share the territory with other species they appear to den separately for hibernation. Both *pyrrhus* and *stephensi* are distinctively snakes of rocky slopes, rarely present on sand flats or level desert areas, and thus they are somewhat segregated from the western diamond-back, the horned rattlesnake, and the Mohave rattlesnake, which inhabit the more level and sandy areas.

Size.—Maximum size of the southwestern speckled rattlesnake 48 inches, 43 inches being an average adult measurement; *stephensi* rarely exceeds 34 inches.

Food.—Mainly small rodents, with occasional birds and lizards. Young specimens probably eat a larger proportion of lizards.

Breeding Habits.—The few references indicate relatively small broods, 3 to 5 young being recorded from the body of females of *pyrrhus,* 6 to 8 from *stephensi.*

Klauber, L. M., *Trans. San Diego Soc. Nat. Hist.,* Vol. 8, pp. 149-184, pl. 19-20, Figs. 1-3, map.

Black-tailed Rattlesnake.—*Crotalus molossus molossus* Baird and Girard.* (Plate 33). Readily distinguished by its black tail, and by the color pattern, in which the rhombic blotches have a pair of light spots. The blotches often connect with lateral spots to make cross-bands extending to the ventrals. The ground color in Texas specimens is distinctly greenish; in Arizona it may be straw yellow.

Range.—Central and western Texas to New Mexico and Arizona, southward on the Mexican Plateau.

The black-tailed rattlesnake is one of the large and aggressive species of the American southwest. Some specimens encountered by the authors in the field were the reverse of aggressive, attempting to escape and even refusing to coil or rattle. It is found in a wide variety of habitats, ranging from the woody thickets of the Edwards Plateau in Texas to the rock slides of the higher mountain ranges in its area, like the Chisos and Huachucas.

Size.—The maximum recorded length appears to be 50 inches. Newly born young measure about 12 inches.

Food.—Doubtless mainly small and medium-sized rodents.

Breeding Habits.—No records of courtship and mating of this species are known to the writers. Broods of young average only 5 (Klauber).

Mohave Rattlesnake.—*Crotalus scutulatus scutulatus* Kennicott. A moderate-sized species with diamond-shaped markings bordered by light scales, black bands around the tail much narrower than the light spaces between them, postocular light stripe passing backward above the angle of the mouth, lower half of first segment of rattle light in color; usually only two scales between the ocular plates.

Range.—From the Mohave Desert in California into the southern part of Nevada and through southwestern Arizona to Mexico.

Size.—Average size of large male specimens 3 feet, 4 inches, of females 35 inches (Klauber).

Food.—Presumably small and medium-sized rodents.

Breeding Habits.—Average brood 8 (Klauber).

Tiger Rattlesnake.—*Crotalus tigris* Kennicott. A pattern of numerous rather narrow but not very sharply defined darker cross-bands on a ground color of gray, buff, or pink-

---

* Another subspecies, *C. m. nigrescens,* occurs in Mexico.

ish gray, about six dark rings on the tail in females and eight in males; head relatively small, and rattle large. The two internasals (instead of three or more) distinguish this form at once from other rattlesnakes which resemble it in pattern.

Range.—South central Arizona southward in Mexico to central Sonora.

This snake appears to inhabit especially the rocky foothills of the mountain ranges of southern Arizona, and the adjacent desert areas. It was long confused with the snake of the Mohave Desert now known as *Crotalus mitchellii stephensi.* The tiger rattlesnake appears to be relatively inoffensive and not prone to rattle or to strike.

Size.—Largest specimen recorded 31 inches.

Food.—Doubtless small mammals and especially rodents.

Breeding Habits.—Unknown.

Klauber, L. M., *Trans. San Diego Soc. Nat. Hist.,* Vol 6, pp. 353-370, pl. 23, map.

Arizona Spotted Rattlesnake.—*Crotalus triseriatus pricei* Van Denburgh. A dorsal pattern of a double row of small more or less squarish spots averaging fifty to fifty-five on the body, distinguishes this small species sharply from all others in our list; it is the northernmost form of a series of subspecies characteristic of the Mexican Plateau.

Range.—Mountains of southeastern Arizona southward into Mexico to the state of Durango, where this subspecies meets *Crotalus t. triseriatus.*

Size.—Maximum length about twenty-four inches; juveniles 5½ to 8 inches long.

Food.—Small rodents probably form the chief food of this species.

Breeding Habits.—Average number of young in a brood 5 (Klauber).

THE PRAIRIE RATTLESNAKES
(*Crotalus viridis*)

Plate 34

The chain of no less than six subspecies into which the prairie rattlesnake is divided forms a somewhat typical example of a series of intergrading subspecies. These forms

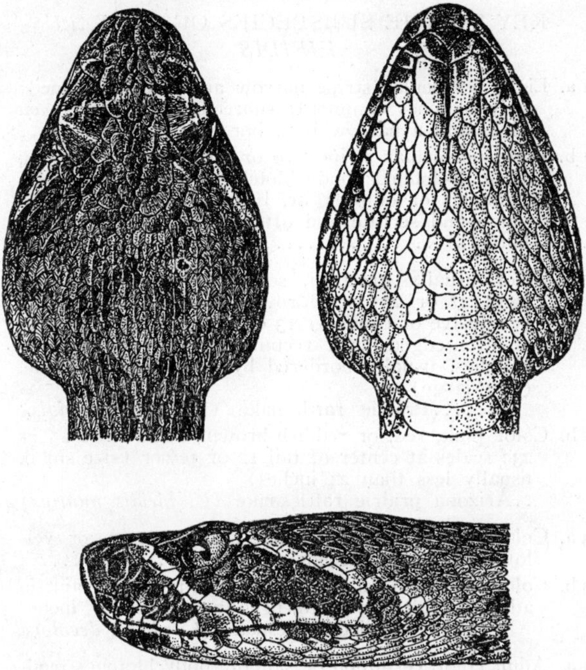

Fig. 101. Prairie rattlesnake (*Crotalus v. viridis*).

present a wide range of size, color pattern, and of scale characters. Klauber's analysis of *viridis* into its component geographic forms is a model of taxonomic study. His detailed statistical studies, especially of the typical Great Plains form, represents a new trend in modern zoological research, applied for the first time to snakes.

Klauber, L. M., 1930. New and renamed Species of *Crotalus confluentus* Say, with Remarks on related Species. *Trans. San Diego Soc. Nat. Hist.,* Vol. 6, pp. 95-144, 4 plates, 1 map—1936-1940. A statistical Study of the Rattlesnakes. *Occ. Papers San Diego Soc. Nat. Hist.,* Nos. 1-6.

KEY TO THE SUBSPECIES OF *CROTALUS VIRIDIS*

1 a. Light postocular stripe narrow and sharply defined; body blotches commonly subrectangular, with even edges and a narrow light border 2

1 b. Light postocular stripe two or more scales in width, often ill-defined; body blotches, if distinct, usually diamonds or ellipses, or, if rectangular, the edges rough and serrate and often without narrow light borders 3

2 a. Color usually greenish, somtimes brownish; scale rows 27 or 25; scale rows around center of tail (exclusive of caudals) 13 or more; pattern usually of even-edged dark rectangular or subhexagonal blotches, usually bordered by a narrow light line (size large)
......Prairie rattlesnake (*C. viridis viridis*)

2 b. Color pink, red, or reddish-brown; scale rows 25 or 23; scales at center of tail 12 or fewer (size small, usually less than 24 inches)
..Arizona prairie rattlesnake (*C. viridis nuntius*)

3 a. Coloration usually dark, not straw, cream, or yellow; adult size exceeds 25 inches 4

3 b. Color straw, cream, or yellow, blotches often faint in adults; adult size small, usually less than 25 inches
......Faded rattlesnake (*C. viridis decolor*)

4 a. Adult color vermilion or salmon, body blotches tending to disappear in the adult
....Grand Canyon rattlesnake (*C. viridis abyssus*)

4 b. Adult color not vermilion or salmon; body blotches well-defined, or body black 5

5 a. Ground color lighter, usually buff or drab; body blotches shorter or about equal to the lighter interspaces; secondary lateral spots not well-defined
......Great Basin rattlesnake (*C. v. lutosus*)

5 b. Ground color darker, with dark brown or black dorsal blotches, which are usually longer than the light spaces between them; a secondary series of lateral blotches well-defined (occasional mountain specimens nearly uniform black)
......Pacific rattlesnake (*C. v. oreganus*)

Prairie Rattlesnake.—*Crotalus viridis viridis* Rafinesque. (Plate 34). A bold pattern of darker squarish or rounded

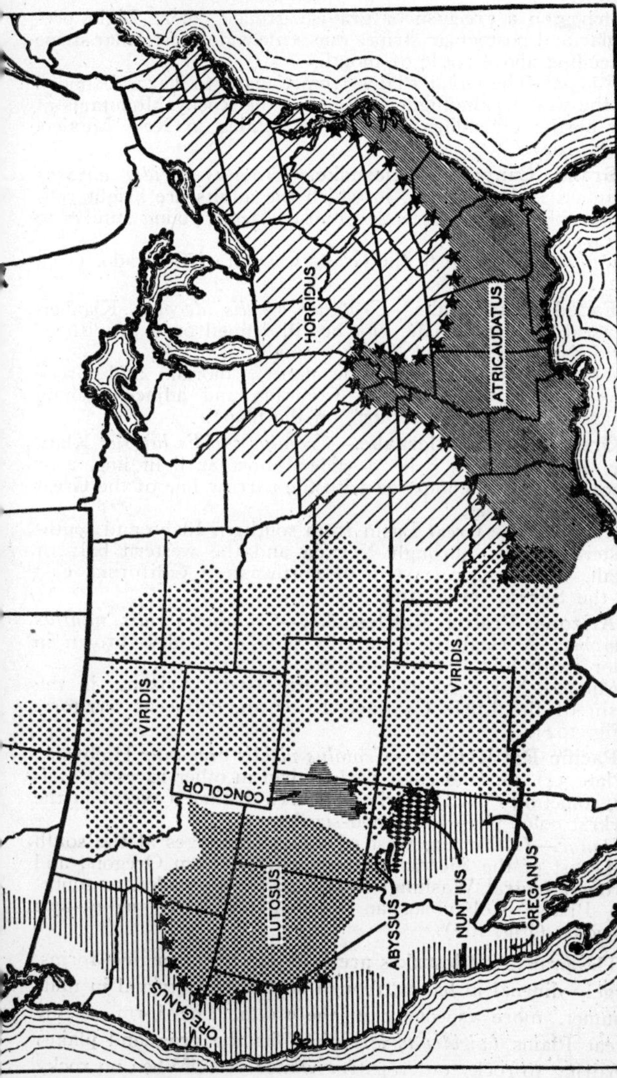

Fig. 102. Distribution of the subspecies of the Prairie rattlesnake (*Crotalus viridis*) and of the banded rattlesnakes (*Crotalus horridus*). The form in eastern Utah labeled "concolor" should be *decolor*. (From Klauber).

blotches on a greenish or grayish ground color. Light preocular and postocular stripes one scale wide; postocular stripe extending above angle of mouth.

Range.—The Great Plains from Canada to Texas, bounded on the west by the higher ranges of the Rocky Mountains at the north; extending into the mountains in New Mexico. (Fig. 102).

Grand Canyon Rattlesnake.—*Crotalus viridis abyssus* Klauber. A large form, in which the adults are bright reddish, with blotches of body almost absent; young similar to *v. viridis.*

Range.—Confined to the Grand Canyon of Colorado. (Fig. 102).

Faded Rattlesnake.—*Crotalus viridis decolor* Klauber. General coloration pale, blotches ill-defined on a grayish or yellowish gray ground color; a small form.

Range.—The basins of the upper Colorado and Green Rivers in extreme western Colorado and adjacent Utah. (Fig. 102, labeled "concolor" on the map).

Great Basin Rattlesnake.—*Crotalus viridis lutosus* Klauber. A large form, with a wide postocular light line, 2 or 3 scales wide, as compared with the narrow line of the Great Plains subspecies.

Range.—The Great Basin from southern Idaho and southeastern Oregon through Nevada and the western half of Utah, with a narrow strip of northeastern California, east of the Sierra. (Fig. 102).

Arizona Prairie Rattlesnake.—*Crotalus viridis nuntius* Klauber. A small race, usually pink or reddish brown in color, with blotches well-defined.

Range.—North central and northeastern Arizona, in the basin of the Little Colorado River and adjacent territory. (Fig. 102).

Pacific Rattlesnake.—*Crotalus viridis oreganus* Holbrook. (Plate 34). Ground color darker than in other races of *viridis,* sometimes black; darker blotches distinct (except in the darkest color phase); a good-sized race.

Range.—California, west of the coast ranges at the south and west of the Sierras at the north; western Oregon; and through central Washington, east of the Cascades, to southern British Columbia; an isolated population in eastern Arizona. (Fig. 102).

The prairie rattlesnakes are bold and wide-ranging forms, largely diurnal in habits, though doubtless nocturnal in midsummer, more especially in the south. The form of the Great Plains (*viridis viridis*) inhabits the grassland plains, repairing to rocky outcrops for winter dens. When no rocky ledges are available, prairie dog dens supply winter refuges. It is this species that has been thought to live in amity with the prairie dog and burrowing owl and it doubtless does often inhabit prairie dog and other rodent burrows. The other races occupy a wide variety of habitats, from desert conditions with *nuntius* and *lutosus* to the forests of the Pacific slope where *oreganus* is found. These snakes are often killed in large numbers at their dens. Hall (1929, *Bull. Antiv. Inst. Amer.*, Vol. 3, p. 79) describes a typical den of *lutosus,* in Nevada, in broken rock at the edge of a butte.

Size.—The largest of the subspecies seems to be the prairie rattlesnake (*viridis viridis*) with a maximum recorded length of 5 feet. The dwarfed forms *nuntius* and *decolor* do not seem to exceed about 30 inches.

Food.—Primarily small rodents.

Breeding Habits.—Klauber has shown that broods of the prairie rattlesnake vary from 4 to 21 (average 12), and that the smaller races tend to have smaller broods.

Willard's Rattlesnake.—*Crotalus willardi* Meek. Characterized by a general brownish color with narrow, widely spaced light cross-bands, and boldly marked light stripes on the head; a vertical light line on the middle of the rostral shield and mental; tail with longitudinal stripes instead of cross-bands.

Range.—Santa Rita and Huachuca Mountains, at higher elevations, southward into the Mexican state of Durango.

Size.—Maximum recorded length 24 inches.

Food.—Doubtless small mammals.

Breeding Habits.—A single record of a brood of 6 young.

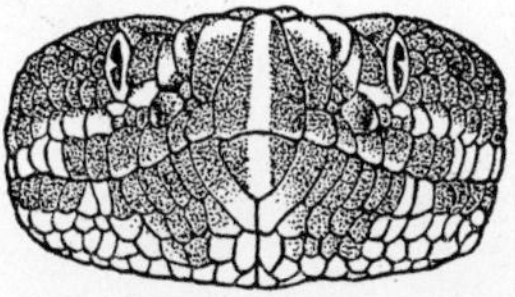

Fig. 103. Willard's rattlesnake (*Crotalus willardi*), to show characteristic line on rostral and mental. (After Klauber).

REFERENCES

GENERAL BOOKS

Hopley, C. C., 1882. Snakes: curiosities and wonders of serpent life, 614 pp., il. (London: Griffith and Farran).——Gadow, H. F., 1909. Amphibia and reptiles, 668 pp., il. (Cambridge Natural History, Vol. 8).——Barbour, T., 1926. Reptiles and amphibians; their habits and adaptations, 125 pp., il. (Houghton Mifflin Co.).——Ditmars, R. L., 1931. Snakes of the world, 207 pp., il. (The Macmillan Co.).——Hoopes, I., 1936. Reptiles in the home zoo., 64 pp., il. *Special Publ. New England Mus. Nat. Hist.*, No. 1——Pope, C. H., 1937. Snakes alive and how they live, 238 pp., il. (Viking Press).——Curran, C. H., and C. Kauffeld, 1937. Snakes and their ways, 285 pp., il. (Harper & Bros.).

NORTH AMERICA

Cope, E. D., 1900. The crocodilians, lizards, and snakes of North America, 1117 pp., il. *Report U. S. Nat. Mus. for 1898.*——Ditmars, R. L., 1936. The reptiles of North America, 476 pp., il. (Doubleday, Doran & Co.).——Conant, R., and W. Bridges, 1939. What snake is that?, 163 pp., il. (Appleton-Century).——Stejneger, L., and T. Barbour, 1939. A check list of North American amphibians and reptiles, 207 pp. (Harvard Univ. Press).——Perkins, C. B., 1940. A key to the snakes of the United States, 63 pp., il. *Bull. Zool. Soc. San Diego, No. 16.*

CANADA

Nash, C. W., 1908. Batrachians and reptiles of Ontario, 14 pp., *in* Vertebrates of Ontario.——Seton, E. T., 1918. A list of the turtles, snakes, and batrachians of Manitoba, *Ottawa Naturalist,* Vol. 32, pp. 79-83.——Logier, E. B. S.,

1939. The reptiles of Ontario, 63 pp., il., *Roy. Ontario Mus. Zool. Handbook No. 4.*

WESTERN NORTH AMERICA

Van Denburgh, John, **1922**. The Reptiles of Western North America, 415 pp., 71 plates. *Occ. Papers Calif. Acad. Sci.,* No. 10, Vol. 2.——Slevin, J. R., **1934**. A handbook of the reptiles and amphibians of the Pacific states. 73 pp., il. (*Calif. Acad. Sci., Special Publ.*).

NEW ENGLAND

Henshaw, Samuel, **1904**. Fauna of New England. 1. List of the Reptilia, 15 pp. *Occ. Papers Boston Soc. Nat. Hist.,* Vol. 7.——Babcock, H. L., **1929**. The snakes of New England, 30 pp., il. *Boston Soc. Nat. Hist., Nat. Hist. Guides,* No. 1.

UNITED STATES

ALABAMA

Löding, H. P., **1922**. A preliminary catalogue of Alabama amphibians and reptiles, 59 pp. *Geol. Surv. Alabama, Mus. Paper No. 5.*——Haltom, W. L., **1931**. Alabama reptiles, 145 pp., il. *Alabama Mus. Nat. Hist., Paper No. 11.*

ARIZONA

Van Denburgh, J., and J. R. Slevin, **1913**. A list of the amphibians and reptiles of Arizona, *Proc. Calif. Acad. Sci.* (*Fourth series*), Vol. 3, pp. 391-454, 12 pls.——Gloyd, H. K., **1937**. A herpetological consideration of faunal areas in Southern Arizona. *Bull. Chicago Acad. Sci.,* Vol. 5, pp. 79-136, 22 figs.

ARKANSAS

Dellinger, S. C., and J. D. Black, **1938**. Herpetology of Arkansas. Part one, The reptiles. *Occ. Papers Univ. Ark.*

Mus., No. 1, 47 pp.——Schwardt, H. H., **1938**. Reptiles of Arkansas. *Univ. Ark. Agr. Exp. Sta. Bull.* No. 357, 47 pp., il.

CALIFORNIA

Grinnell, Joseph, and C. L. Camp, **1917**. A distributional list of the amphibians and reptiles of California. *Univ. Calif. Publ. Zool.*, Vol. 17, pp. 127-208, 14 figs.——Klauber, L. M., **1931**. A statistical survey of the snakes of the southern border of California. *Bull. Zool. Soc. San Diego*, No. 8, 93 pp., il.——**1939**. Studies of reptile life in the arid southwest. *Bull. Zool. Soc. San Diego*, No. 14, 100 pp.

COLORADO

Ellis, M. M., and Junius Henderson, **1913**. The Amphibia and Reptilia of Colorado. *Univ. Colo. Studies*, Vol. 10, pp. 39-129, 8 pls.——Same, **1915**. Part II, *Publ. Colo. Biol. Surv.*, No. 17, pp. 253-263.——Jones-Burdick, W. H., **1939**. Guide to the snakes of Colorado. *Univ. Colo. Mus. Leaflet* No. 1, 11 pp., 6 figs.

CONNECTICUT

Lamson, G. H., **1935**. The reptiles of Connecticut. *Conn. Geol. Nat. Hist. Survey Bull.* No. 54, 35 pp., 12 pls.

DELAWARE

Fowler, H. W., **1925**. Records of amphibians and reptiles for Delaware, Maryland, and Virginia, I. Delaware, *Copeia*, No. 145, pp. 57-61.

DISTRICT OF COLUMBIA

Hay, W. P., **1902**. A list of the batrachians and reptiles of the District of Columbia and vicinity. *Proc. Biol. Soc. Wash.*, Vol. 15, pp. 121-145.

FLORIDA

Carr, A. F., Jr., **1940**. A contribution to the herpetology of Florida. *Univ. Fla. Publ. Biol. Sci.,* Vol. 3, 118 pp.

GEORGIA

No state lists of snakes available.

IDAHO

Stejneger, Leonhard, **1891**. Results of a biological reconnaissance of south-central Idaho. Annotated list of reptiles and batrachians, *N. Amer. Fauna,* No. 5, pp. 109-113.——Erwin, R. P., **1925**. Snakes in Idaho. *Copeia,* No. 138, pp. 6-7.—Tanner, Wilmer W., **1941**. The reptiles and amphibians of Idaho, *Great Basin Nat.,* Vol. 2, pp. 87-97.

ILLINOIS

Garman, H., **1892**. A synopsis of the reptiles and amphibians of Illinois. *Bull. Ill. State Lab. Nat. Hist.,* Vol. 3, 175 pp., il.——Schmidt, K. P., and W. L. Necker, **1935**. Amphibians and reptiles of the Chicago Region. *Bull. Chicago Acad. Sci.,* Vol. 5, pp. 57-77.

INDIANA

Hay, O. P., **1892**. The batrachians and reptiles of the state of Indiana. *Ann. Rep. Dept. Geol. Ind.,* No. 17, 204 pp., il.

IOWA

Guthrie, J. E., **1926**. The snakes of Iowa. *Bull. Iowa State Agric. Exp. Station,* No. 239, 46 pp., il.

KANSAS

Branson, E. B., **1904**. The snakes of Kansas. *Univ. Kansas Sci. Bull.,* Vol. 2, 78 pp., il.——Gloyd, H. K., **1928**. The amphibians and reptiles of Franklin County, Kansas. *Trans. Kansas Acad. Sci.*, Vol. 31, pp. 115-141.

KENTUCKY

Funkhauser, W. D., **1925**. Wild life in Kentucky. *Ky. Geol. Surv.*, (series 6) Vol. 16, 385 pp., il.——Dury, Ralph, and R. S. Williams, **1933**. Notes on some Kentucky amphibians and reptiles. *Bull. Baker-Hunt Mus., Covington,* No. 1, 22 pp.

LOUISIANA

Beyer, G. E., **1900**. Louisiana herpetology, etc. *Proc. Louisiana Soc. Nat.*, 1897-1899, App. 1., 45 pp.

MAINE

Verrill, A. E., **1863**. Catalogue of the reptiles and batrachians found in the vicinity of Norway, Oxford Co., Maine. *Proc. Boston Soc. Nat. Hist.*, Vol. 9, pp. 195-199.——(See also New England).

MARYLAND

Kelly, H. A., A. W. Davis, and H. C. Robertson, **1936**. Snakes of Maryland. *Nat. Hist. Soc. Maryland* (special publ.). 103 pp., il.

MASSACHUSETTS

See New England.

MICHIGAN

Ruthven, Alexander G., Crystal Thompson, and Helen T. Gaige, **1928**. The herpetology of Michigan. *Mich. Handbook Series, Univ. Mich.,* No. 3, 228 pp., il.

MINNESOTA

No state list of snakes available. An account of the herpetology of the state is in preparation by W. J. Breckenridge.

MISSISSIPPI

No state list of snakes available.

MISSOURI

Hurter, Julius, **1911**. Herpetology of Missouri. *Trans. Acad. Sci. St. Louis,* Vol. 20, pp. 59-274, 7 pls.

MONTANA

Coues, Elliott, and H. C. Yarrow, **1878**. Notes on the herpetology of Dakota and Montana. *Bull. U. S. Geol. Survey,* Vol. 4, pp. 259-291.

NEBRASKA

Taylor, W. E., **1892**. The Ophidia of Nebraska. *Ann. Rep. Nebr. State Board Agric.,* Vol. for 1891, pp. 310-357.

NEVADA

Linsdale, J. M., **1940**. Amphibians and reptiles in Nevada. *Proc. Amer. Acad. Arts Sci.,* Vol. 73, pp. 197-257, 29 figs.

NEW HAMPSHIRE

Oliver, J. A., and J. R. Bailey, **1939**. Amphibians and reptiles of New Hampshire, exclusive of marine forms. *Biol. Surv. Conn. Watershed, Surv. Rep.* No. 4, pp. 195-217, 1 pl.

NEW JERSEY

Fowler, H. W., **1907**. The amphibians and reptiles of New Jersey. *Ann. Rep. N. J. State Mus.,* Vol. for 1906, pp. 23-348, il.——Trapido, Harold, **1937**. The snakes of New Jersey, a guide. *Newark Mus.* (*special publ.*), 60 pp., il.

NEW MEXICO

Van Denburgh, John, **1924**. Notes on the herpetology of New Mexico, with a list of species known from that state.

Proc. Calif. Acad. Sci., (Fourth series) Vol. 13, pp. 189-230.

NEW YORK

De Kay, J. E., **1842**. Zoology of New York . . . Pt. 3, Reptiles and amphibians, 104 pp., 23 pls.——Eckel, E. C., and F. C. Paulmeier, **1902**. Catalogue of New York reptiles and batrachians. *N. Y. State Mus. Bull.,* No. 51, pp. 355-414.——Ditmars, R. L., **1896**. The snakes found within fifty miles of New York City. *Abstr. Proc. Linn. Soc. N. Y.,* No. 8, pp. 9-24.——Same, **1905**. The reptiles of the vicinity of New York City. *Amer. Mus. Journal,* Vol. 5, pp. 93-140, il.——Noble, G. K., **1927**. Distributional list of the reptiles and amphibians of the New York City Region. *Amer. Mus. Nat. Hist. Guide Leaflet,* No. 69, 9 pp.

NORTH CAROLINA

Brimley, C. S., **1907**. Artificial key to the species of snakes and lizards which are found in North Carolina. *Journal Elisha Mitchell Sci. Soc.,* Vol. 23, pp. 141-149.——Same, **1926**. Revised key and list of the amphibians and reptiles of North Carolina. *Ibid.,* Vol. 42, pp. 75-93.——(See also "Carolina Tips," Elon College, 1941 on).

NORTH DAKOTA

No state list available.

OHIO

Smith, W. H., **1882**. Report on the reptiles and amphibians of Ohio. *Rep. Ohio Geol. Survey,* Vol. 4, pp. 629-734, il.——Morse, Max, **1904**. Batrachians and reptiles of Ohio. *Proc. Ohio Acad. Sci.,* Vol. 4, (Special papers No. 9), pp. 93-144, il.——Conant, Roger, **1938**. The reptiles of Ohio. *Amer. Midl. Nat.,* Vol. 20, pp. 1-200, il.

OKLAHOMA

Van Vleet, A. H., **1902**. Snakes of Oklahoma. *2nd Bienn. Rep. Okla. Terr. Dept. Geol. Nat. Hist.,* (1901-1902), pp.

167-173.——Ortenburger, A. I., **1926**. A preliminary list of the snakes of Oklahoma, *Proc. Okla. Acad. Sci.,* Vol. 5, pp. 83-87.——Same, **1926**. A key to the lizards and snakes of Oklahoma. *Publ. Univ. Okla. Biol. Survey,* Vol. 2, pp. 209-239, il.

OREGON

Gordon, Kenneth, **1939**. The Amphibia and Reptilia of Oregon. *Oregon State Monographs, Zool.,* No. 1, 82 pp., il.

PENNSYLVANIA

Surface, H. A., **1906**. The serpents of Pennsylvania. *Bull. Div. Zool. Penn. State Dept. Agric.,* Vol. 4, pp. 113-208, il. ——Netting, M. G., **1939**. Hand list of the amphibians and reptiles of Pennsylvania. *Bienn. Rept. Pa. Fish Comm.* for 1936-1938, 26 pp.

RHODE ISLAND

Anonymous, **1918**. The reptiles of Rhode Island. Part II —Snakes. *Park Mus. Bull.,* Vol. 10, pp. 85-88.——See also New England.

SOUTH CAROLINA

Corrington, J. D., **1929**. Herpetology of the Columbia, South Carolina, Region. *Copeia,* No. 172, pp. 58-83.

SOUTH DAKOTA

Over, W. H., **1923**. Amphibians and reptiles of South Dakota, *S. D. Geol. Nat. Hist. Survey, Bull.* 12, 34 pp., 18 pls.

TENNESSEE

Rhoads, S. N., **1895**. Contributions to the zoology of Tennessee. No. 1, Reptiles and amphibians. *Proc. Acad. Nat. Sci. Phila.,* Vol. for 1895, pp. 376-407.——Blanchard, F. N., **1922**. The amphibians and reptiles of western Tennessee. *Occ. Papers Mus. Zool. Univ. Mich.,* No. 117, 18 pp.

TEXAS

Strecker, John K., **1915**. The reptiles and amphibians of Texas. *Baylor Bull.,* Vol. 18, No. 4, 82 pp. (Numerous county lists and other herpetological notes in the same publication, 1915-1935).

UTAH

Woodbury, A. M., **1931**. A descriptive catalogue of the reptiles of Utah. *Bull. Univ. Utah,* Vol. 21, No. 5, 129 pp., il.

VERMONT

No state list available. See New England.

VIRGINIA

Dunn, E. R., **1918**. A preliminary list of the reptiles and amphibians of Virginia. *Copeia,* No. 53, pp. 16-27.

WASHINGTON

Brown, W. C., and J. R. Slater, **1939**. The amphibians and reptiles of the islands of the State of Washington. *Occ. Papers Dept. Biol. Coll. Puget Sound,* No. 4, pp. 6-31.——Owen, R. P., **1940**. A list of the reptiles of Washington. *Copeia,* Vol. for 1940, pp. 169-172.

WEST VIRGINIA

No published list. M. G. Netting of the Carnegie Museum, Pittsburgh, has a mimeographed preliminary list available for distribution (1934).

WISCONSIN

Pope, T. E. B., and Dickinson, W. E., **1928**. The amphibians and reptiles of Wisconsin. *Bull. Publ. Mus. Milwaukee,* Vol. 8, 138 pp., il.

WYOMING

Cary, Merritt, 1917. Life zone investigations in Wyoming. *N. Amer. Fauna,* No. 42, 95 pp., il.

PLATES

Adult Blue Racer
(*Coluber constrictor flaviventris*)

Juvenile Blue Racer

Juvenile Milk Snake
(*Lampropeltis triangulum triangulum*)

Juvenile Fox Snake
(*Elaphe vulpina vulpina*)

Common Coral Snake
(*Micrurus fulvius fulvius*)
Poisonous

False Coral Snake
(*Lampropeltis elapsoides elapsoides*)
Non-poisonous

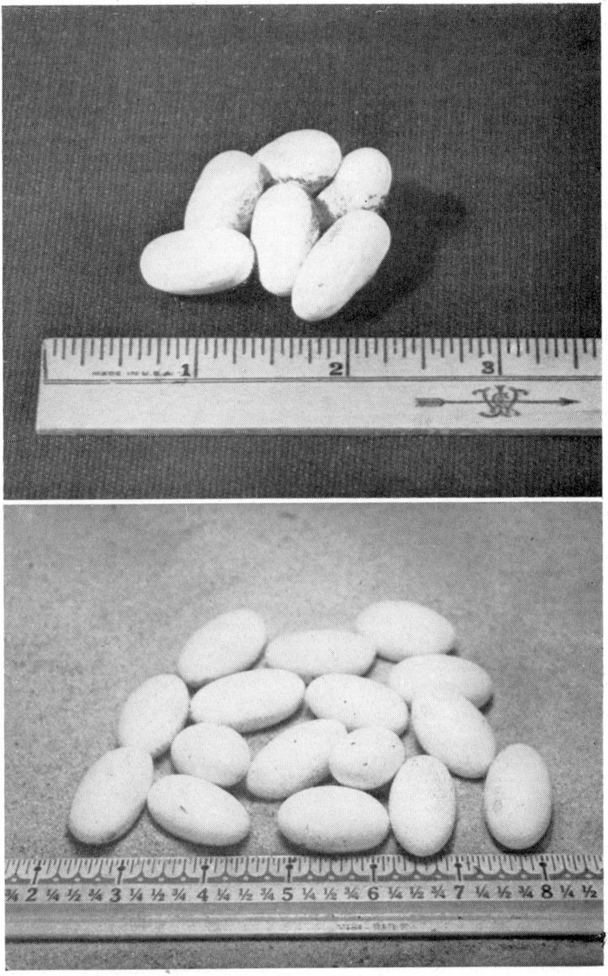

EGGS OF SNAKES.

(**Above**) Eggs of Smooth Green Snake. (**Below**) Eggs of Black snake (photo by Emil Rokosky).

Top: Texas Blind Snake, *Leptotyphlops d. dulcis*. Average length 8 inches.

Center: California Boa, *Lichanura r. roseofusca*. Average length 24 inches (photo by L. M. Klauber).

Bottom: Rubber Snake, *Charina Bottae*. Average length 18 inches.

Above: Mud Snake, *Farancia abacura.* Average length 4 feet.
Below: Yellow-lipped Snake, *Rhadinaea flavilata.* Average length 12 inches.

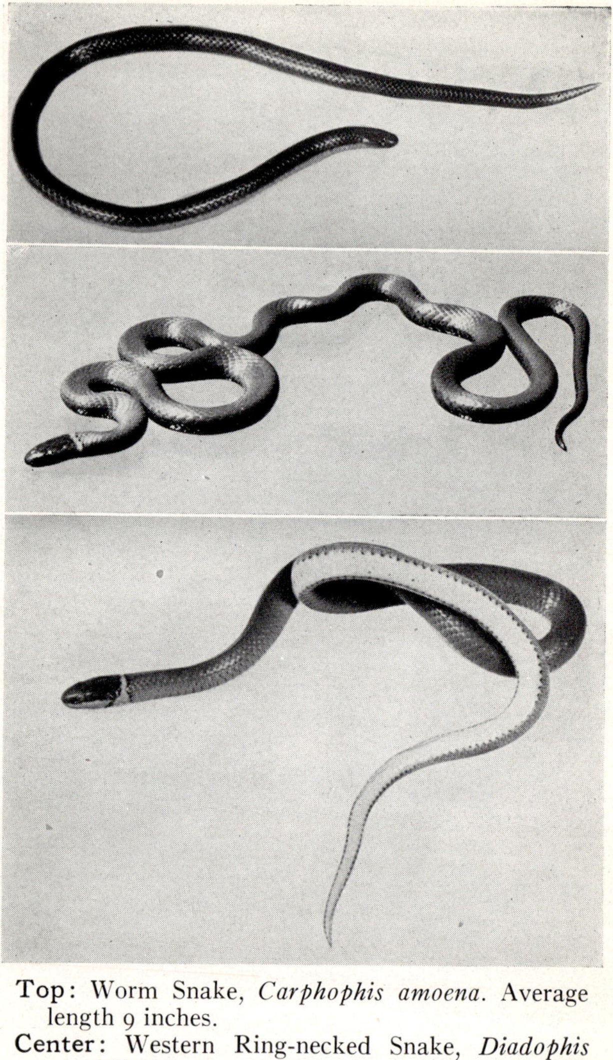

Top: Worm Snake, *Carphophis amoena*. Average length 9 inches.

Center: Western Ring-necked Snake, *Diadophis amabilis*. Average length 16 inches (photo by L. M. Klauber).

Bottom: Eastern Ring-necked Snake, *Diadophis punctatus*. Average length 12 inches.

Above: Common Hog-nosed Snake, *Heterodon contortrix*. Average length 24 inches.
Below: Western Hog-nosed Snake, *Heterodon nasicus*. Average length 18 inches.

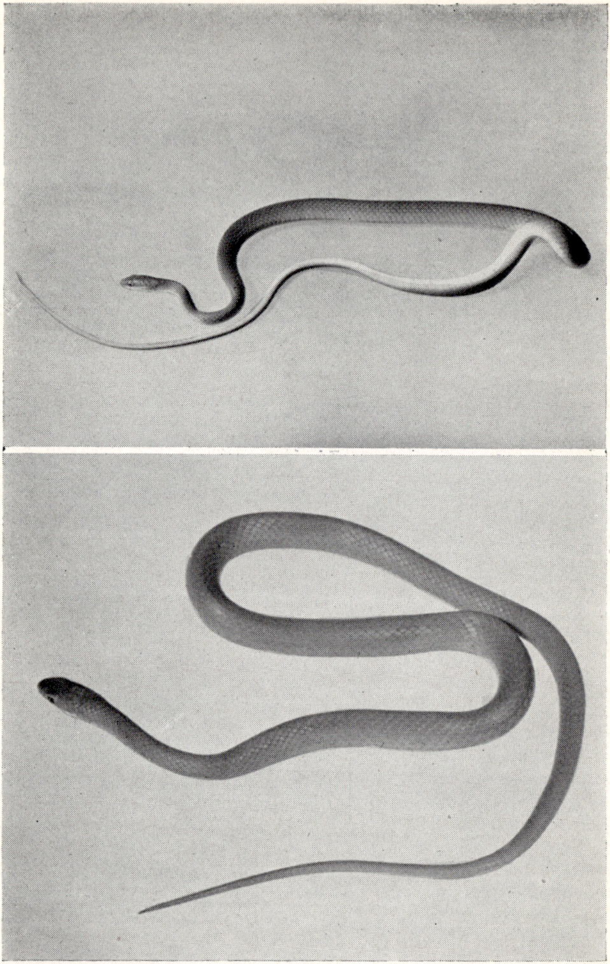

Above: Rough Green Snake, *Opheodrys aestivus.* Average length 28 inches.
Below: Smooth Green Snake, *Opheodrys vernalis.* Average length 15 inches.

Top: Blue Racer, *Coluber constrictor flaviventris.* Average length 4 feet.
Center: Eastern Coachwhip, *Coluber flagellum flagellum.* Average length 4 feet.
Bottom: Red Racer, *Coluber flagellum frenatus.* Average length 4 feet.

Top: Ornate Whipsnake, *Coluber taeniatus girardi.* Average length $3\frac{1}{2}$ feet.
Center: California Striped Racer, *Coluber lateralis.* Average length $3\frac{1}{2}$ feet.
Bottom: Indigo Snake, *Drymarchon corais couperi.* Average length 5 feet.

Above: Patch-nosed Snake, *Salvadora lineata*. Average length 30 inches.

Below: Leaf-nosed Snake, *Phyllorhynchus decurtatus*. Average length 15 inches (photo by L. M. Klauber).

Top: Corn Snake, *Elaphe guttata*. Average length 3 feet.

Center: Pilot Black Snake, *Elaphe o. obsoleta*. Average length 4 feet.

Bottom: Four-lined Chicken Snake, *Elaphe q. quadrivittata*. Average length 4 feet.

Above: Fox Snake, *Elaphe vulpina.* Average length 3½ feet.

Below: Faded Snake, *Arizona elegans.* Average length 30 inches.

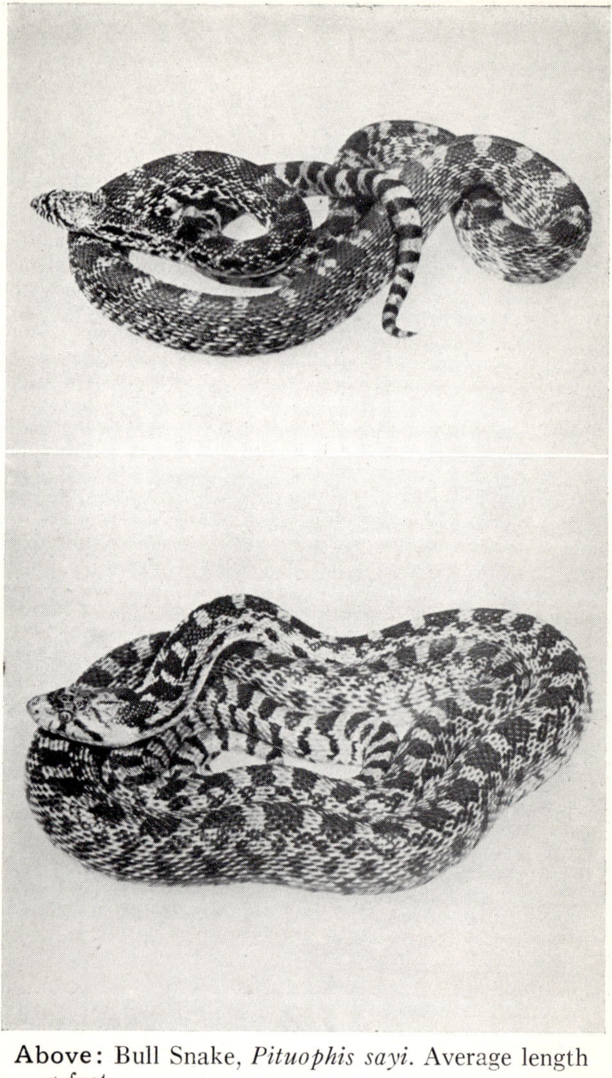

Above: Bull Snake, *Pituophis sayi.* Average length 5 feet.

Below: Gopher Snake, *Pituophis catenifer.* Average length 4½ feet.

Top: Yellow-bellied King Snake, *Lampropeltis calligaster*. Average length 3 feet.
Center: Common King Snake, *Lampropeltis g. getulus*. Average length 3½ feet.
Bottom: Speckled King Snake, *Lampropeltis g. holbrooki*. Average length 3½ feet.

Top: California King Snake, *Lampropeltis g. californiae,* showing the two pattern phases. Average length 3 feet (photo by L. M. Klauber).
Center: Banded King Snake, *Lampropeltis pyromelana*. Average length 30 inches.
Bottom: Milk Snake, *Lampropeltis t. triangulum.* Average length 30 inches.

Top: Short-tailed Snake, *Stilosoma extenuatum*. Average length 18 inches.
Center: Long-nosed Snake, *Rhinocheilus lecontei*. Average length 2 feet.
Bottom: Ground Snake, *Sonora episcopa*, showing two color phases. Average length 10 inches.

Top: Banded Sand Snake, *Chilomeniscus cinctus.* Average length 9 inches (photo by L. M. Klauber).

Center: Kirtland's Water Snake, *Natrix kirtlandii.* Average length 15 inches.

Bottom: Queen Snake, *Natrix septemvittata.* Average length 20 inches.

Top: Green Water Snake, *Natrix cyclopion*. Average length 3 feet.
Center: Brown Water Snake, *Natrix taxispilota*. Average length 3½ feet.
Bottom: Diamond-backed Water Snake, *Natrix rhombifera*. Average length 3½ feet.

Top: Common Water Snake, *Natrix s. sipedon.* Average length 30 inches.
Center: Southern Banded Water Snake, *Natrix s. fasciata.* Average length 3 feet.
Bottom: Mississippi River Water Snake, *Natrix s. confluens.* Average length 30 inches.

Top: Black Swamp Snake, *Seminatrix pygaea.* Average length 12 inches.
Center: De Kay's Snake, *Storeria dekayi.* Average length 10 inches.
Bottom: Southern Ground Snake, *Haldea striatula.* Average length 10 inches.

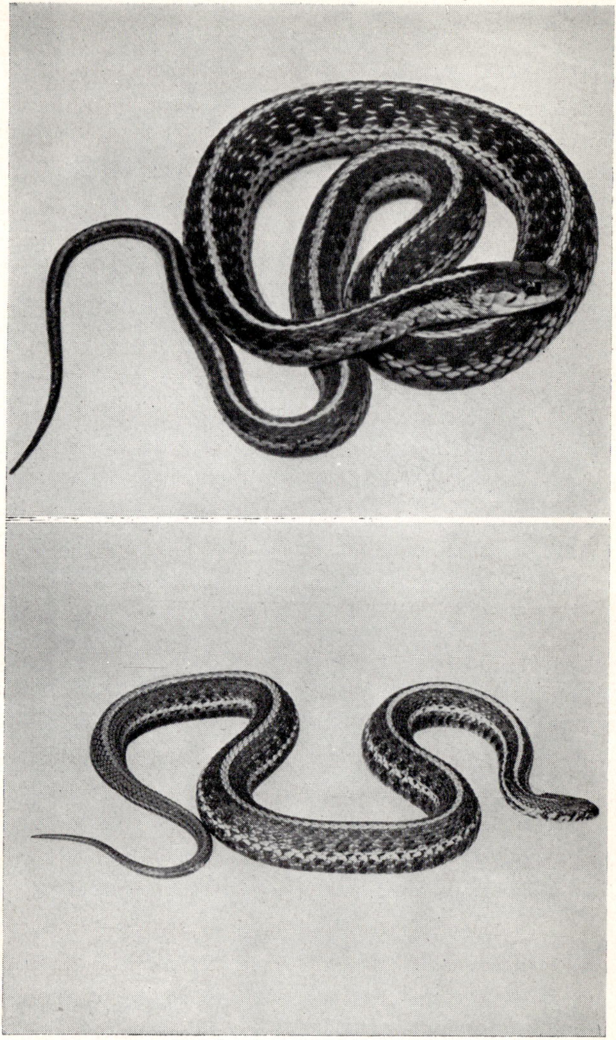

Above: Common Garter Snake, *Thamnophis sirtalis*. Average length 20 inches.
Below: Plains Garter Snake, *Thamnophis radix*. Average length 2 feet.

Above: Pacific Coast Garter Snake, *Thamnophis o. atratus*. Average length 2 feet.

Below: Great Basin Garter Snake, *Thamnophis o. vagrans*. Average length 20 inches.

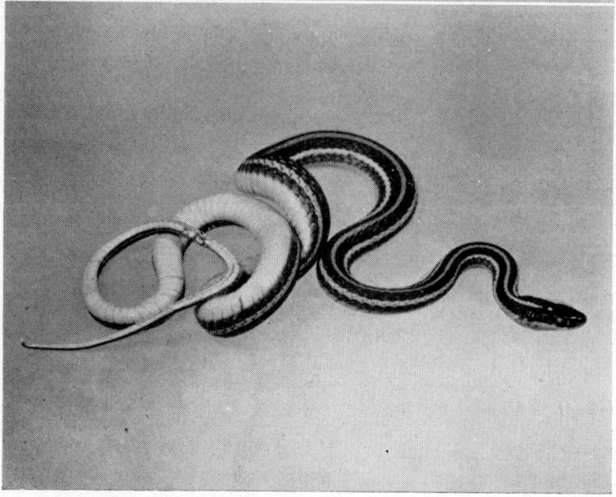

Above: Two-striped Garter Snake, *Thamnophis hammondii*. Average length 2 feet.

Below: Ribbon Snake, *Thamnophis sauritus proximus*. Average length 2 feet.

Top: Lined Snake, *Tropidoclonion lineatum.* Average length 12 inches.

Center: Spotted Night Snake, *Hypsiglena ochrorhyncha.* Average length 15 inches (photo by L. M. Klauber).

Bottom: Lyre Snake, *Trimorphodon lyrophanes.* Average length 3 feet (photo by L. M. Klauber).

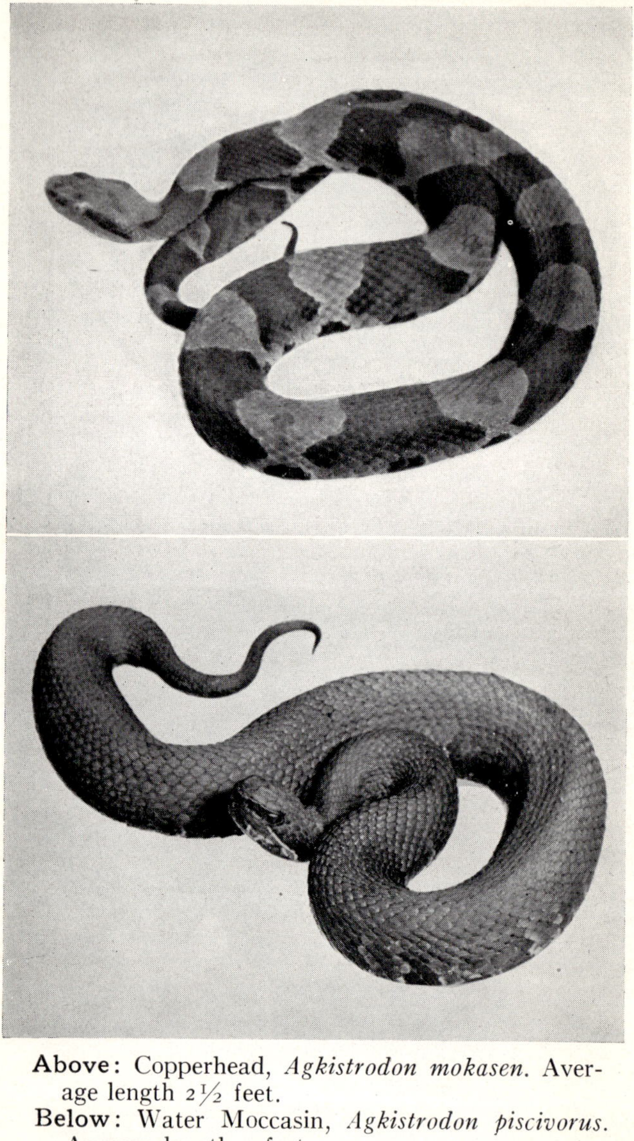

Above: Copperhead, *Agkistrodon mokasen.* Average length 2½ feet.
Below: Water Moccasin, *Agkistrodon piscivorus.* Average length 3 feet.

Above: Pigmy Rattlesnake, *Sistrurus miliarius streckeri*. Average length 18 inches.
Below: Massasauga, *Sistrurus catenatus*. Average length 22 inches (photo by L. M. Klauber).

Above: Western Diamond Rattlesnake, *Crotalus atrox*. Average length 4 feet.

Below: Red Diamond Rattlesnake, *Crotalus ruber*. Average length 4 feet.

Top: Timber Rattlesnake, *Crotalus horridus.* Average length 3½ feet.

Center: Black-tailed Rattlesnake, *Crotalus molossus.* Average length 3½ feet (photo by L. M. Klauber).

Bottom: Sidewinder, *Crotalus cerastes.* Average length 24 inches.

Above: Prairie Rattlesnake, *Crotalus v. viridis*. Average length 3 feet (photo by L. M. Klauber).
Below: Pacific Rattlesnake, *Crotalus v. oreganus*. Average length 3 feet.

INDEX

INDEX